Price $6.50

GOD IS...

Dialogues on the Nature of God for Young People

Kenneth E. Bailey

YOUTH CLUB PROGRAM, INC.

700 Dewberry Road
Monroeville, Pa. 15146

Copyright © 1976 by Kenneth E. Bailey

All rights reserved.

No part of this book may be used or reproduced in any manner whatsoever without written permission, except in the case of brief quotations embodied in critical articles and reviews.

In accord with some of the most recent thinking in the academic press, the Youth Club Program, Inc. is pleased to present this scholarly book which has been prepared from an author-edited and author-prepared camera-ready manuscript.

Library of Congress Cataloging in Publication Data

```
Bailey, Kenneth E
   God is ...

   Bibliography: p.
   1. God--Study and teaching.  2. Christian education
--Text-books.  I. Title.
BT108.B34            231              76-15580
ISBN 0-87808-149-6
```

Published by

YOUTH CLUB PROGRAM, INC.

700 Dewberry Road
Monroeville, Pa. 15146

PRINTED IN THE UNITED STATES OF AMERICA

CONTENTS

FOREWORD	v
PREFACE	vi
CHARACTERS IN THE DIALOGUE	ix

SECTION I. GOD IS GREAT

Lesson

1.	GOD IS SO GREAT THAT HE IS ALL POWERFUL	3
2.	GOD IS SO GREAT THAT HE USES POWER AS A SERVANT OF LOVE	15
3.	GOD IS SO GREAT THAT HE GRANTS US FREEDOM	27
4.	GOD IS SO GREAT THAT HE COMES IN HUMILITY TO REDEEM (1)	39
5.	GOD IS SO GREAT THAT HE COMES IN HUMILITY TO REDEEM (2)	50

SECTION II. GOD IS LIGHT

6.	GOD IS LIGHT AND HE ENLIGHTENS US IN NATURE	63
7.	GOD IS LIGHT AND HE ENLIGHTENS US BY THE PROPHETS	75
8.	GOD IS LIGHT AND HE ENLIGHTENS US IN CHRIST	86
9.	GOD IS LIGHT AND HE WAS FAITHFUL TO HIS PEOPLE IN THE OLD COVENANT	98

Lesson

10. GOD IS LIGHT AND HE IS FAITHFUL TO HIS FAMILY
    IN THE NEW COVENANT 109

11. GOD IS LIGHT AND HE WORKS LIKE LIGHT IN OUR HEARTS 121

SECTION III. GOD IS THREE IN ONE

12. ETERNALLY ONE GOD 135

13. FATHER 149

14. SON 163

15. HOLY SPIRIT 178

SECTION IV. GOD IS HOLY LOVE

16. GOD IS HOLY 195

17. GOD IS LOVE 210

18. GOD IS HOLY LOVE (1) 224

19. GOD IS HOLY LOVE (2) 239

20. GOD WANTS US TO KNOW, ACCEPT, AND RETURN HIS
    HOLY LOVE 253

APPENDIX A. SUGGESTIONS FOR USE IN THE YOUNGER CHURCHES 271

APPENDIX B. NOTE TO THE TEACHER 274

BIBLIOGRAPHY 277

FOREWORD

Kenneth Bailey is a man of prodigious gifts. Musician, poet, scholar, theologian, preacher, teacher, dramatist, writer, he has been prepared in extraordinary ways for his present contribution to the Christian Church. For twenty years he has lived and served in the Middle East in posts ranging from Egyptian villages which have survived almost unchanged through the ages and where attitudes were often older than Abraham, to his present post as Professor of New Testament in the Near East Theological Seminary. He has participated in Holy Week dramatic productions in Jerusalem, and until his evacuation with his family from Lebanon in the midst of the current hostilities there, conducted evangelistic radio broadcasts each week that reached every part of the Arabic speaking world. He has the distinction of having preached to more Middle Eastern listeners than any man in history. He has been frequently published in Arabic, has written and spoken extensively on the theology of mission, and his enormously significant scholarly work, *Poet and Peasant* is soon to be released by Eerdmans Publishing Company.

In *God Is... Dialogues for Young People on the Nature of God*, he combines the richness of Middle Eastern Biblical perspective (the Bible is an Eastern book seen for centuries only through the colored glasses of Western culture), penetrating theological insight, dramatic skill, and gifted teaching. There will be no boredom in classes using *this* book!

The Youth Club Program, Inc. which now services over 2,500 churches of all denominations, currently enrolling over 200,000 young people in what we believe is the most effective Christian Education program in the country, is happy to share in making *God Is... Dialogues for Young People on the Nature of God* available to Christian Education leaders and young people everywhere.

Dale K. Milligan, *Senior Minister, First Presbyterian Church, Oklahoma City, Oklahoma, and President of Youth Club Program, Inc.*

PREFACE

Bishop Steven Neill, in his book *The Unfinished Task*, comments on the village churches of Africa and Asia and says:

> Most preachers in these Churches have few qualifications and fewer books. Demands for sermons and addresses are very heavy. The faithfulness of the majority of the ministers and catechists is beyond praise. Yet there is an almost irresistible tendency for preaching to sink down into the dreariest kind of exhortation. A congregation can endure good advice up to a certain limit; but beyond that limit it ceases to have any effect and results only in weariness. Nothing in the world is easier to produce than conventional exhortations along well-worn lines of the Christian tradition.

The following book is written partly to try and help alleviate the above mentioned distressing situation, and partly to provide a study book for classes of newly literate villagers. *God Is* . . . is a series of twenty dialogues which were originally written to make the Gospel meaningful to the Middle Eastern village Christian.

Two basic problems were encountered in the writing of these dialogues: *selection* and *communication*. Let us look at each of them in turn. First, selection of material:

The church in the Middle East is set in an Islamic context. The thinking of the man in the pew is thereby inevitably colored by that context. Often this influence is unrealized. It is usually strongest in the village. The villager is also influenced from the bottom by his spirit-filled, superstitious village world. In a sense this book could be called "Beginnings in the Doctrine of God for the village church in an Islamic context." The Islamic context is always before us as we move through the book. This is with a view to building a Biblical doctrine of God for the village Christian and also with a view

vi

to Christian Muslim communication horizontally in the village itself. A sculpture is judged on the basis of what is left, not on the basis of what is cut away. I trust this fumbling beginning at theological statement will be judged the same way. For the simple village Christian some of this material will still be too difficult. It will need further simplification by the village pastor. In a sense, it may well be like such so-called "layman's theology" written in this country, which is a bit over the head of many laymen but just hits the spot for many pastors.

On the other hand, some will be disappointed at so much being left out. In painting, Matisse and Picasso deliberately chose two dimensions to paint in rather than three. The fewer lines on the canvas are thus clearer and more striking. The attempt in this direction, though perhaps not the deed, here confronts us.

The second problem has been communication.

The villager is an adult. He is intelligent. But he is unschooled and his frame of reference is *extremely* limited. We again quote from Bishop Neill where he writes, regarding the village Christians of India:

> These poor and disinherited people have lived in a state of almost complete illiteracy. It is no doubt possible to be both illiterate and a very good Christian; but no one who has not personally engaged in the task of instructing illiterate adults can have any idea of the difficulty of making even the simplest religious truth intelligible to them.

This, however, is our task. Illustrations must come from two sources, the Bible and village. Abstractions are meaningless. The Eastern villager must *feel* a thing to be right, not *understand* it to be right, before he will accept it. In Amos 3:3-8 we have, in my opinion, one of the finest illustrations in all of scripture (indeed, in all of literature) of communication to the Eastern village mind. Note this is not a logical movement from "A" to "B" to "C". It is rather an attempt to get the reader to "feel" it to be right by piling up illustrations out of village life with which the villager would be familiar. Christ taught by telling stories. They were simple in form and yet profound in content. The story carries an initial impact, yet holds up under analysis. Thus, regarding method, we have looked to Amos and Christ, not Paul.

The book is written to be translated into Arabic. In many places the style is a bit awkward in English. Sentences are kept purposely short. Words and phrases are often rather monotonously repeated. This also is intentional. Many of the readers will be newly literate. Only someone who has learned to read another language as an adult can appreciate what it

vii

means to find repetition which comes as a refreshing relief, not as boring monotony. Verses are often quoted without the context. The Bible is translated in classical Arabic and often is quite difficult for the villager to read. Thus only the essential quotation itself is listed. Occasionally the reader will run across a seemingly difficult word, and wonder why this word is used if the book is for simple village Christians. Usually in such cases a very simple Arabic word has as its only accurate English equivilant a rather difficult word, thus this word was used.

Qualified teachers in the village church are rare. Therefore, we use dramatics. With these dialogues the lesson teaches itself. Some spiritually sensitive and mature person will be needed to lead the discussion of the questions if they are used. But even he will not need to be the kind of a person that can properly organize and teach a traditionally stated prose lesson.

Discussion centers in three main characters. First is "Yusef, the Wise," who knows the right answers. He is an elder in the village church. Second is "Abdu, the Inquirer," who asks the right questions; and third is "Baseat, the Simple," who never gets the point. Baseat provides some comedy relief (although most of it will be lost to the western reader) and by identification the audience can find it gratifying to be understanding at least more than this dumb fellow.

I am deeply indebted to Dr. Addison Leitch, Professor of Theology at the Pittsburgh Theological Seminary, for his valuable suggestions and invaluable encouragement. Dr. John Bald and Miss Bessie Burrows helped me over many a theological and educational hurdle as the writing progressed. Insights for the Islamic background of the book are almost without exception from my teacher and friend, Dr. Kenneth Cragg.

Words are quite useless in trying to express gratitude to my beloved wife Ethel. She has painstakingly proof-read the manuscript and offered patient and helpful suggestions at many points along the way.

Greatest thanks must go to my many dedicated village friends in the Coptic Evangelical Church of Egypt. They have graciously welcomed me into their Christian fellowship in such a way as to give meaning to the classical definition of grace as unmerited favor.

Yusef the Wise in the play is in reality a character study of my good friend, Elder Musid of Del al Barsha. His life is a living example of the holiness that is fulfilled in righteousness.
      TO HIM THIS BOOK IS DEDICATED
                  Kenneth E. Bailey

CHARACTERS IN THE DIALOGUES

The dialogues have three main characters. First is Yusef the Wise. He is an Elder in the church and is a land owner. He is very wise and he is very pious. All the village respects him. He is dressed in village dress and speaks somewhat slowly. But when he is very anxious to get his point across he speaks rapidly and with great earnestness.

Second is Abd il-Maseeh (called Abdu). He is a villager and can read but he has not had very much education. He is called the Inquirer because he is not satisfied until he understands. He speaks with a village accent and is very earnest in his quest for truth. He is about 35 years old. He owns one acre of land which he works himself.

Third is Baseat. He is a good fellow, but is very simple. He also can read. He is a friend of Abdu, but Abdu mocks him, at least at first. He is not married and he lives with his father. He is about the same age as Abdu. The mayor comes sometimes. Also the carpenter, the builder, the porter and so forth.

SECTION I
GOD IS GREAT

1
GOD IS SO GREAT THAT HE IS ALL POWERFUL

SCRIPTURES TO BE READ: Daniel 4:25, 34-35; I Timothy 6:15-16; Genesis 17:1; II Timothy 2:11-13; Revelation 1:8

STATEMENT OF LESSON

We all know that God is most great. But we do not understand this greatness. This is the first section. In this section we will think about the greatness of God. We will try to understand what it means that God is Most Great. For five lessons we will think about the greatness of our God, to Him be the praise and honor and glory forever and ever. Amen.

In this lesson we will see that God is All Powerful. We will try to see what this means.

OUTLINE

GOD IS SO GREAT THAT HE IS ALL POWERFUL

1. God is indeed All Powerful.
2. God is All Powerful, but God cannot deny Himself.
   a. He cannot be unjust.
   b. He cannot be unwise.
3. God uses His power as a Servant of love.

Now let us turn to the hamlet of light to see what is going on.

THE DIALOGUE

GOD IS . . .

SCENE 1

CHARACTERS:

Elder Yusef

Abd Al-Maseeh, the Inquirer

Baseat, the Simple

Teacher (as Narrator)

Abd Al-Maseeh sat outside his house on his mustaba (a brick bench). He was thinking. He sat alone. He held his head on his chin. Soon Baseat, his friend, comes around the corner and sees him.

THE DIALOGUE

BASEAT: Abdu, why are you sitting alone? Are you angry or something?

ABDU: No, my friend Baseat, I am not angry, only unhappy.

BASEAT: Why are you unhappy?

ABDU: Does not Paul say we should have a reason for the faith that is in us?

BASEAT: Do I know what Paul says?

ABDU: Shame on you Baseat, you should care about these things. But I will tell you my story. This morning I went to town to buy some meat for a banquet for my uncle who has come to visit us. I began talking with the butcher. We talked about many things. Soon we were talking about religion. He asked me "How can God be One if He is Three? The priest says, "In the name of the Father and of the Son and of the Holy Spirit, one God, Amen." "How can this be true?" said the butcher. Then I was ashamed, for I could say nothing to him. For I do not know how God can be One if He is Three. Indeed he asked me many questions about God I couldn't answer. I felt shame!!

BASEAT: This is not our concern.

ABDU: Oh, yes it is! Paul says we must have a reason for the faith that is in us. Listen, Baseat, are you a Christian by birth or by belief?

BASEAT: Do not make yourself the Philosopher of the Age, Abdu.

ABDU: You do not think there is a difference, O Baseat, but there is! You are Baseat! "Baseat" means simple. And a Christian by birth is "Baseat" in his knowledge of

4

ABDU: God. You know nothing! But if you are a Christian by faith then you must be a disciple of Christ. Indeed you must be a student and learn from Christ. But you are hopeless. Your name is Baseat. You had better remain just a Christian by birth. If I were such a Christian I would have said to the butcher this morning, "Go ask the priest." But I could not say this. I know he will not go to the priest. I want to call myself a Christian by faith. This means I must understand these things. I must be able to answer him myself.

BASEAT: Yes, I'm Baseat! My mother called me this when I was born because I was very small. But to sit here alone and angry won't help. I'm not that Baseat!

ABDU: But what can I do? I'll tell you Baseat. Let us go to Yusef, the Wise, Elder of the Church. His house is over on the square in front of the Mayor's house. It is still early and he will be sitting on his mustaba in front of his house. Let's ask him. He is very wise. Maybe he will help us.

TEACHER: Scene 2 - in front of the house of Yusef the Wise. Yusef is sitting watching a builder at work. The builder is building new rooms on the top of the Mayor's house. Next month the Mayor's son will be married. The Mayor is preparing a place for his son.

(Enter Abdu and Baseat)

ABDU AND
BASEAT: Good day, Shiek Yusef.

YUSEF: Good day to you, Abdu, The Inquirer, and to you Baseat.

BASEAT: But Shiekh Yusef, why do you call Abdu "The Inquirer"?

YUSEF: Why, Baseat, do the men of the village call me "The Wise"?

BASEAT: It is because you are very wise.

YUSEF: Why do men call you Baseat?

BASEAT: Because I never understand anything.

YUSEF: Then why do the men of the village call Abdu "The Inquirer"?

BASEAT: It must be because he is always inquiring about things. He always seeks to understand.

YUSEF: Brilliant, Baseat! You are a very clever fellow. If you keep up like that soon we will have to change your name. But, Abdu, is there something? All is well, God willing!

ABDU: Yes, Shiekh Yusef, all is well, praise God. But my name is Abdu, the Inquirer, and I have a question.

YUSEF: What is it, my good friend?

ABDU: Elder Yusef, you who are called "the wise," how can God be One if He is Three? This morning in town the butcher asked me this question and I could not answer him. I was ashamed. Baseat is an idiot. He can't help me. He does not understand. We have come to you.

YUSEF: How strange! I have been sitting here this afternoon thinking about the same question. God showed me part of the answer. But this is a very hard question, Abdu. Listen, O Abdu, where is the elder son of the preacher now?

ABDU: Shukre? He is in the faculty of medicine at the University.

YUSEF: The first day he went there, did they give him a knife and ask him to cut a man's stomach open?

ABDU: No, of course not! He will have to study years before they will let him do operations.

YUSEF: All right. And your son Khaleel, you will want to teach him to buy and sell in the market place, won't you?

ABDU: Of course!

YUSEF: Will you begin by sending him to the grocery to buy 1/2 kilo of sugar, or will you begin by sending him to the city to sell your cotton crop?

ABDU: No. No. O Most respected Elder (Laughing), of course I will begin with the very simple thing and work up to the hard thing. Khaleel is small. They would deceive him. He will not be able to sell cotton for many years.

BASEAT: With me it is all the same. I go to the city to sell cotton - they deceive me. I go to the store to buy 1/4 kilo of sugar, they deceive me! What can I do?

ABDU: Just stay with Elder Yusef, O Baseat, and he will make you wiser than Solomon, the King, . . . maybe.

YUSEF: No Abdu, God can teach us all things, and He alone can make us wise. From man we can learn to be clever. Only God can teach us to be wise. But let us stay with our subject. I am willing to talk to you about the Trinity, but we cannot start with this. We must understand many other things about God first. Are you busy these days?

BASEAT: There is nothing to do in the village - neither in the houses, nor in the fields.

YUSEF: Do you really want to learn about God?

ABDU AND
BASEAT: Yes, sincerely we do!

YUSEF: Very well, you must promise to come to me every evening while it is yet light and we will talk of God, and may His Spirit enlighten us. Do you agree? Will you give me your promise?

BASEAT: Indeed we will, Elder Yusef.

YUSEF: Be sure to bring a Bible with you.

ABDU: We will, Yusef.

TEACHER: The next night comes and Abdu and Baseat return to the house of Elder Yusef.

YUSEF: (Yusef is seated as usual on the mustaba outside his house. He is reading the 8th Psalm out loud as Abdu and Baseat arrive.) "O Lord, our Lord, how majestic is thy name in all the earth! Thou whose glory above the heavens is changed by the mouth of babes and infants. . ."

Welcome! Welcome, my friends, my beloved sons! How are you today?

ABDU AND
BASEAT: We are well, Elder Yusef, only because of your presence among us.

YUSEF: May God keep you, my friends. Are you ready to talk about the deep things of God?

ABDU: We are ready. What will be our first subject as we try to understand God?

YUSEF: We must begin with God's power. John says that God is "Able to do anything," Abdu!

ABDU: Yes, Yusef.

YUSEF: Turn and read Genesis 17:1. Who does God say He is?

ABDU: (Reading) "And He said to him, I am the Lord God Almighty." He calls Himself "The Almighty."

YUSEF: Good. Now turn to Daniel 4:25 and read.

ABDU: (Reading) "....that you shall be driven from among men, and your dwelling shall be with the beasts of the field; you shall be made to eat grass like an ox, and you shall be wet with the dew of heaven, and seven times shall pass over you, till you know that the Most High rules the kingdom of men, and gives it to whom he will."

YUSEF: Very well. Now, Baseat, you read Verses 34 and 35.

BASEAT: (Reading) "At the end of the days, I, Nebuchadnezzar, lifted my eyes to heaven, and my reason returned to me, and I blessed the Most High, and praised and honored him who lives forever; for his dominion is an everlasting dominion, and his kingdom endures from generation to generation; all the inhabitants of the earth are accounted as nothing; and he does according to his will in the host of heaven and among the inhabitants of the earth; and none can stay his hand or say to him, 'What doest thou?'"

YUSEF: Now, Abdu, never mind about the eating grass and all that. What does Daniel tell the king he must learn in the verse you read?

ABDU: He says, "You must know that the Most High rules the kingdoms of men."

YUSEF: Very Good, Abdu. So we see that God is called "The Most High" and also is called "The Ruler of the Kingdom of men." Now Baseat, what does your verse say?

BASEAT: Do I know what it says?

YUSEF: Patience, Baseat, patience! You are a very clever fellow, you can understand this very easily. Do not shame me. If you do not understand, then I am not wise because I have not been able to teach you. Read the verse.

BASEAT: (Reading) "At the end of the days, I, Nebuchadnezzar, lifted my eyes to heaven, and my reason returned to me, and I blessed the Most High, and praised and honored Him who lives forever."

YUSEF: Enough, Baseat. What does Nebuchadnezzar call God?

BASEAT: He calls Him "The Most High."

YUSEF: Good! Good, Baseat. Now what else does he call Him?

BASEAT: He calls Him - "The One who lives forever."

YUSEF: Very good, Baseat. Why are you hiding all of this brilliance under a bushel? You are a very clever fellow.

Very well. We now see that God is "Most High," but He is not a long way off! No. He is here ruling the kingdoms of men and He is the One who lives forever. Very good. Now Abdu!

ABDU: Yes, Yusef.

YUSEF: What does Daniel say about the greatness of God?

ABDU: He says that God is the Most High, and that He rules all men and that He lives forever.

YUSEF: What does God say to Abraham?

ABDU: He says, "I am the Almighty."

YUSEF: Very good. Now let us turn to I Timothy 6:15-16. (Yusef reads) "... and this will be made manifest at the proper time by the blessed and only Sovereign, the King of kings and Lord of lords, who alone has immortality and dwells in the unapproachable light, whom no man has ever seen or can see. To him be honor and eternal dominion. Amen."

Listen, friends. Paul the apostle says of God that He is the "only Sovereign," that He is Lord of lords and King of kings; and that He has immortality and that He has eternal dominion. See, so many things we can say about the greatness of our God. Let us look also at what John says in the Revelation. Abdu, turn to Revelation 1:8 and read.

ABDU: (Reading) "I am the Alpha and the Omega, says the Lord God, who is and who was and who is to come, the Almighty."

YUSEF: Now Abdu, what does John call God?

ABDU: He calls Him "The Almighty."

YUSEF: Good. Good. Baseat, what does Paul call God?

BASEAT: Paul says that God is "King of Kings and Lord of Lords."

YUSEF: Very good, Baseat. Abdu, what about Daniel?

ABDU: He says God is the "Most High" and the "Ruler of the Kingdoms of men."

YUSEF: Good, and what about Genesis?

ABDU: God is called "The Almighty."

YUSEF: So we see that the Scriptures from Genesis to Revelation talk about the greatness and the power of God. But there are two more things we must understand.

ABDU: What are they, O Elder Yusef?

YUSEF: Listen carefully, O Abdu. There are some things God cannot do.

ABDU: (With great indignation and surprise) How can this be, Elder Yusef! God can do everything! If there is something He cannot do, then He must be weak. And if He is weak, then He is not God. I can't get this through my head, Yusef, the Wise!

YUSEF: Don't be angry, Abdu. Just stay with me while I ask you a question. Do you remember the late pastor Hanna?

ABDU: Remember him? My goodness! My grandchildren will know his name! May God have mercy on him! He was a great man!

YUSEF: Tell me what you remember, O Abdu.

ABDU: Indeed, that man was a saint! When he came to our village many years ago, we didn't know anything. We didn't even know the Lord's Prayer! He would come and visit us, and pray with us. He would comfort us and help us in our sufferings and sorrows. When my grandfather died -- indeed, he was an angel to us and our family. He was a saint. May God have mercy on him! There is no one like him. There never will be. He was a good man. He was truly a man of God!

YUSEF: Very well, Abdu. Did the late pastor Hanna ever deceive you or your father's house?

ABDU: (Abdu wide-eyed and nearly exploding) Did he ever deceive us? Pastor Hanna deceive us? Impossible!! Shame on you, Elder Yusef. How can you shame the memory of so great a man? How can you suggest that he would trick us or cheat us or deceive us?

YUSEF: (Trying to calm him) Don't be angry, Abdu. I have a purpose for asking this question. And I will ask another. Could he have tried to deceive you?

ABDU: Impossible! That man was a saint! He couldn't have!

BASEAT: (Insistently) Now, now, Abdu. If he had wanted to, he could have been deceitful.

ABDU: (Firmly) No! Impossible!

BASEAT: (Also firmly) What do you mean impossible? He didn't want to deceive the people, but if he had wanted to, he could have. He didn't choose to be deceitful.

ABDU: (Not backing down) No! Impossible. His nature was not like that. It would have been against his nature to cheat someone! Praise God! Indeed he was a good man!

YUSEF: Do not be angry, my sons. You are both right. If he had had a different nature, he could have cheated men. But with the nature he had, he could not! But let me ask another question. What am I called in the village?

ABDU: We call you Elder Yusef, the Wise.

YUSEF: If my nature is to be wise -- if God has given me some wisdom, though it may be very little, can I speak foolishness?

BASEAT: No. No, Elder Yusef. Even I do not accept that! Let Solomon the King speak foolishness and our Elder Yusef will never speak foolishness!

10

ABDU: Truly! Let the people call us donkeys and do not let them say that Elder Yusef has said or done a foolish thing.

YUSEF: Praise to God. All the blessings of our lives are from God, my brothers! Give thanks to Him. Very well. The wise man cannot act foolishly because it is against his nature. The good man cannot do evil because it is against his nature. Now what about God? Can God act foolishly? Can God do injustice? Will not the Judge of all the earth do right, the Scripture says?

ABDU: I never thought of that!

BASEAT: May you always be present to enlighten us, Elder Yusef.

YUSEF: For example, O Baseat, can fire be cold?

BASEAT: Fire? Cold? (Thinking) No, Yusef, it is impossible.

YUSEF: Abdu, can the water of the river be dry?

ABDU: No, Yusef, it cannot. It is not the nature of water to be dry.

YUSEF: Can the rock be soft like cotton, or can the fresh air be hard like the rock?

ABDU: No, Yusef. These things are not possible.

YUSEF: Why not?

ABDU: The rock is hard. It cannot be soft like cotton. This is not its nature. The fresh air is air, it cannot be hard like the rock. Its nature is like this. It cannot change.

YUSEF: Very well. So it is with God, my friends. God cannot be unjust and He cannot be unwise. The Book says, "He cannot deny Himself." Yes, God can do everything. But He will not change his nature. He cannot be unjust and He cannot be unwise. We must remember this as we think of God's power and omnipotence. God cannot be tricky, deceitful or foolish.

ABDU: We never thought of this, Yusef.

YUSEF: But my friends, there is one more idea we must discuss about the power of God before we say good night. God uses His power as a Servant of love.

BASEAT: My mind is like a bowl of stew now, O Yusef, with the new ideas you have given us already. Will you give us yet another one? Are these not enough! Besides, we have worn you out with much talk. This is enough.

YUSEF: No, my friends, your presence is like a rich perfume. I am ready to talk with you about our God the whole

11

YUSEF: night. But if you are tired, we can stop. (At this point Yusef sees a scorpion crawling out of a hole in the mud brick wall behind Abdu's back. In great agitation he shouts.) Abdu! Give me your staff. Give me your staff! There is a scorpion behind you! Look out! Look out! (Abdu jumps up)

BASEAT: Get back, Elder Yusef! Get back! Give me the stick.

YUSEF: I will kill it. (With a few well-placed strokes, he kills the scorpion) It is finished. Praise God!

ABDU: Praise God.

BASEAT: Praise God, who has saved us from the scorpion by the blessed hand of Elder Yusef.

YUSEF: (Thoughtfully) Sit down again, my friends. It seems that God Himself wanted you to learn the last point about His power. Baseat?

BASEAT: Yes, Elder Yusef.

YUSEF: I see a chain about your neck. It means you have your pocket book with you. Isn't that right?

BASEAT: Yes, Yusef.

YUSEF: And I think you sold a water buffalo in the market last week. Is it not so?

BASEAT: I cannot deceive you, Elder Yusef. It is so.

YUSEF: This means you have at least a hundred pounds in your pocket right now. Is it not so?

BASEAT: (Smiling) A hundred, two hundred? Maybe. I'm not sure.

YUSEF: Who is holding the staff, Baseat?

BASEAT: You are, Elder Yusef.

YUSEF: Then just now if I wanted to, instead of killing the scorpion, I could have hit you over the head and taken your money. Isn't that right, Baseat?

BASEAT: I guess so, Elder Yusef.

YUSEF: Abdu.

ABDU: Yes, Elder Yusef.

YUSEF: The stick in my hands is power, isn't it?

ABDU: Indeed it is, Yusef.

YUSEF: How did I use the power in my hands, Abdu?

ABDU: You used it to help us. You killed the scorpion.

YUSEF: Correct, Abdu. Now think carefully. I used my power as a servant of my love. Is this not true, Baseat?

12

BASEAT: Have pity, O Yusef, I am a very simple man. This philosophy is too much for me.

ABDU: (With great excitement) That's right! That's right! You did, Yusef. The staff is power in your hands. You love us so you used the stick to show your love by killing the scorpion. The staff was a servant of your love.

YUSEF: May God enlighten you, Abdu. I am very pleased with you. The one who seeks, finds. You have sought and you have found. God is all powerful, yes, but He uses His power as a Servant of His love. He never uses it for Himself. The devil tried to get Jesus Christ, Our Savior, to use His power for Himself. On the mount, he tried to get the Son of God to make stones into bread. He tried to get Jesus to jump down from the pinacle of the temple. Jesus refused. This would have been using His power as a servant of Himself. The Jews wanted to make Him show them signs and miracles. He would not use His power in this way. Even on the Cross, they tried to taunt Him into using His power to save Himself. He would not. In all His miracles, He used His power only as a servant of His love. Yes, my friends, God is all powerful. He is the most High. He is able to do anything. But He cannot be unjust and He cannot be unwise for He cannot deny Himself. And He uses His power only as a servant of His love. Now I can say good night for I am finished. But stay, we will talk more.

ABDU: (Slowly and thoughtfully) No. It is enough, O Elder Yusef. We will take our leave. We have learned many things tonight. Our power, too, then must be a servant of our love for our neighbors and for God. Is it not so, Elder Yusef?

YUSEF: It is so, Abdu.

Good night, my friends.

ABDU AND
BASEAT: Good night, Yusef.

QUESTIONS FOR DISCUSSION

1. What does God say to Abraham about Himself?
2. What does Daniel call God? What do these words mean?
3. If God is "The Most High," He must be high in the heavens. Then how can He be here ruling men?
4. What are some of the names Paul uses for the greatness of God? Can you name five of them?
5. What names does John use for the greatness of God?
6. God is able to do everything. Is there anything He cannot do? If so, what? And why cannot he do these things?
7. How does God use His power?
8. What do we mean when we say that for God, power is the servant of love?
9. Give examples from the life of Christ where He uses power as a servant of love.

SUMMARY OF LESSON

God is able to do anything.
But God cannot be unjust.
He cannot be unwise.
These are against His nature.
He cannot deny Himself.

MOTTO: God is most Great. That is, He is always just and always wise.

2
GOD IS SO GREAT THAT HE USES POWER AS A SERVANT OF LOVE

SCRIPTURES TO BE READ: Matthew 11:2-11

STATEMENT OF LESSON

Just at the end of the first lesson, Elder Yusef killed a scorpion. Abdu's staff was power in his hands. He could have used it for himself and taken Abdu's money. He did not. He used His power as a servant of his love. God is all powerful. When he uses his power in this way, this is not weakness. This is great strength. It is easy to use power selfishly. It takes great strength to use power as a servant of love. This is what God does. This is a sign of His great power. He is so strong He is able to use power as a servant of love. In this lesson, we will try to understand this better. We will look first at man. Every man has power. In sin, man uses his power selfishly. But God uses it in love.

OUTLINE

GOD IS SO GREAT THAT HE USES POWER AS A SERVANT OF LOVE

1. Every man has some power. Some of these kinds of power are:
    a. Power of position
    b. Power of wealth
    c. Power of personality
    d. Physical power
2. The sinful man uses this power for himself.

3. God has all power.
4. God uses His power as a Servant of His love. He does this by:
    a. Giving us a fruitful world
    b. Turning aside evil from us
    c. Taking evil and making good out of it
    d. Giving us every good thing, physical and spiritual

THE DIALOGUE

GOD IS . . .

SCENE 2

CHARACTERS:

Elder Yusef

Abdu

Baseat

Mayor Butrus

THE DIALOGUE

TEACHER: The Mayor and Elder Yusef are sitting in front of Yusef's house talking.

MAYOR: Poor fellow. It's a shame he should get sick. Especially now as the yearly flood is approaching.

YUSEF: Yes indeed. Poor man, he has only one acre of ground and his children are too small to help.

MAYOR: Yes and his father is too old to work in the fields. And his brother, the camel driver, is driving his camels way to the south somewhere.

He really is in a bad way.

(Enter Abdu and Baseat)

YUSEF: Welcome, my sons. Or should I say my students? How are you tonight?

ABDU: We are well, professor Yusef. Good evening to our Mayor. How is everything with you? (They shake hands all around)

MAYOR: Praise God. All is well.

ABDU: Mr. Mayor, how soon will the flood come? When will they open the dykes?

MAYOR: In six more days, Abdu. I hope you have all your cotton out of the fields.

ABDU: Yes, praise God, we just finished today. We had no problem. We are many with my cousins and my brothers together.

YUSEF: You are lucky, Abdu. Have you heard about Simaan at the south end of the village?

ABDU: No. What about him?

YUSEF: He's sick.

ABDU: What's wrong with him?

YUSEF: He came in today from the field with a high fever. It seems he has malaria. May it be far from you.

ABDU: Poor fellow. Does he have his crops up off of the land?

MAYOR: Not yet.

BASEAT: Doesn't he have children or brothers or cousins or someone who can do it for him?

MAYOR: He has no one.

BASEAT: God will arrange the matter. He is the one who arranges everything.

YUSEF: (Slowly and thoughtfully) Is that all there is to say about the matter, Baseat?

BASEAT: What do you mean, Yusef? I don't understand.

YUSEF: Nothing, Baseat, nothing. I was just thinking . . . But let us begin where we stopped yesterday. Mr. Mayor, we have decided to meet each night and talk of the deep things of God.

MAYOR: (Emphatically) I know! I know! This is why I have come. I heard about your discussion of last evening and so I invited myself tonight. (Jokingly) Must not the Mayor know everything about the village?

YUSEF: Indeed he must. Our house is always open to you, Mr. Mayor. You have honored us.

MAYOR: May God keep you, Elder Yusef.

YUSEF: Very well. This morning I was thinking about the end of our discussion last night. What was that, Abdu?

ABDU: It was about how God uses His power as a servant.

YUSEF: As a servant of what, Baseat? Be careful - do not shame me before our Mayor.

BASEAT: Servants? Servants? Does God have servants who clean house for Him and so forth?

YUSEF: (Laughing) There is no dust in Heaven, Baseat. But God's power is like a servant to Him. He uses this as a servant of His love. I have been thinking that we must think more tonight about this idea. Last night we learned that God is "Almighty and able to do anything" but He cannot deny Himself. He cannot be unjust and He cannot be unwise. These are against His nature. Every man has some power. Is it not so, Mr. Mayor?

MAYOR: What you mean is not yet clear, Elder Yusef. It seems to me that some men are without power.

18

YUSEF: It is true that some men are weak, but there are different kinds of power. There is the power of position. There is power of wealth. There is power of personality. And there is physical power.

ABDU: Very true, Yusef.

YUSEF: Now let us think of how men have used these different kinds of power. You are a man of a high position in our village, Mr. Mayor. How do men of position use power?

MAYOR: We are all human. Most of them use it for themselves. Look at our fathers, the Pharaohs. They were great men and they had great power. But what did they use their power for? They used it to build great pyramids for themselves. Our people built the pyramids. And did the pyramids do the farmers of Egypt any good? Not at all!

YUSEF: What about today? How do Mayors use their power?

MAYOR: Like in anything else, some are good and some are bad. But man in sin is man in sin. Whatever strength he has he uses for himself.

BASEAT: Very true, Mayor Butrus. Very true!

YUSEF: Exactly right, Mr. Mayor. I have a few acres of land so I will speak of the power of wealth. Take the Turkish landowners a long time ago who used to own much land in our country. Their wealth was power. Did they use their power for themselves or for others?

ABDU: My goodness! They used their wealth only for themselves. We worked for them for 5¢ a day. They were very strong, but now they are gone. Praise God.

YUSEF: Well spoken, Abdu. It is true what you say. They used their power only for themselves. Also today some say that all private property is wrong. They say that it is wrong for any man to own anything! Jesus does not say it is wrong to have property. But He says it is wrong to use it only for yourself. Wealth is power. We can use this power for ourselves only, or we can use it as a servant whom we send to help others. Baseat!

BASEAT: Yes, Yusef?

YUSEF: If I have a servant in my house and I give him an order, does he obey?

BASEAT: Of course! He must obey!

YUSEF: If I know the Mayor has a banquet and needs help to serve the banquet, can I not send my servant to help?

BASEAT: Of course.

YUSEF: And will he not go?

BASEAT: Indeed, he will.

YUSEF: Wealth is like a servant. What I say to my wealth he will do. If I want him to serve only me, he obeys. If I order him to serve others, he obeys. But there is another kind of power. Some men have personal power over other men. Some use this power for good and some use it for bad. We talked yesterday of Pastor Hanna. Did he have the power of wealth, or the power of political position, Abdu?

ABDU: No, Yusef. He had only personal power. But all of us would do anything he said -- anything!

YUSEF: True, Abdu. He had great personal power which he used for good. Now what about Bakhit In-nuri?

BASEAT: Don't mention that man's name -- I am still afraid of him. Praise God he left the village ten years ago and went to the city! My goodness, he used to frighten all of us. I was more afraid of him than of my own father. He was very strong.

YUSEF: Strong? How? Did he have many guns or much wealth or what?

BASEAT: Do I know? He was strong and that's all there is to say.

YUSEF: You are right, Baseat. He was strong indeed. He had a strong personality. He had a strong influence on many people. But -- what a loss -- he used his power only for himself. So he taught people to think only of themselves. He treated people like the players on a chessboard. People were just something for him to use for himself as he wished. But there is another kind of power that we all have. That is physical power. Every man has this. Did you not work in the fields today, Abdu?

ABDU: Of course I did, Yusef.

YUSEF: Did you not use the strength of your body in the field?

ABDU: Naturally, Yusef.

YUSEF: Then this too is power that we can use for ourselves or we can use it for others just like the other kinds of power we have been talking about. Isn't this true, Abdu?

ABDU: (Thoughtfully) I guess so! I never thought about this in this way.

YUSEF: The strength of your body is a servant who does just what you tell him, Abdu. You can use him to serve

YUSEF: only yourself as most men. Or you can use him to serve others, like the good Samaritan.

MAYOR: Your words condemn us all, Elder Yusef.

YUSEF: If there is judgment, it is not from my words, Mr. Mayor. It is from the spirit which speaks to our consciences.

Now, my friends, let us look at Jesus, our Lord. Did He have any power, Baseat?

BASEAT: Him? He had all the power in heaven and on earth.

YUSEF: Right, Baseat. He said before the ascension, "All authority has been given to me in heaven and on earth." Let us look at the kinds of power we have been talking about. Did He have the power of position? He was the Son of God. Did He have the power of wealth? All things were made through Him. Did He have the power of personality? He spoke as one having authority. Even in the Garden of Gethsemane they were afraid of Him. They just looked at Him and were afraid. Did He have physical power? He could work any miracle He wanted. But this is the important point. Did He use His power for Himself?

MAYOR: Never! Only for others.

YUSEF: Exactly right, Mr. Mayor. God has all power, but He uses His power only as a servant of His love. Look around us, Abdu, you were in the fields today. What do you have growing now?

ABDU: Only some clover.

YUSEF: Whose power makes the clover grow?

ABDU: God's power.

YUSEF: Whose power brings the Nile water that we might give the land to drink?

ABDU: God's power.

YUSEF: Whose power brings the sun each day to warm the land?

ABDU: God's power.

YUSEF: Whose power gives you strength to work the soil?

ABDU: God's power.

YUSEF: You see, Abdu, God uses His power as a servant to serve us. But not only in the fields, but in our lives everywhere God is using His power to serve us. Many times He uses His power to serve us by turning aside evil that is about to come upon us. Have you heard the story of the man who didn't believe that all things work together for good for those who love God?

MAYOR: No. We have not heard it. Speak, Yusef.

YUSEF: Once a man had some troubles and he thought God was not being good to him. He kept complaining that he loved God but all things did not work together for good for him. So one night an angel came to him. The angel said to him: "Come with me. Only you must not complain about anything I do until we are all finished. Come and do as I say. Then you will understand something about how all things work for good for those who love God." The man said, "Very well. I will come with you."

So they went off together. At the end of the first day they came to a village. They knocked at one door and asked to be let in. The owner of the house came to the door and did not open it. He shouted: "Who are you and what do you want?" The angel said, "We are strangers in the village and we want some place to sleep the night." The man said, "My house is not a flop house for tramps! Be gone!" So they went on. Down the street, they knocked on the door of another man's house. This man let them in and welcomed them and fed them a banquet. He showed them a special golden cup. It was his most treasured possession. In the morning, as they were leaving, the angel stole the golden cup. He went to the first house. He knocked on the door. The stingy man answered, "What do you want?" The angel said, "Here, take this cup as a present."

"What for?"

"It's all right. I have no need of it and I want you to have it," said the angel.

Our friend was very angry. He shouted at the angel, "Are you an angel or a devil? You take the cup of the generous man who has done everything for us. You give it to the stingy man who gave us nothing -- not even a crust of bread."

The angel answered, "You promised that you would not ask any questions until we are all finished. Now come with me."

So they traveled the second day and at evening they came to another village. The angel stopped at the house of a poor widow who lived in a small house made of cornstalks stuck in the mud. She fed them the best she could. But in the morning the angel, before they left, took out a match and threw it into the cornstalk house of the widow and it burned to the ground.

"You are a devil," cried the man.

YUSEF: "Keep silent," said the angel, "we are not finished with our journey." The end of the third day they came to a third village. They went to the house of a very Godly elder. This man had an only son. For a long time he had had no children. But now, at last, he had a son. The man entertained them royally. Yet in the morning, the angel got up early and went into the room of the sleeping son and struck him and killed him.

Our friend was so angry he could stand it no longer. He said, "You are a devil! I will go with you no longer! All you do is evil! You are a devil!" The angel said, "Wait, my friend. Now I can tell you the rest of the story. The cup the generous man had the first night was filled with poison. His enemies came that day and filled it with poison. The next time he used it he would die. God was tired of the wickedness of the evil man of the village. So God sent me to take the cup to the stingy man that he might drink the poison and die. Under the widow woman's house was a chest of gold. It was the kind of chest that would spring open only if heated. When I burned down her house, the chest under the floor sprang open. Now she will have enough for herself and for her children. With the Godly man's son, God saw into the future. He saw how the devil would enter the boy and lead him into evil ways. God saw how he would bring great shame and suffering to his father and mother and many others. So God took his life to spare him, his parents, and all those he would have harmed." Our friend was ashamed. He said, "I have questioned the goodness of God once. I will not do it again. God's wisdom is too much for me. Indeed, all things work together for good for those who love God."

MAYOR: That was a good story.

ABDU: This story is exactly right. We do not know, but God knows.

YUSEF: You see, Abdu, God uses His power to turn aside evil from us. But more than this, God can also use His power to turn the evil of man into good.

ADDU: Really! You mean God even takes our evil and turns it into good? I cannot understand this. I know He is able to do everything. But how does He do this?

YUSEF: Abdu, do you remember the story of Joseph?

ABDU: Yes, I remember it.

YUSEF: Did Joseph's brothers mean to do good to Joseph, or evil?

ABDU: No doubt they meant to do evil.

YUSEF: But did not God turn it into good?

ABDU: Indeed He did.

YUSEF: And what about Job? The devil meant to do evil to him. Yes, the devil did a lot of evil to him. But God used the evil of the devil to teach Job trust and faith and perfect surrender. This is how God uses His power to bring to us all good things. Baseat!

BASEAT: Yes, Yusef.

YUSEF: Open to Matthew 11, and read verses 2-6.

BASEAT: (Reading) "Now when John heard in prison about the deeds of Christ, he sent word by his disciples and said to him, 'Are you he who is to come, or shall we look for another?' And Jesus answered them, 'Go and tell John what you hear and see: the blind receive their sight and the lame walk, lepers are cleansed and the deaf hear, and the dead are raised up, and the poor have good news preached to them. And blessed is he who takes no offense at me.'"

YUSEF: This was what Jesus did with His power. In the wilderness, He refused to use His power to satisfy even His own desperate needs. But at the wedding feast He used His power as a servant of His love and changed the water into wine. For others He was willing to use His power to satisfy even the extras of life like wine at a wedding feast.

But all this is nothing, my friends, compared to His greatest gift. At the Cross, Christ uses His full power to win a victory for us over sin and death. The Jews said He was weak and had no power. But this great power He would not use even then for Himself. No, He chose to use it to save us. Yes, God is Most Great. Yes, God is All Powerful. But let us never forget that God uses His great power as a servant of His great love for us.

MAYOR: You have made us silent, Yusef. Indeed, How Great is our God that He uses His power in this way.

ABDU: But, Yusef, how can we use our power to show our love for God? We love God, but the only power we have is the power of our bodies. How can we use the power of our bodies to show that we love Him? How can we use the power of our bodies as the servant of our love?

YUSEF: (Shaking his head) Abdu, how many years now have you been going to the Church?

ABDU: Maybe twenty years. Why?

YUSEF: Do you still not understand these things? What does Jesus say?

ABDU: Say What? What do you mean?

YUSEF: Jesus says, "As you have done it unto the least of these, you have done it unto me."

BASEAT: You mean if we serve someone in the village, then we are serving Christ?

YUSEF: Indeed! Indeed!

ABDU: Baseat! Baseat!

BASEAT: Yes, Abdu.

ABDU: Tomorrow we must go to the field of Simaan who is sick. We must use our strength in bringing his cotton crop out of the field onto the dyke to save it from the flood. We do not go to serve Simaan, we go to serve Christ.

YUSEF: (Deeply moved) Go, my sons, and may God go with you. As you labor, remember you are laboring for Him. Good night, my friends.

ALL: Good night, O Elder Yusef.

QUESTIONS FOR DISCUSSION

1. Does every person have power? Explain.
2. What are some of the kinds of power that people have?
3. How do sinful people use these kinds of power?
4. What kinds of power did Christ have?
5. How can we see the power of God around us?
6. How can we see the power of God in the story of Joseph?
7. Tell the story of the man and the angel who came to him at night in your own words.
8. Name some of Christ's miracles. How did Christ here use His power as a servant of love?
9. How did Baseat and Abdu decide to use their power?
10. How can we, every day of our lives, use our power as a servant of love?
11. How did Christ use His power as a servant of love on the Cross?

SUMMARY OF LESSON

All men have some power. Even if we have only the power of our bodies, this is power. Sinners use their power only for themselves. God has all power. All power is given to Christ. He used it only as a servant of His great love for us.

MOTTO: God is All Powerful. But He uses His power always as a servant of His love.

3
GOD IS SO GREAT
THAT HE GRANTS US FREEDOM

SCRIPTURES TO BE READ: John 8:32-36; Galatians 5:1-2;
I Peter 2:16; Philippians 2:12-13

STATEMENT OF LESSON

We know that all is of God. But do we understand that we are created by God as free creatures? We know that God is All Powerful, but do we know that we are responsible for everything we do? God created the animals without freedom. But God created man with freedom. Both of these are proof of His power. Only a strong ruler dares grant freedom. The weak ruler cannot rule if his subjects are granted freedom. God is so mighty that He can grant men freedom and still rule. Thus often we say, "All is of God," and do nothing. Thus we blame God for our mistakes. We do this because we do not accept the freedom God offers us.

God created us because He wanted us to love and serve Him. But real love is possible only in freedom. God grants us freedom so that when we choose to love Him it will be real love. We can love others by command. We cannot get others to love us by command. God wants real love. Thus God gives us freedom. God is so great He granted man freedom. Man chose to sin. Then God in His greatness chose to win us by His love. He could have commanded our obedience, but He chose to win our obedience through an offer of love. Indeed, how great is our God.

OUTLINE

<u>GOD IS SO GREAT HE GRANTS US FREEDOM</u>

1. God created man higher than the animals.

   a. In nature God's power is seen in force.

   b. In man God's power is seen in freedom.

2. Only the weak are afraid to grant freedom

3. To deny freedom is to blame God for our mistakes.

4. God created us because He wants our love and obedience. But He wants friends who have chosen Him for themselves. He does not want the friendship of anyone who has been forced to love Him.

   a. God has the angels around Him, but they must serve Him. They have not chosen to serve Him.

   b. He wants us to choose for ourselves to love and serve Him.

   c. You cannot force someone to love you sincerely.

   d. Out of God's greatness He grants freedom of choice.

   e. Out of His greatness He wins us by His love.

THE DIALOGUE

GOD IS . . .

SCENE 3

CHARACTERS:

Yusef

Mayor

Abdu

Baseat

Siddeek

Narrator

THE DIALOGUE

NARRATOR: Yusef is seated in front of his house reading from Galatians 5.

YUSEF: (Reading) "For freedom Christ has set us free. Stand fast, therefore, and do not submit again to a yoke of slavery."

MAYOR: (Entering) Good evening, Yusef.

YUSEF: Good evening, Mayor Butrus, my good friend. How are things with you?

MAYOR: All is well. Praise God. And with you?

YUSEF: It has been a good day. Praise God.

MAYOR: Yusef, my uncle, I have a problem.

YUSEF: All will be well, if God is willing.

MAYOR: Since my father passed away, may God have mercy on him, you have become my father. I can speak only to you of my problems.

YUSEF: Your father, Butrus, was a great man. I cannot take his place, but I am proud that you can come and talk with me.

MAYOR: The problem, as you know, Yusef, is with my guard, Habib.

YUSEF: Yes, I know, Butrus. There is trouble between our house and his house. Do not tell me, for I know. There was anger between his father and your father, the former mayor. Habib, your guard, hates you because of this trouble.

MAYOR: Yes, Uncle, this is true. And I do not know what to do with him. He is obedient, but he does not love me.

MAYOR: He is very polite, but I know in his heart there is hatred.

ABDU: (Entering) Good evening, Elder Yusef. Good evening, Mr. Mayor.

YUSEF: Welcome, my friends. Are you ready again to talk of the things of God?

BASEAT: We are ready, Yusef, and we are glad that our great Mayor has again honored us this evening.

MAYOR: It is my privilege.

ABDU: Elder Yusef, what is our subject for tonight?

YUSEF: We must still talk together about the greatness of God. But tonight let us think of how God is so great that He grants us freedom of choice.

BASEAT: This is a very hard subject, Yusef.

YUSEF: But, Baseat, there is no benefit from things that are easy, so let us begin. Abdu?

ABDU: Yes, Yusef.

YUSEF: Do the animals have freedom?

ABDU: I do not know, Yusef. The horse in the pasture is free to turn any way he wishes.

YUSEF: Can the horse choose to act like some other animal?

ABDU: No, he cannot.

YUSEF: Must not the horse always act like a horse?

ABDU: Yes, he must, Yusef.

YUSEF: Baseat, if you plant date seeds along the dyke, can the date seeds come up as fig trees? Or if you plant cotton in the field, can cotton seeds choose to come up as corn?

BASEAT: No, Yusef. Of course not. These things cannot choose.

YUSEF: Correct, Baseat. The plants and the animals cannot choose. They live and grow by the command of God. In this command, we see the greatness of God. But you see, Abdu, God has created man higher than the animals. The Psalmist says, about man, "Thou hast made him a little less than the angels and dost crown Him with glory and honor." Now, my friends, one of the big differences between men and animals is that animals cannot choose for themselves, but men can choose. They can choose good, or evil. Abdu, open and read Galatians 5:1-2.

ABDU: (Reading) "Live as free men, yet without using your freedom as a pretext for evil, but live as servants of God."

MAYOR: This is right, Yusef. If we say we have no freedom, if we say we cannot choose for ourselves, then we are lowering ourselves to the level of the animal. Baseat, do you see the point?

BASEAT: Of course I see the point. The horse can go whichever way he likes and I can go whichever I like.

MAYOR: No. No, No, Baseat. This is not the point at all. Baseat, do you have a donkey?

BASEAT: Yes, Mr. Mayor, and it is a very naughty donkey.

MAYOR: Did your donkey choose to be naughty or did it just come out this way?

BASEAT: Most honorable Mayor, she is a donkey and she is naughty. It is no use. A donkey is a donkey.

MAYOR: I see you do understand, Baseat. If your donkey is naughty, it cannot change, but if a man is evil, can he change?

BASEAT: God knows all things.

YUSEF: Stay with us, O Baseat, and you will understand even this too. Now, Abdu, pay close attention. The point is the weak are <u>afraid</u> to grant freedom and the strong <u>want</u> to grant freedom.

ABDU: How, Yusef, I do not understand?

YUSEF: Do you not have a son, Abdu?

ABDU: Indeed I do.

YUSEF: His name is Khalil, is it not? And how many years old is he now?

ABDU: Let's see - about ten years.

YUSEF: Is he free to run about in the village streets, Abdu?

ABDU: Of course he is.

YUSEF: Why do you let him? Maybe a water buffalo will step on him.

ABDU: Yes, maybe this could happen.

YUSEF: Maybe he will learn bad talk. Maybe he will take his manners from the boys in the village and not from you. Maybe he will learn immorality. Maybe the wall of someone's house will fall on him. Maybe he will get into a fight and get hurt. May God move all of these things from him, but they could happen, Abdu.

ABDU: The Lord protects us all.

YUSEF: Maybe he will grow up and no longer obey you. Maybe he will bring shame upon your father's house. I have an idea, Abdu.

ABDU: What is it, Yusef?

YUSEF: I think it is better, Abdu, that you always keep Khalil in the house. All of his life you must keep him in the house. This way no harm will come to him and you will always be able to control him.

ABDU: No, Yusef. This has never happened in the village. If I did this, he would never grow up to be a man. If I did this, he would always be a child. If he is to be a man, he must be free to go and come. I am not afraid of what he will do when he becomes a man. He is a good boy. He will bring honor to his father's house.

YUSEF: Excellent, Abdu. This is the point exactly. God is our Father. He wants us to grow up to become men. To do this, He must grant us freedom. But He is so great that when He grants us freedom, He is still in control -- In your house, Abdu, your boy, Khalil, has freedom, has he not?

ABDU: Yes, he does, Yusef.

YUSEF: But still you, Abdu, are in control of your house. With God it is like this.

ABDU: (Turning to Baseat) Do not worry, Baseat. I will explain everything to you afterwards.

BASEAT: I am not worried. I just do not understand.

YUSEF: Never mind, Baseat. After awhile you will understand everything, but let us take another idea. (Turning to the Mayor) Mr. Mayor --

MAYOR: Yes, Elder Yusef.

YUSEF: You are building new rooms of stone on top of your house. Is this not true, Mr. Mayor?

MAYOR: Yes, it is true. Soon my son Magdi is to be married and I am preparing rooms for his family.

YUSEF: And what is the name of the builder?

MAYOR: His name is Siddeek. And he is from the next village. (Yusef stands up and goes over to the window. He calls to Siddeek through the windows)

YUSEF: Strength to you, Uncle Siddeek.

SIDDEEK: (Answering from the outside) All is of God, Elder Yusef.

YUSEF: Uncle Siddeek, come and talk to us for a minute.

SIDDEEK: (Again from the outside) Your command I will obey, Elder Yusef. (Siddeek enters) All is well - God willing?

YUSEF: Yes, all is well. Praise God. Sit down, friend.

SIDDEEK: No, it is impossible. I can never sit down before you and the Mayor.

MAYOR: No. No. Sit down, Siddeek. We are all one.

YUSEF: Yes, sit down, friend. There is nothing. (Siddeek with great reluctance, sits down)

YUSEF: Uncle Siddeek?

SIDDEEK: Yes, Yusef.

YUSEF: When I called to you just now and said, "Strength be upon you," what did you answer?

SIDDEEK: I answered, "All is of God," of course. What else is there to say?

YUSEF: All movement is of God. I see. Then if you make a mistake in building the Mayor's house, you are not responsible? Is this what you mean, Siddeek? If you make a mistake in building and waste the Mayor's money, are you responsible, or is God responsible?

SIDDEEK: (Somewhat confused) Do I understand these things? I am a poor man. The people say "all is of God." This is all I know.

YUSEF: Very good, Uncle Siddeek. You are a good man. Thank you very much for stopping to talk with us.

SIDDEEK: I have done nothing, but -- excuse me, I must go before my mortar dries. Good day, all of you.

ALL: Good day, Siddeek.

YUSEF: Now, Abdu!

ABDU: Yes, O Yusef.

YUSEF: Open Philippians 2 and read verses 13 and 14.

ABDU: (Opens and reads) "Therefore my beloved, as you have always obeyed, so now not only as in my presence, but also much more in my absence, work out your own salvation with fear and trembling. For God is at work in you, both to will and to work for his good pleasure."

YUSEF: Now, Abdu, Paul says, "Complete your own salvation." This means it is up to you. Is this not true, Abdu?

ABDU: It seems to be true, Yusef.

YUSEF: Then he says, God is at work in you. You see, Abdu, God works and we work. Abdu, do you know Elder Latif?

ABDU: Yes, all of us know Elder Latif.

YUSEF: How did Elder Latif begin twenty years ago?

ABDU: He began as a camel driver, and a very poor man.

YUSEF: Is he still a camel driver?

ABDU: No. No indeed, he now owns twenty acres of land.

YUSEF: Very well. Whenever anyone asks him to do anything, what does he answer?

ABDU: I never noticed, Yusef.

YUSEF: He answers, "Rely on God and rely on me." And this is the right answer. When someone says to you, "Strength upon you," you should answer, "All is of God and all is of me."

ABDU: But how can this be true?

YUSEF: We do not understand how this can be true, we only know that it is true. Sunday morning when I go to invite people to Church, I say to them, "Come to Church this morning." They answer, "If God wills." But you see Abdu, they are using God for an excuse for laziness. They are lazy and do not want to move. They do not intend to go. They are ashamed to say this, so they say, "I will go if God wills it." But they are blaming God for their laziness. We can find out God's will only when we move. We cannot find out God's will when we only sit and do nothing. If you made a mistake, Abdu, then blamed me, would not it be a great shame?

ABDU: Yes, it would be a great shame indeed.

YUSEF: Well, what if you make a mistake and then blame God? Would this not be a greater shame?

ABDU: It would be a terrible shame indeed.

YUSEF: But you see, my friends, many times we do this. We say, "If God wills," and do nothing to find out what God's will really is. We are blaming Him for our mistakes. We say, "All is of God." We must also say, "All is of us." These are like light and heat. They are always together. If there is light there is heat. They are two things, but they are not separate. Abdu, when you light a village lamp to see your way in the house at night, do you understand how light and heat are together?

ABDU: No, Yusef, I do not understand these things.

YUSEF: But they are together, are they not?

ABDU: Yes, indeed they are.

YUSEF: Even so, Abdu, we cannot understand how it can be true that all is of God and all is of us, but it is true and the two are together and cannot be divided.

YUSEF: But I have another question. Why did God create us? What does He want from us that He does not have from the angels? If He wants friends and servants, He has the angels. What does He want from us that they cannot give?

BASEAT: Maybe there aren't enough angels and He wants more!

ABDU: O come on now, Baseat, don't be stupid! He wants us to love Him and serve Him maybe?

YUSEF: Indeed He does, but do not the angels love Him and serve Him?

ABDU: True, they do.

MAYOR: Ah, my friends, but the angels have no choice. They did not <u>choose</u> to serve Him out of freedom, they had no choice. God must want from us that we love and serve Him from ourselves. Not because we have to but because we want to.

YUSEF: Exactly right, Mr. Mayor. I will tell you a story. Once there was a village called the Hamlet of Ignorance.

BASEAT: (Clapping his hands in delight) Very good.

YUSEF: (Continuing) And in this village one of the men of the village was angry with the Mayor. The Mayor was building a wall around his garden and this man came and asked if he could have the new-made bricks of the Mayor to complete the second story of his house. Of course, it was not good that this man should ask such a thing of the Mayor. The mayor said "No." The man was angry and stayed angry for a long time. The Mayor tried to make a reconciliation with him, but it was no use. Then one day the Mayor was thinking. He said to himself, "I am the Mayor! I have power in this village. It is not right that anyone in the village should not like the Mayor. I must use my power to solve this problem. I know what I will do. I will give an order that everyone in the village must love the mayor. I will order them to love me and everything will be well." So the Mayor gave the order. The people did not know what to do at first. They talked together for many hours. Many nights they sat together trying to decide what to do. In the end, they all knew there was only one thing to do. They must please the Mayor. So from then on, every time the Mayor passed in the streets, the people shouted, "Here comes our beloved Mayor. Here comes the great man. Mr. Mayor, you have taken away our loneliness. You have given the air a pleasant smell with your presence. All was darkness, but now that you have come, all is light. In your person Christ has visited us." For a while the Mayor was very pleased, but he

YUSEF: found he still was not happy. He went on like this for some time. Then one cold day he thought he would sit out in the sun to get warm. He put on his cloak and put it up over his head to keep out the wind and sat outside his house. As he sat there a small boy came up and began to talk to him. The small boy was too young to know how to be polite. Also he did not recognize the Mayor because the Mayor's head was covered and he did not see his face. Finally the small boy said very plainly, "Mister, why do all the people in the village hate the Mayor?" The Mayor was shocked, stunned. He thought for a while and finally said, "But my son, all the people have been commanded to love the Mayor and everywhere he goes they say nice things about him."

The boy said, "Yes, but they all hate him just the same. Why?"

The Mayor said, "Do you see that man sleeping over there in the sun? Run over and wake him up and ask him the same question. But do not say who sent you. Come back and tell me what he says and I will give you a coin."

The boy ran over across the open space in front of the Mayor's house and woke the man up and asked him, "Mister, why do all the people in the village hate the Mayor?"

The man was angry to be awakened and tried to dismiss the boy by shouting at him. When the boy kept poking him and persisting, he finally said gruffly, "We hate him because he has ordered us to love him and love is not by command -- now leave me alone."

The boy went back and told the Mayor. Then the Mayor gave him a coin and said, "I see then that this village is not a Village of Ignorance, but it has a Mayor of Ignorance." And so by the plainness and sincerity of a little boy, the mayor learned a great truth.

ABDU: This is a good story, Yusef.

YUSEF: Indeed, Abdu, love is not by command, but there is something there we must understand. Jesus says: "A new commandment I give you that you love one another." If love is not by command, why does Jesus command us to love one another?

ABDU: (Slowly) I am not sure.

MAYOR: Ah, this is different, Abdu.

ABDU: How do you mean - different? Mr. Mayor?

MAYOR: By command from Jesus I can love. I have been commanded to love you. Even if I do not want to love you I can love you by command. But by command I cannot get you to love me. This is the difference.

YUSEF: Exactly right, Mayor. You have understood the point exactly. God loves us and He commands us to love others. But by command we cannot get others to love us. By command, even God cannot get us to love Him, so He must give us freedom. If we do not have freedom to choose to love Him from ourselves, then our love will be empty. So God gave men freedom to choose to love and serve Him, or to hate and disobey Him. Then what did men choose?

MAYOR: Men chose to hate and disobey.

YUSEF: Now what can God do? He gives man freedom to choose to obey or to disobey. Man disobeyed. Can He use His power to force us to obey?

ABDU: He can if He wishes.

YUSEF: But is this the way He chooses?

(All are silent. They are confused. After a brief pause Yusef continues)

Don't you see it, my friends? God uses His great power in love to redeem us. He comes Himself to win us back to Himself by suffering for us in the Cross of our Saviour Jesus Christ. O how great a God we worship that in His power He was willing to come in humility and redeem. But we must talk more of this again.

MAYOR: Yes, indeed we have delayed long enough. We must go.

ABDU AND
BASEAT: Yes indeed. Good night, Yusef.

YUSEF: Good night, my friends.

(Exit Baseat and Abdu - the Mayor remains for a while)

MAYOR: I am beginning to see what I must do with my guard Habib. This is very hard, Yusef.

YUSEF: Did anyone ever say it would be easy?

MAYOR: No.

YUSEF: Yes, it is a hard way, but it is the only way. Think on these things, Butrus, and we will talk further. Good night.

MAYOR: Good night, Uncle.

QUESTIONS FOR DISCUSSION

1. Go back and pick out some of the questions from lessons one and two and ask them for review.
2. What is one of the differences between man and the animals?
3. Is nature free or is nature not free? Explain?
4. Why is Yusef telling Abdu to keep his son at home?
5. What has freedom to do with strength and weakness?
6. All of us say "All is of God." Is there anything wrong with this? If so, what?
7. How can a man blame God for his mistakes? Do we do this? Think of illustrations.
8. Is love by command or not? What kind of love is by command? What kind of love is not by command?
9. Tell the story of the Mayor of the Hamlet of Ignorance. What is the point of the story?
10. Why does God grant us freedom?
11. What happened when He did? After God granted freedom to men, how did He use His power?

SUMMARY OF LESSON

God is so great, He gives us freedom.
God wants us to truly love and serve Him.
So He gives us freedom.

MOTTO: All is of God and all is of me.

4
GOD IS SO GREAT THAT HE COMES IN HUMILITY TO REDEEM: PART 1

SCRIPTURES TO BE READ: Matthew 18:1-4; Matthew 23:1-12; John 13:3-4; Philippians 2:6-11

STATEMENT OF LESSON

In this lesson we will try to understand that God is so great that He comes to man to redeem man. Some think that if God becomes a man, God is very small and very weak. But this is not true. In this lesson, we will try to see how great God is. God is so great He redeems man in Christ. If we wish to see how strong a man is, we must give him something very heavy to lift. So with God. The hardest thing God has done is proof of how great He is. The hardest thing God has done is to redeem man on the Cross of Jesus Christ. God has given man law. Man disobeyed these laws. So God, because He is great, must do something. He can if He wishes, punish men and be finished. This is the easy way, the way of the weak. Or God can try to win them back. This is the hard way, the way of the strong. This is the way of the great, the way God chose. But this is so hard a task, God must do it Himself. He cannot do it by command or by force. He can only do it by love. So God comes in Christ to men. Right away, the devil tries to get Christ to choose the way of the weak. The devil says to Christ, "Give the people something, and they will follow you. Pay them and they will follow you." Christ knows this is the way of the weak and He refuses. Then the devil tries to get Christ to give a great sign and win all the people to follow Him. Christ refuses. Christ knows this is the way of the weak. Then the devil tries to get Christ to seize political power. Christ refuses. He knows this is the way of the weak. Christ chose the way of the strong, the way of true greatness. This is the way of self-emptying, the way of service. This is the way of choosing to suffer in order to redeem. So we see God is so great that He comes to redeem.

OUTLINE

GOD IS SO GREAT THAT HE COMES IN HUMILITY TO REDEEM

1. A strong man proves that he is very strong by lifting something very heavy.

2. We understand the greatness of God by looking at the hardest thing He has done.

3. What is the hardest thing God has done?

    a. Creation of the earth? No!

    b. Creation of man? No!

    c. Redemption of men on cross? Yes!

4. The King gives an order and the people disobey. He must do something or he is weak.

    a. He can punish, but this is the easy way, the way of the weak.

    b. He can win back. This is the way of the strong, the way of the great.

5. How does the strong King win back allegiance? This cannot be done by force. This cannot be done by command. It is so difficult, he must do it Himself.

    a. The devil showed Christ three ways to win people to follow him.

        (1) Give them something material. Christ says, "No, this is the way of the weak."

        (2) Show them a great sign so that they will know you are from God; then they will have to follow you. They will have to believe and accept you. Christ says: "No, this is the way of the weak."

        (3) Use earthly power. Seize political power, then men will have to follow you. Christ says: "No, this is the way of the weak."

    (The subject is continued in the next lesson)

THE DIALOGUE

GOD IS . . .

SCENE 4

CHARACTERS:

Yusef

The Mayor

Baseat

Abdu

Subhi, the Peasant

Narrator

THE DIALOGUE

Yusef and the Mayor are seated in Yusef's sitting room.

MAYOR: It is a good idea that we sit inside here today, Yusef. The wind is very strong outside.

YUSEF: I thought it would be better inside.

MAYOR: But, Yusef, why did you ask Abdu and Baseat last night to bring Subhi with them tonight?

YUSEF: I have heard that Subhi is physically a very strong man. He is, isn't he?

MAYOR: Yes indeed. He is the strongest man in the village, but why do you want him to come here tonight?

YUSEF: Patience is beautiful, Mayor.

MAYOR: (Laughing) Very well, Yusef. I will wait. But I will not have to wait long, for I hear the voices of our friends coming down the street.

Enter Abdu, Baseat and Subhi, the peasant.

ALL: Good evening. Welcome. You have honored us. How are things today? Praise God. (Finally, they all sit down.)

SUBHI: Abdu came to me today, Mr. Mayor. He said you wanted to see me. I was very busy. If anyone else had asked me to come, I would have said "no." But I said to myself, "If Elder Yusef wants me, then I will go -- I must go." It is a great honor to be asked to go to the house of Elder Yusef.

YUSEF: Thank you, Subhi. We have been a great burden to you.

SUBHI: The burden you put upon me, Yusef, is a pleasure. Only say your request.

41

YUSEF: I hear, Subhi, that you are a very strong man.

SUBHI: Indeed, I am, Yusef.

YUSEF: I hear that you are the strongest man in the village.

SUBHI: That's true too.

YUSEF: Very well. I wish to prove your strength tonight.

SUBHI: Give me something to lift. I am so strong I am able to carry even a whole mountain!

YUSEF: Very well, Subhi, here is a piece of paper. See if you can lift this piece of paper.

SUBHI: (Subhi stands up and takes the sheet of paper very slowly. Unbelievingly he looks around the circle and turns to the Elder and says...)

What is this, Yusef? Is this a game of children? If you want proof of my strength, you must give me something heavy.

YUSEF: Very well, Subhi, here is a book.

SUBHI: (Complaining) This is ridiculous, Yusef. If you wish proof of my strength, you must give me something heavy.

YUSEF: Very well, see if you can lift that chair.

SUBHI: A small boy can lift that chair. Give me something heavy.

YUSEF: Very well, pick up this couch on which I am sitting.

SUBHI: My goodness! Baseat here can pick up that couch, and he is Baseat in his body and in his mind.

YUSEF: (Reprimanding) Now - Subhi. Baseat is a very good fellow. He is learning many good things about God. Already he probably knows more about God than you. But I see you want something heavy. Very well, in the courtyard of my house, behind us here, there is a wagon. And on top of the wagon there is a threshing sledge. Abdu, you and Baseat go with Subhi. Go and see if he can pick up the heavy end of the wagon, where the threshing sledge is laid.

(Baseat, Abdu, and Subhi go out)

MAYOR: Do you think he can lift it, Yusef?

YUSEF: I think he can. Let us listen.

ABDU: Strength on you, Subhi.

(Voices from outside the room)

SUBHI: All is of God.

BASEAT: No, Subhi, do not say "All is of God," say, "All is of God and all is of me."

SUBHI: Say it yourself, if you are so smart.

(Sounds of great grunting, shouting and cheering. Finally loud clapping and congratulations all around for Subhi who has lifted the wagon. They all return to the room)

ABDU: (In great excitement) He lifted it! He lifted it, Yusef!

BASEAT: Yes indeed, he lifted it.

YUSEF AND MAYOR: Congratulations, Subhi. You are a very strong man.

SUBHI: It was nothing. Did I not tell you I was able to carry a whole mountain?

YUSEF: Indeed, you are a very strong man. Now, sit down, all of you, and let us think of God. I have a question. What is the hardest thing God has done?

ABDU: Why do you ask, Yusef?

YUSEF: You see, Abdu, Subhi proved that he was very strong by lifting something very heavy. So if we would understand the greatness of God, we must look at the hardest thing that He has done. The hardest thing He has done is proof of how great He is.

ABDU: Yes, I am with you, Elder. This makes sense.

YUSEF: Very well. Now what is the hardest thing that God has done?

ABDU: Creation of the heavens and the earth.

MAYOR: No, Abdu, the Psalmist says this is the work of His fingers. This is so easy, He did not need His hands and His arms. He needed only His fingers. I think the creation of man in His own image must have been much harder. Is it not so, Yusef?

YUSEF: Yes, this was harder, Mayor, but God has done something much harder than this. What do you think it is?

ABDU: I . . ah . . . I don't know, Yusef.

BASEAT: If Abdu doesn't know, of course I don't know either. But Subhi here is a very clever fellow. You tell him, Subhi.

SUBHI: (Fumbling) This is indeed a hard question, Yusef. I do not know the answer.

YUSEF: The hardest thing that God has ever done, my friends, was the redemption of man on the Cross. <u>This</u> is proof of His greatness.

ABDU: How is this true, Yusef?

YUSEF: I will explain it to you, my friends. Subhi?

SUBHI: Yes, Yusef.

YUSEF: If our honorable Mayor here gives a command, and if the people in the village do not obey, must he not do something about it?

SUBHI: Yes, indeed he must. He must act.

YUSEF: Correct. If he does nothing, then he is weak. Abdu, do you remember Daniel in the Old Testament?

ABDU: Yes, indeed I do, Yusef.

YUSEF: What did Nebuchadnezzer, the King, say to Daniel?

ABDU: He told him that he and his friends must worship the image that the King had set up.

YUSEF: And when Daniel disobeyed, did the King Nebuchadnezzer say, "Never mind, it doesn't matter." Did he do nothing?

ABDU: No, indeed. He must act. He must do something or he is weak.

YUSEF: Suppose you are in the fields, Abdu. Suppose the mother of Khaleel is baking. You know she cannot bring your lunch to you. You send Khaleel to get the bread and cheese. Then he runs off to play and does not bring your lunch. He does not obey you. Do you let it go? Do you say, "Never mind." Or must you do something about it?

ABDU: Of course, I cannot leave the matter. I must do something. If I do nothing, then Khaleel will think I am weak. He will not respect me.

YUSEF: What is the easiest thing to do with him, Abdu?

ABDU: The easiest thing, Yusef, is to beat him.

YUSEF: That's right, Abdu. It is the easiest thing. And excuse me for saying this. Because it is easy, it is not the way of the great. Of course with children, sometimes it is the only way. Even so Nebuchadnezzer the King decided that he must punish Daniel. But there is a better way, my friends. This better way is the way of the strong -- the great.

MAYOR: What is it, Yusef?

YUSEF: You give an order to your guards, Mayor, and one of them disobeys. Does he not have a reason?

MAYOR: Indeed he does, Yusef.

YUSEF: Does he not think it is a good reason, even if it is a bad reason?

MAYOR: Indeed he does, Yusef.

YUSEF: Is it easier then, to punish him and make him fear and hate you, or is it easier to win him back so that he will love and respect you?

MAYOR: It is much, much easier to punish him than to try to win his love.

YUSEF: Exactly right, Mayor. This is the hard way. When the people of a great king are disobedient, the great king tries to win them back. A weak king can only punish them. To win them back is much harder than to punish them. This is very hard and it cannot be done by force or command. It is so hard the king must do it himself. Isn't that right, Mayor?

MAYOR: Yes indeed, Yusef.

YUSEF: (Very emphatic) You see, my friends, this is the way God chose. God gave us laws. Many disobeyed the laws. God, because He is great, must do something. He can punish us and be finished. But He chose to try to win us back. This is so hard, He must do it Himself. So God came in Christ to win us back to Himself.

ABDU: I am just beginning to understand, Yusef.

YUSEF: You see, my friends, as soon as Christ began His ministry, the devil tried to get Him to use the way of the weak.

MAYOR: How is this, Yusef?

YUSEF: Think of how the devil tried to tempt Christ in the wilderness. Think. What was the first temptation?

BASEAT: I think it was to turn stones into bread, Yusef.

YUSEF: Very good, Baseat. Very good indeed! But pay close attention to what the devil is really saying to Jesus. "Give the people something, and they will follow you." The devil says to Jesus, "You want the people to follow you. Give them bread and they will follow you. They will not follow you for nothing. If you want friends, you must give them something. Then they will be your friends." Is this not true with many people, Abdu?

ABDU: Many, many people are this way. Give them something, they will be your friend. If you do not give them anything, they will not be your friend.

YUSEF: Ah, but Jesus will not choose this way. This is the way of the weak. Next the devil says to Him, "Show the people a great sign. Do something very marvelous. Jump down from the temple. They will know that only God can do this and not be hurt. Then they must follow you. The people will ask you for a sign. Give them a great sign and they will all follow you. This is the way you must choose," says the devil. And what does Jesus answer to this, Subhi?

SUBHI: He said, "No."

YUSEF: Why?

SUBHI: I don't know.

YUSEF: The reason is clear, Subhi. If Jesus wins people by great miracles, many will follow Him.

SUBHI: Many, indeed.

YUSEF: But Subhi, if Jesus does this, people will follow Him because they have seen a great sign. They will say to themselves, "This Man must be from God. Only God could do these things." They will be convinced in their minds that this is from God. They will follow Him. But will they be changed within themselves.

SUBHI: I don't understand.

YUSEF: That is -- in their hearts will they be changed?

SUBHI: (Thinking) I do not think so, Yusef.

YUSEF: You are right, Subhi. Selfish men will still be selfish. Proud men will still be proud. A hypocrite will still be a hypocrite and the envious man and the adulterer will still be just the same. They will be following Jesus, but they will be just the same as they were before. They will not be changed in their hearts. Mr. Mayor, why did Jesus not appear to the Jews after the resurrection? That is, the Jews that killed him . . . ?

MAYOR: I have always wondered this question myself. Why not?

YUSEF: For this same reason. Suppose he had appeared to them after the crucifixion. They knew that they had killed Him. If they saw Him alive, they would have to accept Him. They would accept Him against their wills. They would accept Him and they would still be just as proud, selfish, and self-righteous. Jesus wants men to follow Him, but He does not want men to follow Him in this way. This is the way of the weak. Jesus is too strong to choose this way. Abdu, then what did the devil do?

ABDU: He took Jesus on a high mountain and offered Him the kingdoms of the world. He asked only that Jesus serve him, the devil.

YUSEF: Did Jesus agree?

ABDU: No, of course not.

YUSEF: What does the devil mean when he asks Christ to serve him?

ABDU: I do not know, Yusef. Explain it to us.

YUSEF: It is very simple. All he means is that he wants Jesus to use the way of the power of the earth, that is, the power of men. He says to Jesus, "You must become a political power. If you are the head of a great government, the people will have to follow and serve you."

ABDU: But is this not true?

YUSEF: Yes, it is true. If Jesus had done this, the people would have had to have served Him. But they would serve Him and they would not be changed. Do you remember the last night when Jesus was with Judas in the Upper Room?

MAYOR: Yes, we remember the night and the story.

YUSEF: Very well. Did Jesus know that Judas would betray Him?

BASEAT: Of course.

YUSEF: Were the disciples armed?

MAYOR: Yes, we know that Peter at least had a sword.

YUSEF: Now, what if Jesus had said to Peter, "This man will betray us. Do with him as you wish." What would Peter have done?

MAYOR: He would have drawn his sword and killed him straight away.

YUSEF: Then Jesus could very easily have slipped out of the city at night. He could have fled away into Galilee. He could have raised a great army. All the people were with Him.

ABDU: Yes indeed they were. Did they not sing "Hosanna! Hosanna!" as He entered Jerusalem on the day of Triumphal Entry?

YUSEF: Yes indeed. So we see that even at the very last Jesus would not choose the way of earthly power. This is the easy, weak way. Jesus chose the great, strong way.

ABDU: (Thinking) I used to think this was the way of the strong because it is the way that many use. But now I see it is the easy way. The easy way is the way of the weak.

YUSEF: Exactly right, Abdu. You understand very well indeed.

ABDU: But, Yusef, if Christ refuses this way, what way can He choose? He will not give the people something so they will follow Him. He will not show them a sign so that they will accept Him and follow Him. He will not seize power, power of the earth, to get men to follow Him. What way is there left? If these are the ways

47

ABDU: of the weak, what are the ways of the strong? What is the way of true greatness?

YUSEF: (Very slowly) The way of true greatness, my friends, is clear. Christ chooses to win us back to Himself by humility and self-emptying. Christ redeems us through suffering. This is the way of true greatness. But this is a big subject, my friends. It is late. We cannot finish it tonight. We must take this subject tomorrow.

MAYOR: It is true, Yusef, and besides we already have enough to think about. The greatest thing God has done is the hardest thing that He has done, and the hardest thing He has done is to come in Christ to redeem us. <u>This</u> is the sign of His greatness. We never thought of it this way.

YUSEF: As we turn to sleep tonight, let us think of this great God. Goodnight, my friends. You have honored us.

ALL: Goodnight, Yusef: May God honor your ways.

QUESTIONS FOR DISCUSSION

1. What must the strong man do to prove that he is strong?
2. God is great. Do we understand this by looking at the easy things that He has done, or at the hard things that He has done? Why?
3. Was the creation of the heavens and the earth very hard for God?
4. Was the creation of man very hard for God?
5. Was the redemption of man on the cross the hardest thing that God has ever done? If this is true, how is it true?
6. If a king makes a law and the people disobey, what must the king do? What does a weak king do? What does a strong king do?
7. If God wishes to win man back to Himself, why must He come and do it Himself?
8. The devil tries to get Christ to use the ways of the weak to win men. How is the first temptation the way of the weak?
9. How is the second temptation the way of the weak?
10. How is the third temptation the way of the weak?
11. Say in your own words the important point of the lesson.

SUMMARY OF LESSON

God is so great He chooses to redeem. We see how really great God is by looking at the hardest thing He has done. Man has disobeyed. God must act. To punish is the answer of the weak. To redeem is the answer of the strong. God is great. Thus He chooses to redeem.

MOTTO: A truly great God redeems.

5
GOD IS SO GREAT THAT HE COMES IN HUMILITY TO REDEEM: PART 2

SCRIPTURES TO BE READ: Proverbs 18:12; Proverbs 15:33;
                         Matthew 18:1-4; Matthew 23:11-12;
                         John 3:3-4; Philippians 2:6-11

STATEMENT OF LESSON

Lesson four and Lesson five are one subject. In Lesson four, we understand how really great God is by looking at the hardest thing He has done. Creation was easy for God. Redemption of man was very hard. God gave man rules. Man disobeyed those rules. God had to do something or He would be weak. He could punish man or try to win man back. God chose to try and win us back. But this was so hard, He had to do it Himself. He had to come in Christ to save us. The devil tried to get Christ to win men by using the ways of the weak. But Christ would not. This lesson we will see the way Christ chose, even the way of the strong, the way of true greatness. Christ's disciples could not understand. They thought true greatness was in being lifted up, but Jesus said true greatness is in humility and self-emptying. The disciples said true greatness was in being served, but Jesus said true greatness is in serving. The disciples said that Christ is so great that He cannot suffer, but Christ said that Christ is so great that He must suffer in order to redeem. God is so great He comes in humility to redeem.

OUTLINE

<u>GOD IS SO GREAT THAT HE COMES IN HUMILITY TO REDEEM</u>
Christ chose the way of true greatness

1. True greatness is in humility and self-emptying
    a. The disciples say, "Greatness is in being lifted up."
    b. Christ says, "Greatness is in humility and self-emptying."
2. True greatness is in service
    a. The disciples say, "Greatness is in being served."
    b. Christ says, "Greatness is in serving."
3. True greatness is in choosing to suffer in order to redeem
    a. The disciples say that Christ is so great that He cannot suffer.
    b. Christ says, "The Christ is so great that He must suffer in order to redeem."

THE DIALOGUE
GOD IS . . .
SCENE 5

CHARACTERS:

Yusef

Abdu

Baseat

Mayor Butrus

(Abdu, Yusef and Baseat are seated in Yusef's front room. Yusef is reading from Matthew 18.)

THE DIALOGUE

YUSEF: "At that time the disciples came to Jesus, saying 'Who is the greatest in the kingdom of heaven?' And He called to Him a child and put Him in the midst of them and said, 'Truly I say unto you, unless you become like children, you will never enter the kingdom of heaven. Whoever humbles himself like this child, he is the greatest in the kingdom of heaven.'"

MAYOR: Good evening, my friends.

ALL: Good evening, Mr. Mayor.

MAYOR: Yusef, I have been waiting all day to come and sit with you. The subject last night was wonderful. I yearn to hear the end of the subject tonight.

YUSEF: I hope you will not be disappointed, Mayor Butrus.

MAYOR: I am not afraid, Yusef. Let us begin. Last night we learned that the way of punishment is the easy way and that the way of redemption is the hard way, but yet it is the great way.

ABDU: Explain to us, Yusef, the way of true greatness.

YUSEF: The way of true greatness, my friends, is very simple. It is the way of humility, the way of service, and the way of suffering which redeems.

ABDU: But how is this greatness?

YUSEF: I will tell you. Abdu, open and read from Proverbs 18:12.

ABDU: (Opens and reads) "Before destruction a man's heart is haughty. But humility goes before honor."

YUSEF: Very well, Abdu. Now read Proberbs 15:33.

ABDU: (Reading) "The fear of the Lord is instruction and wisdom, and humility goes before honor."

YUSEF: So you see, my friend, humility goes before honor, but humility also goes before greatness. Baseat, read Matthew 18:4.

BASEAT: (Reading) "Whoever humbles himself like this child, he is the greatest in the kingdom of heaven."

YUSEF: You see, my friends, Solomon says the <u>honorable</u> man is the humble man, and Jesus says the <u>great</u> man is the humble man. Mr. Mayor.

MAYOR: Yes, Yusef.

YUSEF: You have read some history, have you not?

MAYOR: (Unduly modest) Some, not too much.

YUSEF: Who was greater, Mr. Mayor, Abraham Lincoln or Fat Boy Faruk?

MAYOR: Abraham Lincoln was much, much greater than Fat Boy Faruk.

YUSEF: Why, Mayor?

MAYOR: It is very clear, Yusef. Fat Boy Faruk had nothing to do with the people. He built big palaces for himself. He did not serve the people. He made himself great, rich, and high. He did not even learn good Arabic. He did not care about the people. Therefore, he was not great.

YUSEF: So what was great about Lincoln?

MAYOR: He was very different, O Yusef. He mixed with the people. He helped the people. He served the people. He spoke with the people. He worked with the people. Indeed he suffered for the people. He freed the slaves. He was a very great man.

YUSEF: Baseat!

BASEAT: Yes, Yusef.

YUSEF: Pay close attention, Baseat. You must understand this point. Who is the greater king, Baseat? The king who sits in his palace and has nothing to do with the people, or the king who comes in humility to serve the people?

BASEAT: In any case, the one who comes in humility must be greater.

YUSEF: Exactly right, Baseat. But do the disciples like this idea?

BASEAT: Do I know what the disciples liked?

YUSEF: Abdu. What about you?

ABDU: I'm not sure, Yusef.

YUSEF: They thought greatness was in being honored. Don't you remember? They were always arguing about who was the greatest. They thought Jesus was going to set up a great earthly kingdom so they argued. This one wanted to be prime minister. That one wanted to be minister of foreign affairs. This one wanted to be minister of interior.

ABDU: You mean they thought they would get very high positions?

YUSEF: So it seems. They argued many times about it. But Jesus says, "The first shall be last, and the last shall be first." Mr. Mayor!

MAYOR: Yes, Yusef.

YUSEF: Be kind enough to read Matthew 23:11-12 for us.

MAYOR: (Reading) "He who is greatest among you shall be your servant. Whoever exalts himself shall be humbled, and whoever humbles himself shall be exalted."

YUSEF: The disciples didn't like this either. They thought if they joined Jesus and Jesus began a great kingdom, then people would serve them. But what does Jesus say, Abdu?

ABDU: He says the greatest shall be a servant.

YUSEF: An important man has a servant to serve him at meals, doesn't he, Baseat?

BASEAT: Of course, Yusef.

YUSEF: Very well, Baseat. Who is greater, the man who sits at the table or the waiter, who serves him?

BASEAT: The man who sits at the table, of course.

YUSEF: You are sure, Baseat?

BASEAT: Of course I'm sure.

YUSEF: Very well, Baseat. Open your Bible and read Luke 22: 24-27.

BASEAT: (Reading) "A dispute also arose among them, which of them was to be regarded as the greatest. And He said to them, 'The kings of the Gentiles exercise lordship over them, and those in authority over them are called benefactors.'" (By this time, Baseat has done such a poor job in reading that Abdu takes over.)

ABDU: Never mind Baseat, I'll finish! (Reading) "But not so with you. Rather let the greatest among you become as the youngest, and the leader as one who serves. For which is the greater, the one who sits at table, or

ABDU: the one who serves? Is it not the one who sits at table? But I am among you as one who serves."

YUSEF: Never mind, Baseat, don't get upset. You read very well. But you see, my friends, we think like the disciples. We do not think like Christ. Jesus says to his disciples, "You think the man who sits at table is the greater, but I am among you as a waiter." You heard about Louis XIV of France?

MAYOR: I've heard of him, but speak on, Yusef.

YUSEF: He was king of France a long time ago. He was very rich. Many, many people served him. He lived in a great palace. He even had great princes who worked as servants in his house. But he cared nothing for the people. They say once the people ran out of bread. They came to him and said, "The people have no bread." He answered, "Give them cake." Of course there was no cake either. He thought he was a very great man. But now we judge him as a very small man, because he did not serve his people. But I once read another story, about Abraham Lincoln.

MAYOR: Tell it to us.

YUSEF: It seems once Abraham Lincoln, when he was President of America, was riding in his special coach outside Washington. He was riding just to relax and enjoy the countryside. As they were riding along, he saw a mud hole at the side of the road. In the mud hole there was a pig that was stuck. Mr. Lincoln called to the carriage driver and said, "Stop!" The carriage driver said, "Why stop here? There is nothing to stop for!" Mr. Lincoln said, "No, we must stop here." Mr. Lincoln got out. He took off his coat and shoes. He rolled up his pants, and started walking into the mud hole. The driver called to him, "No, no, Mr. Lincoln! This is not right for you to do this. This is terrible, Mr. Lincoln." Mr. Lincoln walked into the mud hole, pulled the pig out and set the pig free on its way. He was very humble. He was ready to serve the smallest person in his country. Very well, Abdu, who was greater, Mr. Lincoln or Louis XIV of France?

ABDU: This is a very strange story, Yusef. Mr. Lincoln must have been a very great man. Indeed he was much greater than the King of France.

YUSEF: And what did Jesus do to the disciples the night of the Last Supper?

MAYOR: He washed their feet, Yusef.

YUSEF: Yes, Mayor, but what does He say? What does John say about it? Open, Abdu, and read John 13:3-4.

ABDU: (Reading) "Jesus, knowing that the Father had given all things into his hands, and that he had come from God and was going to God . . . "

YUSEF: (Stopping him) Abdu, after an introduction like this, what do you expect Jesus to do?

ABDU: We expect Him to do something great.

YUSEF: Exactly right. Jesus knows He has all power in His hands. He knows that He has come from God and is going to God. We expect Him to declare a great kingdom. We expect Him to launch a great movement, or step up and sit on a great throne.

MAYOR: Or perhaps to declare victory over His enemies.

YUSEF: Right! But what does He do, Abdu?

ABDU: He washes their feet.

YUSEF: Do you see, Abdu? Do you see? Greatness is in service.

ABDU: I am beginning to understand just a little.

YUSEF: But this is not all, my friend. God is even greater than this. He is so great He chooses to suffer in order to save.

BASEAT: This is a very hard idea, Yusef. How can this be?

YUSEF: I will explain it to you, Baseat. I think you have a camel, don't you?

BASEAT: Yes, Yusef. I have a camel.

YUSEF: Now suppose your camel goes mad and tramples you under its feet. Then suppose Subhi, the strongman, chooses to step in to save you from the mad camel. If he did this, he might get hurt.

BASEAT: He would get hurt for sure. My donkey is naughty but my camel is a beast. My camel is mean even when he feels good. I'm afraid to think what he would be like if he were mad.

YUSEF: Very well, Baseat. Supposing Subhi were badly hurt trying to save you from the camel. Would this be a sign that he was weak because he chose to save you and got hurt?

BASEAT: No, this would be a sign that he was very strong -- very great.

YUSEF: Now, Abdu, supposing Khaleel, your son, falls into a well. Then you jump down into the well to save your son. Your son is saved, but part of the well falls in upon you and your foot is crushed. So you are badly hurt, saving your son from the well. You yourself,

YUSEF: chose to save him. You got hurt. Would this be a sign that you are weak?

ABDU: Oh, Yusef. This would be a sign of greatness.

YUSEF: Very well, my friends, now what about Jesus? Sin is like a great, fierce, wild male camel. This camel has trampled men under its feet. Jesus chooses Himself to save us. He saves us from the wild camel which is sin. The camel is so strong and so wild that only Jesus can save us. He saves us, but the camel hurts Him very badly. Is this a sign of His weakness or of His greatness, Mr. Mayor?

MAYOR: Indeed, (Very thoughtfully) indeed, if He chooses to suffer for us, to save us, this is a sign that He is the greatest of the great.

YUSEF: Exactly right, Mayor. But you see, my friends, the disciples could not accept this. They thought Jesus must win the way the world wins. When Jesus told them that He must suffer, what did Peter answer, Mayor?

MAYOR: He said, "Be it far from thee, O Lord."

YUSEF: Right, Mayor, they thought it was impossible! -- impossible! -- that this should happen. But Jesus knew you cannot redeem unless you suffer. After the resurrection, Jesus talked to men on the way to Emmaus. Open, Abdu, to Luke 24:25 and see what Jesus says to them.

ABDU: (Reading) "And he said to them, 'O foolish men and slow of heart to believe all that the prophets have spoken. Was it not necessary that the Christ should suffer all these things and enter into His glory?'"

YUSEF: The important thing, my friends, is that if Jesus Himself chose to do this, then this is a sign of His strength, of His greatness. No one made Him go to Jerusalem. But He chose to go.

ABDU: Your thoughts run very deep, O Yusef.

YUSEF: We worship a God who is very great, Abdu. Tonight my friends, we have entered a subject that is so great and marvelous that we can understand only a little of it. We have spoken of the suffering of Christ, and I am not able to speak more. But before you go, Abdu, read to us Philippians 2:5-11. Let us return to our homes tonight, thinking about our great God who out of His greatness has come to us in humility to serve and to save. Read, Abdu.

ABDU: (Reading) "Have this mind amongst yourselves which you have in Christ Jesus, who, though He was in the form of God did not count equality with God a thing to be grasped, but emptied Himself, taking the form of

ABDU: a servant, being born in the likeness of men, and being found in human form; He humbled Himself and became obedient unto death, even death on a cross. Therefore God has highly exalted Him and bestowed on Him the name which is above every name, that at the name of Jesus every knee should bow in heaven and on earth and under the earth, and every tongue confess that Jesus Christ is Lord to the glory of God the Father."

QUESTIONS FOR DISCUSSION

1. Turn back and ask at least two questions from each of the first four lessons. We have now finished the first section of the book. It is time to review the whole section.
2. What does Solomon say about humility and honor?
3. What kind of a king is the greatest king?
4. Jesus says greatness is in humility. Did the disciples like this idea? What was their idea of greatness?
5. Tell Jesus' story about the man who sits at meat. What is the point Jesus is trying to make?
6. What is Jesus trying to show when He washes the disciples' feet?
7. If a man suffers, he must be weak. Is this statement true or false? Explain.
8. Tell the example of Baseat and the camel. What is the point Yusef is trying to make?
9. Tell the example of Abdu and Khaleel and the well. What is the point Yusef is trying to make?
10. Do the disciples like the idea that Jesus must suffer? What do they say? What does Jesus answer?
11. How does a suffering servant reveal an almighty God?

SUMMARY OF LESSON:

True greatness is in humility.
True greatness is in serving.
True greatness is in choosing to suffer in order to save.

MOTTO: A truly Great God comes to Redeem!

SECTION II
GOD IS LIGHT

6
GOD IS LIGHT AND HE ENLIGHTENS US IN NATURE

SCRIPTURES TO BE READ: I John 1:5; Genesis 1:3; Romans 1:19-20; Psalm 19:1-4; Psalm 33:6-9; Genesis 8:22; Job 38:36-38; James 1:17; Jeremiah 10:10

STATEMENT OF LESSON

With this lesson we begin a new section. We learned first that God is great. Now in this section we will try to understand the meaning of "God is Light." God wants us to love and obey Him. But we cannot love and obey an unknown God. God knows this and God is Light. Because God is Light He wants to enlighten us concerning Himself. God does this first in nature. We do not look about us to see God in nature. But God has created the natural world, thus the natural world can teach us something about God. Think of the furniture made by a good carpenter. As you look at the furniture, you can tell something about the carpenter. You can tell whether or not he is skillful, honest, and careful. So with God. We look at the handiwork of God and we can tell something about God. In the natural world we can see that God is powerful, orderly, and generous. We can see that God is a living God.

OUTLINE

GOD IS LIGHT AND HE ENLIGHTENS US IN NATURE

1. God wants us to love and obey Him.
2. We cannot love and obey an unknown God.
3. God is light and so He enlightens us concerning Himself.

4. God enlightens us concerning Himself first in nature.
   a. The words of the Psalmist - Psalm 19:1-4
   b. The words of Paul - Romans 1:19-20
5. From nature we learn that God is:
   a. A powerful God
   b. An orderly God
   c. A generous God
   d. A living God

THE DIALOGUE

GOD IS . . .

SCENE 6

CHARACTERS:

Yusef

Abdu

Baseat

THE DIALOGUE

NARRATOR: Abdu and Yusef are seated talking in Yusef's sitting room.

YUSEF: You see, Abdu, the problem is that half an acre of ground down by the river to the south.

ABDU: I know very well where it is, Yusef.

YUSEF: It is right beside the Village of Knowledge. I do not want to rent the ground. I want to grow cucumbers.

ABDU: This is a very easy matter, Yusef. Find someone reliable in the Village of Knowledge to work the ground for you.

YUSEF: Do you know of anyone, Abdu from the Villege of Knowledge whom I can trust - whom I can rely upon?

ABDU: (Thinking) I think Kamel would be a very good man.

YUSEF: Kamel? I don't know him.

ABDU: Don't worry, Yusef, I know him very well. He took to wife Meriam, daughter of the man who is married to the cousin of the girl whose brother's wife is related to Jude here in the village.

YUSEF: Oh, yes! Very well. Do you think I can rely upon him?

ABDU: Indeed you can.

YUSEF: Bring him to see me some day, Abdu.

ABDU: At your service, Yusef.

(Baseat enters)

ABDU: Baseat, you're late. Where have you been?

BASEAT: I have been here a long time. And where have you been?

YUSEF: Never mind, my friends. We have lots of time. Let us begin. Our subject for five nights has been what - Baseat?

BASEAT: We have been talking about God.

YUSEF: Good! Very good, Baseat. You're right.

ABDU: You certainly are, Baseat, you are the cleverest fellow I ever laid eyes on. (To Yusef) We have been talking, Yusef, about the greatness of God.

YUSEF: Exactly! For five nights we have talked about how God is great. Now for many nights we must think about another great subject. We must think of light. John says in his first letter, "This is the message that we have heard from Him and proclaim to you that God is . . ." Finish, Abdu.

ABDU: "God is Light and in Him is no darkness at all."

YUSEF: Good, Abdu. We must think of light and learn of God. What will we be doing, Baseat?

BASEAT: We will think of God and learn of light.

YUSEF: (Patiently) No, Baseat, we will think of light and learn of God. Now what will we do?

BASEAT: We will think of light and learn of God.

YUSEF: Very good! Now, Abdu, what does God want from us?

ABDU: He wants us to love Him and to obey Him.

YUSEF: Now Abdu, can I love and obey someone whom I do not know?

ABDU: No, I don't think so, Yusef.

YUSEF: What were we talking about just before Baseat came in?

ABDU: We talked about getting Kamel to work your half-acre of ground to the south by the river.

YUSEF: Very well, Abdu. Does Kamel know me?

ABDU: (Thinking) He has heard of you, of course, Yusef, but I do not think he knows you.

YUSEF: Very well. If I do not go and make myself known to him, can he obey me?

BASEAT: How can he obey you if he does not know you?

YUSEF: Can he love me if he does not know me?

BASEAT: That's not possible at all. How can anyone love somebody they do not know?

YUSEF: Good! Now - Kamel has heard about me, but he does not know me. If he is to work my land, he must obey me. I want him to love me, thus I must make myself known to him. Am I making good sense, Abdu?

ABDU: Very good sense.

YUSEF: It is so with God also. God wants us to love and serve Him so He must make Himself known to us. Now

YUSEF: do we go to Him, Abdu, to understand Him, or must He come to us?

ABDU: I do not know.

YUSEF: This is **very** important, my friends. God must come to us to explain Himself. When man, by himself, tries to understand God, he ends up worshipping idols. This is how idolatry begins. Each man has a different idea about God, so each man builds a different idol to worship. So in the old days, the land was full of idols, but praise God, He has come and made Himself known to us. What is the verse you just quoted, Abdu?

ABDU: "God is light and in Him there is no darkness at all."

YUSEF: Very well, Abdu. What does light do?

ABDU: Light enlightens.

YUSEF: Must the light enlighten? Cannot the light make darkness?

BASEAT: Of course not! Light makes light.

YUSEF: Now, Baseat, when I came into the room tonight, I opened the shutters. Why?

BASEAT: Do I know why you opened the window? Maybe there was a rat in the room and the rat wanted to run out, so you opened the window.

ABDU: (Reprimanding) Shut up, Baseat, you impolite fellow. Yusef's house is very clean, he has no rats. Use your brains. Elder Yusef opened the shutters because he wanted to let the light in. We couldn't see.

BASEAT: O-h-h- was that the reason? I see.

YUSEF: Do not be angry, Abdu, Baseat is trying. Let him say what he likes. It doesn't matter. But you are right, Abdu. I opened the shutters to let the light in so that we can see. God is light. He enlightens us so that we can see. But what is it He wants us to see, O Abdu?

ABDU: (Thinking) I'm not sure.

YUSEF: Very soon it is dark and I will call for a light. If I call for a light, what do I want you to see when they bring the light?

ABDU: You will want us to see you, of course.

YUSEF: Exactly right, Abdu. If I do not wish to be seen, I will not call for a light. But if I call for a light, this means I wish to be seen. Now - Baseat -- what is the first thing that God says in the Bible?

BASEAT: I do not know. Does He say "good morning" or something like that?

67

ABDU: (With great impatience) You are hopeless, Baseat! Hopeless! Open up your Bible, stupid, and look and see what God says first.

BASEAT: I never thought of that! Where shall I open it?

ABDU: (In complete impatience and exasperation) It's no use. It's absolutely no use.

YUSEF: Patience, Abdu, patience. Baseat, open your Bible to the very beginning. At the very beginning we will see the first thing that God says.

BASEAT: (As though a profound thought had just been suggested to him) Hey - that's a good idea! I will open the Bible at the beginning and see.

YUSEF: Read Genesis 1, the third verse, Baseat.

BASEAT: (Reading) "God said 'Let there be light' and there was light and God saw that the light was good."

YUSEF: You see, Baseat, this is the first thing that God says. He says "Let there be light." If I call for light here in the room, this means I want people to see me. God calls for light at the beginning of the world. This means He wants to be known. God is light. God enlightens us so that we can know Him. When we know Him, we can love Him and obey Him. We cannot love and obey a God that we do not know - an unknown God. Now our question is "How does God enlighten us so that we might know Him?" Abdu, open and read Romans 1:19-20.

ABDU: (Opens and reads) "For what can be known about God is plain to them, because God has shown it to them. Ever since the creation of the world His invisible nature, namely, His eternal power and deity, has been clearly perceived in the things that have been made."

YUSEF: Now Baseat, read Psalm 19: 1 through 4.

BASEAT: (Opens and reads) "The heavens are telling the glory of God and the firmament proclaims His handiwork. Day to day pours forth speech, and night to night declares knowledge. There is no speech, nor are there words; their voice is not heard; yet their voice goes out through all the earth, and their words to the end of the world."

YUSEF: Now, Abdu, what is the first way God uses to enlighten us about Himself?

ABDU: The Bible says that God can be known through the things that have been made.

YUSEF: Yes, God shows himself through nature. What other ways does He have, Abdu?

ABDU: I'm not sure, Yusef.

YUSEF: Very well, Abdu, open to John, the first chapter, and read until I stop you.

ABDU: (Abdu opens and begins reading) "In the beginning was the Word, and the Word was with God, and the Word was God. He was in the beginning with God; all things were made through Him, and without Him was not anything made that was made."

YUSEF: (Cutting in) Stop. Only this far! What is this about, Abdu?

ABDU: This is about the creation.

YUSEF: Very good. God is light, and He makes Himself known through the creation. Now read verse 6.

ABDU: (Reading) "There was a man sent from God, whose name was John. He came for testimony, to bear witness to the light, that all might believe through him. He was not the light, but came to bear witness to the light."

YUSEF: Very good. Now Abdu, what is John called?

ABDU: He is called a man sent from God.

YUSEF: Very good. Now what do we call the men sent from God?

BASEAT: The men of God.

YUSEF: What is another name?

ABDU: The Prophets.

YUSEF: Exactly right. This is the second way God uses. Now Abdu, read verse 14.

ABDU: (Reading) "And the Word became flesh and dwelt among us, full of grace and truth; we have beheld His glory, glory as of the only Son from the Father."

YUSEF: Very good. Very good! This is the third way God has used. First God enlightens us through nature. Then He enlightens us through the prophets. Finally, He comes Himself in his Word to enlighten us. Now Abdu, what are these three ways?

ABDU: God enlightens us through nature.

YUSEF: Right.

ABDU: God enlightens us through the prophets.

YUSEF: Very good.

ABDU: And God enlightens us Himself, through His Son.

YUSEF: Excellent. This is a big subject, my friends, and we must study it for three nights, but tonight let us take the first. God is light and God enlightens us about Himself in nature. Now Baseat, what does David say the heavens do in Psalm 19? What does he say they do?

BASEAT: I can't remember.

ABDU: Well, look it up, you fool.

YUSEF: Be patient, Abdu. Baseat is a very clever fellow. He just can't remember things very long.

ABDU: He has no brains. That's all that's wrong with him.

BASEAT: It says here, "Day to day pours forth speech, and night to night declares knowledge . . ."

YUSEF: Yes, yes. Go on.

BASEAT: (Reading) "There is no speech, nor are there words; their voice is not heard; yet their voice goes out through all the earth, and their words to the end of the world."

YUSEF: You see, my friends, David says the world of nature speaks night and day. Day and night nature speaks telling of the glory of God. But nature speaks using no words. Nature speaks but you hear no voice. The question is - "What does nature say when she speaks about God?"

ABDU: (Thoughtfully) This is right. Nature does speak telling about God, but we do not listen to her. Always we are talking. Always we are making noise. We are not ready to listen to the voice that speaks without words.

YUSEF: (Also thoughtfully) How true this is, Abdu. Every morning I go to my garden at the back of the house. I sit there alone because I wish to hear the clear voice of God speaking to me through nature. David says the voice goes out through all the world. But it is a voice which we must learn to hear. But right now I must ask "What does this voice say?"

ABDU: I have never listened to this voice, Yusef, therefore I do not know what it says.

YUSEF: My sons, you must learn to listen to this voice. It says many things. I will tell you what it says. First, it says that God is powerful. All the world says this, and it says it very clearly. Baseat, read Psalm 33:6 through 9.

BASEAT: (Reading) "By the word of the Lord the heavens were made, and all their host by the breath of his mouth. He gathered the waters of the sea as in a bottle; he put the deep in storehouses. Let all the earth fear the Lord, let all the inhabitants of the world stand in awe of him! For he spoke, and it came to be; he commanded, and it stood forth."

YUSEF: Baseat, all of nature says that God is powerful. Have you stood in the river at flood time?

BASEAT: Yes, I have.

YUSEF: The river is very strong at flood time. Its strength is the strength of God. Abdu, have you felt the heat of the sun at noon?

ABDU: Yes, I have, Yusef.

YUSEF: Have you seen the strength of the wind in the palm tree?

ABDU: Yes, I have, Yusef.

YUSEF: Have you seen the power of the flash flood as it comes in from the desert to destroy?

ABDU: Yes, I have, Yusef.

YUSEF: Have you seen the strength of the sun which rises each morning?

ABDU: Yes, I have, Yusef.

YUSEF: Then have you not thought of the strength of the Creator who did all of this?

ABDU: I am ashamed. Every day I walk in the fields, but I have not thought of these things.

YUSEF: (Compassionately) All of the created world speaks to us, my friends. We must learn to hear its voice. But it speaks also of order. Baseat, read Genesis 8:22.

BASEAT: (Reading) "While the earth remains, seedtime and harvest, cold and heat, summer and winter, day and night, shall not cease."

YUSEF: Abdu, read Job 38: 36 through 38.

ABDU: (Reading) "Who has put wisdom in the clouds, or given understanding to the mists? Who can number the clouds by wisdom? Or who can tilt the waterskins of the heavens, when the dust runs into a mass and the clouds cleave fast together?"

YUSEF: Order, my friends, order. God gives order to all things. If we wish to grow wheat, what must we have, O Baseat?

BASEAT: We must have land.

YUSEF: What else?

BASEAT: Water.

YUSEF: What else, Abdu.

ABDU: You must have seeds, and you must have sun for you cannot grow anything in the shade.

YUSEF: This is correct. We must have all four of these things. Let us look to see how God has ordered them. The seeds of plants will stay for a long time without

71

YUSEF: being planted. The cotton seeds are like the children of the cotton plant. We can keep these seeds for months -- even years -- if we wish before we plant them. The seeds of animals are not so. If we put the seeds of animals in a room by themselves for a long time, they would die. Is it not so?

ABDU: Of course.

YUSEF: What if the seeds of plants were like this? What if we had to plant the cotton seeds right away or they would die? What if we could not store them?

ABDU: My goodness. You would not be able to farm at all.

YUSEF: God has ordered this for us. But think also of the land. The land is flat and rich. Can we grow cotton in the sand?

ABDU: No, it is impossible.

YUSEF: Can we grow cotton on the mountainside?

BASEAT: No.

YUSEF: God has made the land flat. He has made the land rich. Think also of the sun. If the sun does not warm the land, what happens?

ABDU: The plants would die from the cold.

YUSEF: And if the sun is too hot, what happens?

BASEAT: The plants die from the heat.

YUSEF: God has ordered the sun for us. Think also of the water. Can we grow cotton with salty water?

ABDU: No. We must have sweet water. Salty water would not do.

YUSEF: God has ordered the water for us. God has ordered all things for us, my friends. He has ordered the seeds, the land, the sun and the water. The voice that speaks to us without words also tells us that God is gracious. Abdu, read James 1, verse 17.

ABDU: (He opens and reads) "Every good endowment and every perfect gift is from above, coming down from the Father of lights with whom there is no variation or shadow due to change."

YUSEF: Every good and perfect gift is from above. The voice of nature - the voice that speaks with no words - tells us this every day if we will learn to listen. The sun, the river, the blue sky by day, the bright stars by night -- all of these speak and tell us that God is gracious to us. All that we have, whether it be little or much, has been given to us by Him. But I think of something else, my friend. A carpenter

YUSEF: makes a table. Who is greater, the table or the carpenter?

ABDU: This is very easy to see, Yusef. The carpenter must be greater than the table.

YUSEF: Why, Abdu?

ABDU: He could not make it unless he were greater than the table.

YUSEF: You are right, Abdu. God has created life, therefore He must be living. Only if He is a living God could He create life. Can the dead bring forth life?

BASEAT: No, this is impossible.

YUSEF: Abdu, read Jeremiah 10:10.

ABDU: (Reading) "But the Lord is the true God; he is the living God and the everlasting King."

YUSEF: In nature all about us we see life. This means that God is living, for the living bring forth the living.

ABDU: Indeed, indeed, O Yusef. Every morning I go to the fields early. For years I have done this, but I have never heard this voice that speaks without words.

YUSEF: I know. I know. You speak of "How much did I pay for it? How much did you pay for it? How much did so and so get it for? What price was it last week? And, I think I can get it for you for less. How much! How much!" This is what we talk of all day long. We must learn to be silent, and meditate in the night. We must learn to listen to the voice that speaks without words. This voice -- the voice of the heavens and the earth is speaking of the glory of God. We must learn to listen to it.

QUESTIONS FOR DISCUSSION

1. What does God want us to do?
2. Is God an unknown God? If not, why not?
3. God says "Let there be light." What is it He wants us to see?
4. What is the voice that speaks without words?
5. God tells us of Himself in three ways. What are they?
6. What are the four things that Yusef learned about God from the voice that speaks without words?
7. Give examples of each of these four.
8. What other lessons can we learn about God from nature?
9. Give other examples of the order of God as we see it in nature.
10. What can we do to learn to listen to the voice that speaks without words?

SUMMARY OF THE LESSON

God is light.
He wishes to enlighten us.
He speaks to us in nature.
He tells us about Himself.

MOTTO: Have you heard the voice that speaks without words?

7
GOD IS LIGHT AND HE ENLIGHTENS US BY THE PROPHETS

SCRIPTURES TO BE READ: Genesis 1:1;
Nehemiah 9:6, 9, 15, 22, 26-30, 31;
Isaiah 5:16; Isaiah 43:10-11;
Isaiah 44:6.

STATEMENT OF LESSON

God is light. This means He wants to enlighten us. In Lesson 6 we saw that God enlightens us in nature. In this lesson, we will see that God enlightens us by the prophets. The prophets teach us about God. Nature was not enough. God wants to teach us more about Himself. The prophets teach us many things about God. We can study only a few of them. We learn first that God is One, and second that he is a living Person. Some people believe that God is only a general power, but the prophets teach that God is a living Person. Third, the prophets teach us that God is Master of history. We live in a world that makes us afraid. We are afraid of what will happen. We forget that God rules history. Fourth, the messengers of God teach us that God is Holy. But what does holiness mean? Some men thought holiness meant certain things are holy. The priests knew that certain things and places were called holy. But the prophets said that holiness means righteousness. God is holy. This means that God is pure and purity means righteousness. All men understand sacred things and places. Even idol worshippers have such things. The prophets teach us that holiness means righteousness.

OUTLINE

GOD IS LIGHT AND HE ENLIGHTENS US BY THE PROPHETS

1. God is holy.
2. God is a living Person.
    a. God is not a general power.
    b. God is a living Person.
3. God is Master of history.
    a. God rules history.
    b. Therefore, we need not fear.
4. God is holy.
    a. The priests say, "Holiness means holy places and things."
    b. The prophets say, "Holiness means righteousness."

THE DIALOGUE

GOD IS . . .

SCENE 7

CHARACTERS:

Yusef, the Wise

Abdu, the Inquirer

Baseat, the Simple

THE DIALOGUE

(All three characters are seated together out in front of Yusef's house.)

YUSEF: The matter is not settled, Abdu.

ABDU: What matter, Yusef?

YUSEF: The arrangements about the land to the south.

ABDU: Oh, you mean the half-acre down by the river.

YUSEF: Yes, the land that is next to the Villege of Knowledge. You remember. Last night you told me about Brother Kamel.

ABDU: Oh, yes, I remember.

YUSEF: Have you gone to see him yet?

ABDU: No, I'm sorry I have not been down to see him yet.

YUSEF: Well - it doesn't matter. Any time will do.

BASEAT: But what is our subject for tonight, Yusef.

YUSEF: What was our subject last night, Baseat?

BASEAT: Ah - ah - ah - h. The greatness of God.

ABDU: No. No, Baseat. Last night we began a new subject. We talked about God is light.

YUSEF: Good, Abdu. What did you learn?

ABDU: I learned that God is light. This means God wants to enlighten us. Because He is light He wants us to know about Him. Only if we know Him can we love Him and serve Him. So He tells us about Himself in nature. Nature is the voice that speaks without words and tells us about God.

YUSEF: (Delighted) Very good, Abdu. You have learned your lesson well. God is light and He wants to enlighten us. He does this in three ways. We see these three ways in the first verses of the first chapter of John. What are they, Abdu?

ABDU: He enlightens us in nature. He enlightens us by special messengers and He enlightens us by Christ.

YUSEF: You are a good student, Abdu. You must have been reading your Bible today to remember this.

ABDU: Yes, Yusef, I read these first verses from John. Today I began to understand them for the first time.

YUSEF: Very well. Tonight we talk about God's messengers. Now, Baseat.

BASEAT: Yes, Yusef.

YUSEF: I want Kamel down in the Village of Knowledge to serve me by farming a piece of ground for me. To do this he must know and understand what I want. Right?

BASEAT: Right!

YUSEF: Very well. Do you see this cloak, Baseat?

BASEAT: Indeed I do. It is a very fine cloak.

YUSEF: Very well. I will send this cloak down to Kamel and he will know exactly what I want him to do. Right?

BASEAT: (In surprise) No. How is this? You send him your cloak? The cloak won't tell him anything.

YUSEF: But you see, Baseat, I made this cloak myself.

BASEAT: Yes, I know, Yusef.

YUSEF: If I send this cloak to Kamel, he will learn many things about me. He will look at the cloak. He will see that the thread is very fine. He will say, "The maker of this cloak is very skillful." What else will he say, Abdu?

ABDU: He will see that the thread is the same thickness all the way along. He will say, "The maker of this cloak pays very close attention to what he does." He will see that the cloak is clean. It is not torn. He will say, "The maker of this cloak is careful with his things."

YUSEF: You see, Baseat, I have made the cloak. If I send the cloak to Kamel, he will learn many things about me.

BASEAT: But this is not enough if you want him to serve you. Even I understand this.

YUSEF: Very good, Baseat. Very good. That's exactly right. So it is with God. We look at what God has made - the world of nature. This teaches us many things about God, but this is not enough. If I want Kamel to serve me I must show him many more things about myself and what I want. If God wants us to love and serve Him, He must show us more about Himself. What He teaches

YUSEF: us about Himself in nature is not enough. So what does He do, Abdu?

ABDU: He sends us prophets.

YUSEF: What do you mean by prophets?

ABDU: Prophets? Special messengers from God, as John says.

YUSEF: Very good. Now let us think of some of the things that the prophets teach us about God. They teach us many, many things. We can think of only a few. The first is - they teach us that God is One. How does the Bible begin, Abdu?

ABDU: "In the beginning, God created the heavens and the earth."

YUSEF: Very well, in the beginning one God creates, not many. Then the prophets teach us that God is One. In Deuteronomy we read, "The Lord our God is one God." Abdu, last week I heard the drum beating in your end of the village. There must have been a wedding.

ABDU: Yes, it was a very good wedding. The bride was from our section of the village.

YUSEF: Did the bride have many things?

ABDU: Very many.

YUSEF: How did they take her things to the house of the bridegroom?

ABDU: On a camel, of course.

YUSEF: Were all of these things tied very neatly on the camel?

ABDU: (Laughing) No, of course not. There were ten men all trying to tie the things on the camel. All of the men of her family and half of the men of his family tried to load up the camel. There was much noise and confusion. Each man was sure he knew best how to load the camel. They got the camel loaded, but of course it was not orderly.

YUSEF: Very good, Abdu. Yesterday we thought together about the world which God has created. We saw that it was very orderly. This means that God, the Creator, must be one. If there were many Gods, creation would be as confused as all the stuff on that camel. Baseat, what does the proverb say about two captains?

BASEAT: Put two captains in the boat and the boat sinks.

YUSEF: Very good, Baseat. Our world is the same way. We only have one captain in the boat. The trouble is that lots of people do not obey Him. Abdu, open to Isaiah 43, and read verses 10 and 11.

ABDU: (Reading) "Thus says the Lord. I am the first and I am the last. Beside me there is no God."

YUSEF: All the prophets teach this. God is one. But they teach us something else, my friends.

BASEAT: Say on, Yusef. We are listening.

YUSEF: They teach that God is not just a general power that fills the earth. They teach that God is a Person and He deals with us as a Person.

ABDU: How is that Yusef?

YUSEF: I think you have a young son?

ABDU: Yes. Hakiem.

YUSEF: May God keep him for you, Abdu. How old is he now?

ABDU: Oh - about a year.

YUSEF: Then he must need someone to watch him and care for him?

ABDU: Of course.

YUSEF: Very well. How far is my irrigation pump from your house?

ABDU: It is in the field at the edge of the village near our house. I can walk there in ten minutes.

YUSEF: Would you say the engine is powerful?

ABDU: Yes, it is indeed - very powerful.

YUSEF: Very well, Abdu, you need someone to guard and care for Hakiem. Every night why not tell your wife to take Hakiem and leave him in the pump house. Then I will go and turn on the pump. The pump is very strong. Hakiem needs something strong to guard him and care for him, so you leave him in the pump house. The pump will be just right for him.

ABDU: No! No! It is impossible. Hakiem does not need a great pump to take care of him. He needs a person to take care of him. If he cries, what can the pump do? If he falls, can the pump pick him up? The pump can do nothing for him. What is this story all about, O Yusef, I don't understand.

YUSEF: I will explain, my sons. The people are like your son, Hakiem, Abdu. We as men are weak and we need someone to care for us and help us. A general power through the world is not enough. God is not a general power - but rather a special Person. The prophets understood this. The Bible says "As a father pitieth his children, so the Lord pitieth them that serve Him." God is a special Person. Power is not enough.

ABDU: That's exactly right, Yusef. This is a great idea.

YUSEF: Yesterday we said that God creates life. This means God must be alive. Do you follow me?

BASEAT: Indeed I do.

YUSEF: Very well. God also creates personality. This means God must be a person. Does this not make sense, Abdu?

ABDU: (Thinking) Yes, this makes sense, Yusef. I never thought of this.

YUSEF: Open, Abdu and read Hosea 11: verses 3 and 4.

ABDU: (Reading) "Yet it was I who taught Ephraim to walk, I took him up in my arms; but they did not know that I healed them. I led them with cords of compassion, with the bands of love, and I became to them as one who eases the yoke on their jaws, and I bent down to them and fed them."

YUSEF: So the messengers of God teach us that God is One and that He is a living Person. But the prophets noticed something else.

ABDU: What else, Yusef?

YUSEF: They saw that God is Master of history.

BASEAT: This is well known, O Yusef. Everyone knows this.

YUSEF: Yes, we know it because God has taught us through his prophets. Without them, we would not know it. Baseat, open Nehemiah to the 9th chapter. Let us read a few verses from that chapter. Begin, O Baseat, with verse 6.

BASEAT: (Reading) "And Ezra said: 'Thou art the Lord, thou alone; thou hast made heaven, the heaven of heavens, with all their hosts, the earth and all that is on it, the seas and all that is in them.'"

YUSEF: God is Master of creation. Now read from verse 7.

BASEAT: (Reading) "Thou art the Lord, the God who didst choose Abram and bring him forth out of Ur of the Chaldees and gave him the name Abraham."

YUSEF: And God is the one who directed Abraham. Now read verse 9.

BASEAT: (Reading) "And thou didst see the affliction of our fathers in Egypt and heard their cry at the Red Sea, and didst perform signs and wonders against Pharoah and all his servants. . ."

YUSEF: So God brought the people out of Egypt. Now read verse 15.

81

BASEAT: (Reading) "Thou didst give them bread from heaven for their hunger and bring forth water for them from the rock for their thirst, . . ."

YUSEF: God also directed them while they were in the wilderness. Now Baseat, read verse 22.

BASEAT: (Reading) "And thou didst give them kingdoms and peoples, and didst allot to them every corner;"

YUSEF: God gave them land. Now verse 26.

BASEAT: (Reading) "Nevertheless they were disobedient and rebelled against thee and cast thy law behind their back and killed thy prophets, who had warned them in order to turn them back to thee, and they committed great blasphemies. Therefore thou didst give them into the hand of their enemies, who made them suffer;"

YUSEF: Notice this also! God punishes them for their sins. What do we learn from all this, Abdu?

ABDU: The lesson is very clear. God is the Master of history.

YUSEF: He was the Master of history then, but is He the Master of history now?

ABDU: Of course.

YUSEF: Then why are we afraid of the future?

BASEAT: Do I know - we just are.

YUSEF: The prophets saw that God is Master of history. They teach us that God is the one who arranges history. We read of atomic bombs. We hear of nitrogen bombs. We hear talk of wars. We hear of trouble in many parts of the world. We are afraid, but the Psalmist says, "Surely the wrath of men shall praise thee."

ABDU: This is true, we should not be afraid if God is really Master of history.

YUSEF: God is light. He enlightens us by his prophets. The prophets teach us about Himself. They teach us great lessons. Let us take one more. This is a very important idea. This idea only the prophets saw. They taught that God is holy.

ABDU: This is not strange, Yusef. Everyone knows that God is holy.

YUSEF: Ah, but Abdu, the question is, "What is holiness?" In the Old Testament, the priests said one thing. The prophets said something else.

BASEAT: You mean the priests and the prophets fought?

YUSEF: Yes, indeed. All through the days of the Kings, the priests said one thing. The prophets said something else.

ABDU: What did the priests say, Yusef, about holiness?

YUSEF: The priests said holiness means "holy things." They said the things that belonged to worship are set apart. These things are holy. The priests said the places where we worship are "holy."

BASEAT: They were right weren't they?

YUSEF: Listen carefully, Baseat. The priests said God is holy. Holiness means "set apart." The priests said certain things and certain places were "set apart." The priests said holy robes, incense, sacrifices, lampstands -- these things were holy things. They said the Temple where they worshiped was a holy place. The priests said holiness, thus, is to respect holy things, and holy places.

ABDU: Of course, this is what holiness is. Respect for holy things and holy places.

YUSEF: Ah, but my son, the prophets said, "Holiness is <u>more</u> than this."

ABDU: In what way more?

YUSEF: Very well, Abdu, open up and read Isaiah 5 verse 16.

ABDU: (Reading) "But the Lord of hosts is exalted in justice, and the Holy God shows himself holy in righteousness."

YUSEF: Do you see, Abdu? Isaiah, the prophet, says the Holy God shows Himself holy in righteousness. What does this mean?

ABDU: (Very much confused) I don't understand. What has righteousness to do with holiness?

YUSEF: This is a big, big subject, my friends. After some time, we must talk about the holiness of God. Tonight we can only begin in this subject. I will try to explain what the prophets meant. The prophets said God is holy. All right thus far, Abdu?

ABDU: Thus far is fine.

YUSEF: (Very slowly) Now, the prophets said holiness means purity.

ABDU: (Thinking) Holiness means purity. Holy things are pure. Yes, this is fine.

YUSEF: (Very slowly) Now, the prophets said, "Holiness means purity. Purity means righteousness."

ABDU: I am trying to understand, but this is a very hard idea.

83

YUSEF: It is very hard, but it is very important. You must think about this. Holiness means purity; purity means righteousness.

ABDU: But I do not understand. Is it not true that some things are holy? God gave us the Bible. We call it the Holy Bible. Is this wrong?

YUSEF: No, it is not wrong, but it is not enough. Who gave us the palm tree?

ABDU: The palm tree? God gave us the palm tree.

YUSEF: Very good. Then if the palm tree is the gift of God, the palm tree is holy, too. Who gave us the earth which we farm?

ABDU: God gave it to us.

YUSEF: Then the earth is holy. Everything that God has made is holy. When you go to work in the fields, O Abdu, do you not take off your shoes.

ABDU: Yes, of course. This is so they will not get dirty.

YUSEF: From now on, Abdu, as you go to your fields, take off your shoes because the ground is holy ground. Everything God has made is holy.

ABDU: My goodness! This explanation has not reached our ears. I don't know what to say.

YUSEF: Think, my friends, of the words of the prophet Isaiah. "The holy God shows Himself holy in righteousness." We must think of these things.

QUESTIONS FOR DISCUSSION

1. God reveals Himself in nature. Why is this not enough?
2. What does Genesis 1:1 teach about God? How does this teach that God is One?
3. What is the point of Yusef's example of the bride with her camel?
4. Is God a Person, or just a Power?
5. Does God treat His people like a Person, or like a Power only?
6. God creates personality. From this what do we know about God?
7. Why did Yusef suggest that Abdu take his son, Hakeim, and leave him in the pump house?
8. What did the prophets believe about God and history?
9. Is history by chance, or does God rule history?
10. What did holiness mean for the priests in the Old Testament?
11. What did holiness mean for the prophets in the Old Testament?
12. Yusef says the palm tree is holy. Explain.
13. What has holiness to do with righteousness?

SUMMARY OF LESSON

God is One and He is a living Person.
God is holy and He is Master of history. We learn this from the prophets.

MOTTO: The Creator of personality must be a Person.

8
GOD IS LIGHT AND HE ENLIGHTENS US IN CHRIST

SCRIPTURES TO BE READ:　John 3:16; Luke 14:11-13; John 13:21-26; Isaiah 53:4-6; I Corinthians 15:54-57

STATEMENT OF LESSON

God is light and He wishes to enlighten us about Himself in nature. We learned how God teaches us about Himself by the prophets. In this lesson, we will see how God teaches us about Himself by Himself. He does this in Jesus Christ, the Word of God. God is a Person. We cannot really know any person closely by hearing about him. We must come to know the person ourselves. God wants us to know what He is like, so He comes in Christ to show us. This is a very deep lesson. We can understand only a small part. As we study the teachings of Christ, we see that God loves all people, not just good people. We see also from the teachings of Christ that God is not angry with sinners, He is broken-hearted over them. We learn about God also from the Cross of Christ. Here we see that God does not want us unless we come responding to His love. We see also how God destroys evil by bearing evil Himself. In the resurrection of Christ we also learn about God. Here we see love united with power. The love of God in the Cross is united with the Power of God in the resurrection. We see also the victory of sacrificial love.

OUTLINE

GOD IS LIGHT AND HE ENLIGHTENS US IN CHRIST

1. We learn about God from the teachings of Christ.
   a. God loves all men.
   b. God is not angry with sinners, He is broken-hearted.
2. We learn about God from the Cross of Christ.
   a. God wants us to come to Him only if drawn by His love.
   b. God destroys evil by bearing evil.
3. We learn about God from the resurrection of Christ.
   a. Love unites with Power.
   b. The victory of sacrificial love.

THE DIALOGUE

GOD IS . . .

SCENE 8

CHARACTERS:

Abdu

Baseat

Yusef

Mayor Butrus

(Abdu, Baseat and Yusef are present talking together in Yusef's front room.)

THE DIALOGUE

YUSEF: Did you get down to see Kamel today?

ABDU: Yes. Baseat and I went down to visit him in the Village of Knowledge.

YUSEF: Did you explain to him what I want?

ABDU: Yes, I explained to him. I said you want him to farm your half-acre of ground down by the river. I told him you want to grow cucumbers.

YUSEF: What did he say?

ABDU: He said, "Yusef, the Wise. I don't know Yusef, the Wise. I have heard about him, but I do not know him."

YUSEF: Did you not explain to him who I was?

BASEAT: Yes, we explained everything about you.

YUSEF: When you finished, what did he say?

ABDU: He said, "I must see Yusef and talk to him myself."

YUSEF: Why did he ask that?

ABDU: I don't know. He said to understand you he must know you personally.

YUSEF: Very well. I will go and see him tomorrow.

(The Mayor comes in. Everyone rises to their feet.)

YUSEF: Welcome, Mr. Mayor. We have missed you.

MAYOR: Welcome to all of you. I was very sorry to miss your last two meetings. I was gone out of the village. Abdu?

ABDU: Yes, Mayor.

MAYOR: Sometime you must explain to me what Elder Yusef has said.

ABDU:	I will do my best. We have talked of great things.
MAYOR:	I am sure of this, but Yusef, what is the subject tonight?
YUSEF:	Our subject is "God is light." We have been talking about this for three meetings. Do you remember, Mayor, I talked to you about Kamel down in the next village?
MAYOR:	Oh yes, I remember. Is he going to farm that half-acre for you?
YUSEF:	If God wills. But he says he wants to see me so he will understand exactly what I want.
MAYOR:	That is only natural.
YUSEF:	I sent Abdu, but he says he wants to see me, myself. This is a good beginning, my friends, for our subject tonight. God is light. He enlightens us in Christ. Abdu, what did we talk about the last two meetings?
ABDU:	We talked about how God teaches us of Himself in nature, and through His prophets.
YUSEF:	Tonight we talk about the third way God used. God is light, and He enlightens us in Christ. Abdu, what did the prophets teach about God?
ABDU:	(Thinking) Let me see. The prophets teach us that God is One and God is Holy.
YUSEF:	Very good, Abdu. What else?
ABDU:	They teach us that God is Master of history . . . let me see . . . Oh yes, and that God is a Person.
YUSEF:	Now Abdu, how does a person get to know another person? Can you do it by sending someone else to the person you want to know?
ABDU:	No. You must sit and get to know the person yourself if you wish to know him truly. Like Kamel down in the next village. He wants to know you. I went to him, but this was not enough. He said, "I want to see him and talk to him." I did my best to explain to him what you want, Yusef.
YUSEF:	I'm sure you did, Abdu. And this is the important point. God is a Person. He wants us to know Him. We can know Him only through a person, so God comes in Jesus Christ.
MAYOR:	That follows. If God is a Person, we can know Him only if He comes to us as a Person. We cannot know any person unless we come to know him personally. This must be true of God too.
YUSEF:	Good Mr. Mayor. Now we must look at three things. We must look to see what we can learn from the teachings

YUSEF: of Christ about God, from the Cross of Christ, and from the resurrection of Christ. Baseat!

BASEAT: Yes, Yusef.

YUSEF: How much water is there in the Nile River?

BASEAT: Very much.

YUSEF: How long would it take you to dip out the Nile River with a soup ladle?

BASEAT: My goodness! If all the people in our country started dipping altogether with soup ladles, they could never dip out the Nile River.

YUSEF: Correct, Baseat. My friends, our subject tonight is like this. God enlightens us in Christ. This is a great mystery - God in Christ. We will talk about this theme admitting what little we understand. It is like what a man can dip out of the river with a soup ladle. Compared with what is there, it is nothing.

ABDU: But even this little, Yusef, is very helpful to us.

YUSEF: This is why we must try. From the teachings of Christ about God, I have picked two ideas. First, Christ teaches that God loves all men.

ABDU: (In surprise) Was this a new idea, Yusef?

YUSEF: Indeed it was, Abdu. In the Old Testament, the Psalmist was always calling, asking that the enemies of God be destroyed.

MAYOR: I always worried about that. The Psalmist seems to hate his enemies. He asks that God shall kill and destroy them.

YUSEF: "God so loved . . ." what? The sons of Abraham?

BASEAT: No. "The world."

YUSEF: Right, Baseat. But the Jews of His day could not accept this. They did not want God to love the Romans or any Gentiles. They wanted God to love only them. But Jesus taught that God loves all men. Tell me, Mayor.

MAYOR: Yes, Yusef.

YUSEF: Do the people of this village love the people in the Village of Knowledge.

MAYOR: No, I'm sorry to say. They hate them.

YUSEF: What if a new preacher came to our village. What if he kept preaching again, and again, and again that this village must love the Village of Knowledge. What would happen?

ABDU: The people would get tired and angry because they do not want to love them.

YUSEF: This is what happened with Jesus. But the second thing -- He taught that God loves all men. He taught also that God is not angry with sinners.

ABDU: (With great agitation) What do you mean? God **must** be angry with sinners! Of course He is angry with sinners.

YUSEF: In a way He is angry. But really He is broken-hearted. Listen Abdu, when Khaleel, your son, disobeys you, you get angry, do you not?

ABDU: Of course.

YUSEF: Very well. One day, if God wills, he will be forty years old. He will be a man. What if he disobeys you then? What if he brings shame upon your house? Will you be angry, or will you be broken-hearted?

ABDU: I'm not sure, O Yusef, but I think I would be broken-hearted. Now he is a boy. He understands nothing, so when he disobeys, I am angry. One day he will be a man, then he will know what he is doing. If he chooses as a man to bring shame upon my house, it is true, I would be broken-hearted.

BASEAT: I am a man and my father gets angry with me.

ABDU: That's another story. You are an idiot.

YUSEF: Shame, Abdu. Don't talk that way.

MAYOR: Continue on, Yusef.

YUSEF: Very well, I will ask you a question, Mayor. Was the father of the prodigal son angry, or broken-hearted, when his boy left him?

MAYOR: If he had been angry, he would not have welcomed him when he came back. Surely he was broken-hearted.

YUSEF: Exactly right, Mayor. Do you remember David?

ABDU: Of course, we remember him.

YUSEF: Was he mad at Absalom?

ABDU: No, he wept over him. In great sorrow he said, "My son, Absalom my son, would that I had died for thee."

YUSEF: Exactly right. When we sin we reject God. God is not angry, but He is broken-hearted. God suffers the pain of one whose love is refused.

MAYOR: There is no pain deeper than this pain.

YUSEF: This is what Jesus taught, my friends. We are proud and self-righteous. Each man looks to see how to help himself, not his neighbor. These things cause God pain. When we see the Cross of Christ, we learn of God.

YUSEF: Christ on the Cross teaches us at least two ideas about God. First, God wants us to come to Him only if drawn to Him by His love. Christ does not try to win us by any other way. What were the three temptations, O Abdu?

ABDU: Stones to bread, the pinnacle of the Temple and the kingdoms of this world.

YUSEF: Very good. Now we said that there were three ways to win people. We said they were three ways Jesus refused to use. What are these three ways? Do you remember, Mayor?

MAYOR: I think so. Stones to bread means the way of giving the people something.

YUSEF: Very good. Go on.

MAYOR: The pinnacle of the temple means proving without doubt that you have authority and must be obeyed. Oh yes, and the third is easy. It is the use of earthly power to get men to follow you.

YUSEF: Very good. Now, my friends, think of the Last Supper. Does Jesus know Judas will betray him?

BASEAT: Of course He does.

YUSEF: Very good, Baseat. Now all of you listen closely. That night, the same three temptations were before Him. Jesus is in the Upper Room with the disciples. He knows Judas will betray Him. Now, what is He going to do about this? What can He do?

ABDU: I never thought about it. I do not know what He might do.

YUSEF: Think with me. Judas is angry because he has taken nothing. So Jesus could say to him, "Judas, I see you are angry. You have worked hard and have not been paid. You have a right to be angry. Here is a thousand pounds for you. This will show you how happy I am with you."

BASEAT: My goodness - a thousand pounds.

YUSEF: Now, would Judas have continued following Jesus if He had done this?

MAYOR: Of course. Of course. But Jesus does not want disciples of this kind.

YUSEF: Jesus could have done something else. He could have said, "Judas, I see that you are angry. It seems you are not sure I am the Son of God. If you were sure I was the Son of God, you would not be planning what you are now planning. Very well. I will prove it to you. What great miracle do you want me to do, to prove that I am the Son of God?"

YUSEF: Then Judas could have asked for a great sign. He could have asked to have his grandfather back alive and there in the room, or something like that. But Jesus did not choose this way. Why?

ABDU: Would it not have saved a lot of trouble if He had done something like this?

YUSEF: Pay close attention, Abdu. Jesus does not want people to come to Him if they come in spite of their wills - in spite of themselves. The Jews mocked Jesus and tried to get Him to come down from the Cross. Why did He not come down, Abdu?

ABDU: He did not come down because he wanted to suffer and save us.

YUSEF: But, Abdu, He could have stepped down from the Cross to prove that He was the Son of God, then He could have gone back up to finish our salvation. This way He could have stopped their talk. Why did He not do this?

ABDU: I do not know, Yusef.

YUSEF: (Very insistent) You must understand this, Abdu. Jesus wants people to come to Him only if drawn to Him by love. If He had done this, they would have had to have followed Him, not because they wanted to -- not because they were changed within themselves by His love. But they would be coming because their talk was silenced. They would have seen proof and become false disciples.

MAYOR: (Shaking his head) Indeed. Indeed. Most of us follow Him because we know He is the Son of God and has the authority. We do not follow Him because we are drawn to Him by His love.

YUSEF: Exactly right, Mayor. Let us go back to Judas. Jesus refused to win him by giving him something. He refused to win him by showing him a sign to prove that He was the Son of God. What was the third temptation, Mayor?

MAYOR: The temptation to use earthly power.

YUSEF: Right. Now were the disciples armed, or not?

BASEAT: Peter was armed. After a while, he cut off the priest's ear so we know he was armed.

YUSEF: Very good. So Jesus could have used this way. He could have said to Peter, "This man will betray us. Be a man. Do the expected thing." Then what would Peter have done?

MAYOR: My goodness, he would have jumped up and killed Judas right there on the spot.

YUSEF: Right. And then they could have planned to escape. Jesus could have begun a great political movement. He would have been very successful for all the people were with him. But again, my friends, Jesus does not want political powers. He wants men to come to Him only if drawn to Him by love. So what did He do with Judas?

ABDU: He passed to him the sop.

YUSEF: What did this mean?

ABDU: It meant showing him great honor.

BASEAT: Do you mean He honored him when He knew that Judas would betray Him?

YUSEF: Yes. Even then He tried to win him by love. If He cannot win him through love, He does not want him.

MAYOR: Indeed. We have not understood these things, Yusef.

YUSEF: But also Jesus teaches us about God on His Cross. God destroys evil by bearing evil.

ABDU: What do you mean, Yusef.

YUSEF: I will try to explain, my friends. Way down south in the middle of Africa the people have a game they play. They take a big stone and put it in the fire and heat it. Then a group of men stand in a circle. One man takes the stone out of the fire. He cannot hold it, so quickly he throws it to the next man and so on around the ring. If you do not throw the stone very quickly, you will be burned. As fast as they can, the men throw the stone one to another.

BASEAT: I don't want to play that game.

YUSEF: The point is -- evil is like this stone. It burns us so we pass it one to another quickly. Abdu, what do you do when a man insults you?

ABDU: I insult him.

YUSEF: What if he is too important a man to insult?

ABDU: Oh, I insult Baseat.

BASEAT: That's for sure.

YUSEF: Then what do you do, Baseat?

BASEAT: I insult my donkey. The proverb says, "He could not beat his donkey so he beat the saddle."

YUSEF: Ah, this is the point exactly. When evil comes upon us, quickly we throw the evil to someone else. But God takes the evil and destroys it by bearing it Himself. When He does this He gets hurt. Supposing you were playing the game of the hot stones. You decide

YUSEF: you will not take the stone and throw it to your neighbor to burn his hands. You decide to hold the stone. What will happen, Abdu?

ABDU: You will be very badly burned.

YUSEF: This is the way God destroys evil. He takes evil to Himself. He is very badly hurt, but evil is destroyed. Once I read about a group of soldiers who were fighting in the war. They were all together in a narrow ditch. They were very close to the enemy. Those days in the war, they used small bombs which you throw with your hands. It seems one of the enemy came very close to this ditch. He threw one of these hand bombs into the ditch. The officer saw the bomb fall into the ditch. He knew that in just a minute it would explode and kill all of the soldiers. So he threw his body over the bomb. He took all the power of the bomb into his own body. He saved the lives of all his friends.

MAYOR: This was a great sacrifice for the man to make.

YUSEF: This is what God does in Christ on the Cross. The bomb is like evil. Christ takes evil to Himself and destroys evil. He destroys evil by bearing evil in His own body. Baseat, can you put out a fire by beating on it with a hammer?

BASEAT: No. Of course not. This would only spread the fire to other places.

YUSEF: Evil is like the fire. It cannot be destroyed by force. It can only be destroyed by being borne away. Abdu, what does the 53rd chapter of Isaiah say?

ABDU: (Reciting) "Surely He has borne our griefs and carried our sorrows, yet we esteemed him stricken, smitten by God and afflicted, but he was wounded for our transgressions. He was bruised for our iniquities. Upon him was the chastisement that made us whole and with his stripes we are healed. All we, like sheep, have gone astray. We have turned every one to his own way and the Lord hath laid on him the iniquity of us all."

YUSEF: You see, my friends, even the prophet Isaiah saw and understood these things. Christ on the Cross teaches us two very important things about God. God wants us to come to Him only if drawn to Him by love, and God destroys evil by bearing evil away. But Christ also teaches us about God in the resurrection.

MAYOR: This is right. We have looked at the life of Christ and at the death of Christ, now we must look at the resurrection of Christ.

YUSEF: Here too, we see two things. In his resurrection, Christ shows us love united with power. Without the resurrection all is false, all is lost. Without the

YUSEF: resurrection God has been defeated. If we think only of the Cross, if we do not see the resurrection, then yes, we must say that Christ was defeated.

ABDU: But He was not defeated. He was victorious.

YUSEF: Indeed, He was victorious over sin and death. So in the resurrection, we see love united with power. Many good men have died for things they believed in. This was nothing new.

MAYOR: But only Christ rose from the dead.

YUSEF: Right. So in the resurrection we see perfect love united with perfect power. That is power over sin and death. In the resurrection we see the victory of the love which sacrifices. When Jesus rose from the dead, Abdu, did He go back and show Himself to the priests who had killed Him?

ABDU: No. He showed Himself only to the disciples who believed in Him.

YUSEF: Why did He not show Himself to the priests?

ABDU: If He had, they would have had to have believed on Him in spite of themselves.

YUSEF: Did He not want this?

ABDU: I am beginning to see that He did not. You have taught us that Christ wanted men to follow Him only if drawn by His perfect love.

YUSEF: I am happy that you have begun to see, O Abdu. The resurrection is the victory of love which draws us by love. Baseat, open and read First Corinthians 15, verses 54 through 57. Let us close tonight thinking about these verses.

BASEAT: (Reading) "When the perishable puts on the imperishable, and the mortal puts on immortality, then shall come to pass the saying that is written:

'Death is swallowed up in victory.
'O death, where is thy victory?
O death, where is thy sting?'

The sting of death is sin, and the power of sin is the law. But thanks be to God, who giveth us the victory through our Lord Jesus Christ."

QUESTIONS FOR DISCUSSION

1. What are the three ways God reveals Himself to us?
2. God wishes to teach us about Himself. He sends prophets to us. Why is this not enough?
3. Jesus teaches that God loves all men. Where do we read this in the teachings of Jesus?
4. Jesus teaches that God loves all men. Was this what the prophets taught? Explain.
5. Yusef says Christ teaches us that God is not angry with sinners. How can this be? Explain.
6. What are the two lessons we learn about God from the Cross of Christ?
7. Christ tries to win us to Himself. He uses only one way. What is this way?
8. Christ wants to win us to Himself. What are the ways he rejects?
9. How does God destroy evil?
10. The Cross of Christ shows us the love of God. What does the Resurrection show us?
11. There are three ways Christ did not use to try and win people. Do we follow Him for any of these reasons? Discuss and explain.
12. The Resurrection was a great victory. What kind of a victory was it?

SUMMARY OF LESSON

God is light. He enlightens us in Christ. From the life of Christ we learn that God loves all men. From the death of Christ we learn that God destroys evil by bearing evil. From the Resurrection of Christ we learn that God wins a great victory of love.

MOTTO: God destroys evil by bearing evil.

97

9
GOD IS LIGHT AND HE WAS FAITHFUL TO HIS PEOPLE IN THE OLD COVENANT

SCRIPTURES TO BE READ: I Corinthians 1:9; James 1:17; Psalms 33:4; Psalms 89:31-33; Lamentations 3:22-23; Deuteronomy 7:9; Genesis 17:1-4; II Timothy 2:15

STATEMENT OF LESSON

God is light. Light is always the same. It never deceives us and never changes. God is like this, too, because God is light. This means that God is faithful. We can trust Him. When we say God is faithful we mean He is unchanging. Some think this means He is unmoving. They think all is fixed and cannot be changed. This is not what God means. God is unchanging in His purpose. His purpose is to tell us of His love for us. We know that God is love. Love wants to show itself to the beloved. He is faithful and unchanging in this purpose. We see His unchangingness in the Old Testament. He made a Covenant with Abraham. God promised blessing. Abraham promised obedience. Abraham fulfilled his promise and was obedient. God was faithful in His promise and He blessed Abraham. Then God made a Covenant with a special people through Moses. Again God promises to bless and He asked His people to promise to be obedient. They promised but they were not obedient. Because they were not obedient, God raised up Babylon to destroy them. The Covenant of the Law was not enough. There had to be a New Covenant. The Old Covenant failed, but God remained faithful. He remained faithful to His purpose to show men His love to them. So we see in the Old Testament that God was faithful even when men were faithless and disobeyed.

OUTLINE

HE WAS FAITHFUL TO HIS PEOPLE IN THE OLD COVENANT

1. God is faithful. That is, He is unchanging.

    a. Unchanging does not mean unmoving.

    b. He is unchanging in His purpose to reveal Himself.

2. God is faithful. That is He keeps His promises (Covenants) no matter what happens.

    a. What is a covenant?

    b. What Covenants did God make?

    c. What happened?

THE DIALOGUE

GOD IS . . .

SCENE 9

CHARACTERS:

Yusef, the Wise

Abdu, the Inquirer

Baseat, the Simple

Attalla, Abdu's brother

THE DIALOGUE

(The dialogue opens with Yusef and Baseat sitting in front of Yusef's house, talking.)

YUSEF: Baseat, where is your friend, Abdu?

BASEAT: He will be here right away. His brother, Attalla, the clerk in the county offices, is here to visit him.

YUSEF: I hope he will come.

BASEAT: Sure, he will come. Abdu and I have been telling Attalla about our discussions here together.

YUSEF: What did Attalla think?

BASEAT: Attalla was very pleased. He wants to come tonight.

YUSEF: Good. We will be glad to have him.

BASEAT: Here they come now. (Enter Abdu and his brother Attalla).

YUSEF: Welcome, my friends! How are you, Attalla? It has been a long time since I have seen you. How are you?

ATTALLA: Praise God, all is well. My brother Abdu has been telling me about your discussions. If you don't mind I wish to join you tonight.

YUSEF: You are most welcome, but let us begin. Attalla, we have been talking about the subject "God is light." We said God enlightens us about Himself. He does this in three ways. I will show you how clever your brother Abdu is. Now, Abdu, tell me what are the three ways.

ABDU: He enlightens us about Himself in nature, in the prophets and in Christ.

YUSEF: Very good, indeed. Now we must take a new subject. We must understand more about God who is light. God is light. This means He is faithful. Baseat, read James 1, verse 17.

100

BASEAT: (Reading) "Every good gift and perfect gift is from above, coming down from the Father of lights with whom there is no variation or shadow due to change."

YUSEF: Now, Baseat, tell me what color the clover is.

BASEAT: Green.

YUSEF: Is the clover always green?

BASEAT: Of course.

YUSEF: Maybe tomorrow the light will deceive you. Maybe the light will make the clover look black.

BASEAT: Impossible. Light does not deceive us.

YUSEF: What color is the soil, Baseat?

BASEAT: Brown.

YUSEF: What color is the sky, Baseat?

BASEAT: Blue.

YUSEF: Maybe tomorrow morning the sky will be brown, the soil will be blue.

BASEAT: No. This does not happen.

YUSEF: Maybe the light will trick you.

BASEAT: No. No. Natural light does not trick us.

YUSEF: Very well. Abdu?

ABDU: Yes, Yusef.

YUSEF: Do you think maybe tomorrow when the sun rises the sun will give out cold light rather than warm light.

ABDU: No, Yusef. If the sun rises, it must give off warm light.

YUSEF: Very good, my friends. So we see. Light never changes. It never deceives us. We can trust the light. It will always be the same. That is, the light is faithful. Do you agree Abdu?

ABDU: Indeed.

YUSEF: Now, God is like the light. God never changes. God never deceives us. We can trust God. This means that God is faithful. Brother Attalla, read for us I Corinthians 1:9.

ATTALLA: (Reading) "God is faithful, by whom you were called into fellowship of His Son, Jesus Christ, our Lord."

YUSEF: Very good. God is faithful, for God is light. This is a big subject, my friends. I think we had better divide this subject into two. Tonight let us talk about how God was faithful to His people in the Old Covenant. Tomorrow we will take how God is faithful

YUSEF:	to His family in the New Covenant. Is this all right with everybody?
ALL:	Very good. Yes. Of course. Fine.
YUSEF:	Very well. God is faithful. We said this means He is unchanging. In the verse that Baseat read, James says that God does not change, but my friends, everyone understands this verse wrong. They say God does not change, but what they really believe is that God does not move. Baseat, do you know Mabrook here in the village?
BASEAT:	Mabrook, the lazy?
YUSEF:	Yes, he's the one. Why do men call him "the lazy."
BASEAT:	Go to him in the morning, you find him asleep before his house. Go to him in the afternoon, you find him asleep before his house. Go to him after sunset, you find him asleep within his house. He is the laziest man I know.
YUSEF:	You mean he doesn't change?
ABDU:	Change! He doesn't even move.
YUSEF:	But some people, my sons, make God to be like this. They say God does not change, but what they really believe is God does not move. They say, "All is the will of God." God does not change. This means, we can do nothing. Nothing can change, so there is no use to try to change anything. Surrender. That's all - just surrender. Say, "O Lord, O Lord," then sleep. God does not change. The world does not change. This means we cannot change anything. The rich are the rich, the poor are the poor. The wicked are the wicked. The righteous are the righteous. The saints are the saints, and the sinners are the sinners. But you see, Abdu, if we think this way, this means that God is like Mabrook, the lazy. This is not what we mean when we say, "God does not change."
ATTALLA:	What do we mean?
YUSEF:	We mean that God is faithful like the light. Attalla, my friend, does light change?
ATTALLA:	No, it does not.
YUSEF:	But is light working?
ATTALLA:	Yes, light works all the time.
YUSEF:	Abdu, open and read from Psalm 33:4.
ABDU:	(Reading) "For the word of the Lord is upright and all His work is done in faithfulness."
YUSEF:	God is at work all the time and God is faithful. This means you can rely on God. You do not find Him

YUSEF: faithful today and deceitful tomorrow. No, He is unchanging. Like the light is always faithful. He is faithful in His work. He is faithful in His purpose toward men. Now Abdu, what _is_ His purpose toward men?

ABDU: We learned that His purpose toward men is to tell men about Himself.

YUSEF: Very good. Let us put it in another way. God's unchanging purpose is to tell us of His love for us. Now let us put this together. God is faithful. That is, He does not change. He does not change in His purpose to tell us of His love for us. Does everybody understand so far?

BASEAT: Ah, I understand everything.

ABDU: If you understand everything, Baseat, maybe you had better begin to explain these things to us.

BASEAT: I mean - I understand everything he has said so far.

YUSEF: Good, Baseat. You will understand the rest too. Now, Abdu.

ABDU: Yes, Yusef.

YUSEF: I see you have brought your brother Attalla tonight.

ABDU: Yes indeed, Yusef.

YUSEF: Do you love your brother, Abdu?

ABDU: Of course I love him. This is my older brother, I love him very much.

YUSEF: Attalla, if you get sick, does your brother, Abdu, come to see you.

ATTALLA: He comes at once.

YUSEF: Very well, in the days of the Feast, does he send a remembrance to you?

ATTALLA: Of course!

YUSEF: If he goes to town, does he stop to ask about you?

ATTALLA: Sure he does.

YUSEF: But Attalla, you know that he loves you. Why must he do these things?

ATTALLA: My brother Abdu loves me very much. He wants always to show how much he loves me.

YUSEF: I see. Then the one who loves always wants his beloved to know that he loves him.

ABDU: Of course.

YUSEF: Very well, God is like this. God loves us. Because God loves us He wants us to know that He loves us. But man in sin refuses God's love. Man in sin does

YUSEF: not understand God's love. Man in sin does not respond to God's love. God is faithful in that He continues faithfully to try to make clear His love and to win men by love. God does not change in His purpose to show us that He loves us. God was faithful in this purpose with His people in the Old Testament. Let us look to see indeed how faithful He was. With Abraham, God made a Covenant. Now what is a covenant?

ABDU: It is not a promise, or something like that?

YUSEF: Yes, it is a promise, but it is a special kind of promise. When two men make a promise, each man chooses to make a promise to the other man, but with a covenant, God chooses man. Man does not choose God. With a covenant, two things happen. God promises a blessing. Man promises obedience. Baseat, read Deuteronomy 7:9.

BASEAT: (Reading) "Know therefore that the Lord your God is God, the faithful God who keeps covenant and steadfast love . . ."

YUSEF: (Interjecting) That's far enough, Baseat. It says God is a faithful God who keeps covenant and steadfast love. Now what must man do? Read on, Baseat.

BASEAT: (Reading) "..who keeps covenant and steadfast love with those who love Him and keep His commandments."

YUSEF: I see. There is a condition. Man must obey the commandments. Now, Abdu, what is a covenant? What does God promise and what does man promise?

ABDU: God promises blessing. Man promises obedience.

YUSEF: And who chooses to make the covenant?

ABDU: God chooses man.

YUSEF: Very good. Now - God's unchanging purpose - is to let sinful man know God and His love. So He begins by making a covenant with Abraham. Now, Attalla, my friend, read Genesis 17, verses 1 through 4. This is the story of God's covenant with Abraham. Then tell me what God promises and what man promises.

ATTALLA: (Opens the Bible, reads the verses, thinks for a minute and finally says.) It says God promises that Abraham will be the father of many nations.

YUSEF: Very good. And Abdu, what does God ask of Abraham?

ABDU: (Thinks and reads and finally says) God says, "Walk before me and be blameless."

YUSEF: You see. In a Covenant God promises blessing, man promises obedience. Now, was Abraham faithful to this covenant? Was he obedient?

BASEAT: He was the most obedient of all.

YUSEF: Good, Baseat. Now, was God faithful to bless Abraham?

ATTALLA: Indeed, God blessed him many times over.

YUSEF: So God was faithful. Now let us look at the next covenant. The first Covenant was with one man. The next Covenant was with a whole people at the time of Moses. Abdu, where did he make this covenant?

ABDU: He made it with the people at Mt. Sinai in the desert after they had crossed the Red Sea and escaped from Pharoah.

YUSEF: Now with this Covenant, what did God promise, Abdu?

ABDU: I'm not sure, Yusef.

YUSEF: God promised He would make them a great nation. The people promised they would obey the commandments of God. But then what happened, O Attalla?

ATTALLA: I don't know, Yusef, but my brother Abdu here reads the Bible and understands many things. You must ask him.

YUSEF: Very well, Abdu, what happened then?

ABDU: The people obeyed for a while and then they disobeyed.

YUSEF: Right. With Abraham, it was very easy. Abraham fulfilled his promise. He obeyed. So God fulfilled His promise. He blessed Abraham. But with the second Covenant, the people disobeyed the Law. Now what can God do? He cannot bless them as He wishes. But God is faithful. What shall He do?

BASEAT: Let God go home and the people go home and the matter is finished.

YUSEF: He could have done this. But what is God's unchanging purpose, did we say?

ABDU: It is to reveal His love.

YUSEF: Right, Abdu, and God is faithful to His purpose. Baseat, read Psalm 89, verses 31 through 33.

BASEAT: (Reading) "If they violate my statutes and do not keep my commandments, then I will punish their transgression with the rod and their iniquity with scourges, but I will not remove from Him my steadfast love or be false to my faithfulness."

YUSEF: You see, my friends, God is still faithful. God is still determined to reveal His love, even after men are faithless. Men break the covenant and God remains faithful. Do you know the story of Hosea the prophet?

ABDU: I read it once, but I did not understand it. Tell us the story, O Yusef.

YUSEF: Very well, my friends. This is a great story. Hosea was one of the prophets of Israel. He took to wife a woman who was called Gomar. When he married her, he thought she was a pure woman. After some time, God blessed them with a son. But soon after that, Gomar began to go to other men. Then when she gave birth to a daughter, the prophet was not sure whether the child was his or not. After a time she became with child again. She bore a son. This time, the prophet was sure it was not his child. So he named the boy "Not My People." After this, Gomar went into the world to work for the idol worshippers who used adulteresses in worship. Of course Hosea's heart was broken. "Why," he kept asking, "why has God done this to me? Why did He ask me to marry this woman? Why did this women destroy our home?" Then one day Hosea was walking in the market. He went by the place where they were selling slaves. He saw them selling a woman who looked to be very old. Her face was very hard. Suddenly he saw that this woman was Gomar who used to be his wife. He stepped quickly into the crowd and bought Gomar back. It seemed she had become old very quickly and was no longer of any use to the idolators who used her. So she was sold as a slave and Hosea paid the price to buy her back. Then God said to Hosea, "Go again. Love a woman who is beloved of a paramour and is an adulteress, even as the Lord loves the people of Israel though they have turned to other gods." Little by little, Hosea began to understand. The great suffering which he endured was like the suffering of God. God had loved His people. His people were like a young bride. This young bride went after many lovers. God out of His love buys her back. Hosea understood that he and Gomar were like God and the people of God. Gomar had become an adulteress and had gone after other men. The people of God had become an adulteress and gone after other gods. As Hosea suffered, so God suffered. Hosea still loved his wife. Even so, God still loved his sinful people.

ATTALLA: Indeed. This is a great story.

YUSEF: God is faithful, the people are unfaithful. But even after the people are unfaithful, God is still determined to make His love known to men. Perhaps Jeremiah understood this best of all. Abdu, read Lamentations 3:22 and 23. Pay attention, my friends. Jeremiah has watched the Babylonians come and destroy the City of God -- Jerusalem. He has watched the people of God go away into slavery. He is very sad and his heart is broken. He knows the people have sinned and must be punished, but what does he say of the Lord? Read Abdu.

ABDU: (Reading) "The steadfast love of the Lord never ceases. His mercies never come to an end. They are new every morning. Great is Thy faithfulness."

YUSEF: What if you sat and watched our village destroyed and all our people carried away into slavery? Could you write these words?

ABDU: Indeed. Indeed. I could not write them. Jeremiah must have been a great prophet.

YUSEF: He was indeed a great prophet, my friends. He was so great he saw that the Old Covenant was not enough. The Covenant with Moses was a covenant of law. The Law told men what to do, but men are weak and fail. They do not have the power to obey the law. Every man knows what he should do but he does not do it. Jeremiah was so great he saw that one day God would make a New Covenant. He saw the Old Covenant destroyed. He saw the Old Covenant only condemned men in their weakness. He said one day God will make a new Covenant and write it on the hearts of people, not on tablets of stone. Then people will do good not because they have to, but because they want to. Perhaps Jeremiah understood better than anyone else how great is the faithfulness of God. He knew that when men are faithless, God is still faithful.

QUESTIONS FOR DISCUSSION

1. Does the light ever deceive us?
2. God is light. God is faithful. What is the connection between these two?
3. God is unchanging; this means God does not move. Is this right or wrong? Explain.
4. God does not change. Does this mean nothing in the world changes?
5. God does not change. What is the proper way to understand this?
6. What is God's unchanging purpose towards men? In a Covenant God promises something, and men promise something. Explain.
7. Was Abraham obedient to the Covenant he made with God?
8. God made a Covenant with the people at the time of Moses. What did God promise? What did the people promise?
9. Did the people fulfill their promise?
10. When the people are faithless, what does God do?
11. Tell the story of Hosea.
12. Jeremiah saw the Old Covenant destroyed. He saw the people destroyed. Then what did he say about the faithfulness of God?
13. What did Jeremiah say was needed?

SUMMARY OF THE LESSON

God is light.
God is faithful and God does not change.
He does not change in His purpose to show His love to men.
God made a Covenant with Abraham, and Abraham was faithful.
Then God made a covenant with the people at the time of Moses,
   but the people disobeyed and were not faithful, but God did
   not turn aside from His purpose.
He was faithful to His purpose.
His purpose was to show His love.

   MOTTO: God is faithful. He does not change in His purpose to show His love.

10
GOD IS LIGHT AND HE IS FAITHFUL TO HIS FAMILY IN THE NEW COVENANT

SCRIPTURES TO BE READ: Psalm 143:1-2; Matthew 7:7-11;
Matthew 26:26-28; Romans 8:37-39;
I Corinthians 1:8-9; I Corinthians 10:13;
I Thessalonians 5:23-24;
II Thessalonians 3:3; Hebrew 8:6-10

STATEMENT OF LESSON

God is light. This means that He is faithful. We have seen that He was faithful in the Old Covenant. But the Old Covenant was not enough. It was a Covenant of Law which condemns us. The Law failed to redeem. The Law did not give power for obedience. God was faithful in the Old Covenant. The people were faithless. They had no power to obey the Law. So God made a New Covenant with them in Jesus Christ. God is faithful to this Covenant. He is faithful to forgive us through the sacrifice of Christ if we seek forgiveness. But God does not forgive us and then leave us. He is also faithful to establish us in faith. He asks only that we rely upon Him. If we rely upon ourselves, He cannot establish us in faith. God is light and He is faithful. In faithfulness, He strengthens us for temptation. God does not allow us to be tempted beyond our strength. Finally, God is faithful to answer our prayers. Sometimes His answer is "No," but this is an answer. When He says "No," we think He has not answered. God does not call us His people, He calls us now His family. We see that in many ways He is faithful to us. We are His family.

OUTLINE

<u>GOD IS LIGHT</u>

<u>HE IS FAITHFUL TO HIS FAMILY IN THE NEW COVENANT</u>

1. God is faithful to forgive. He forgives in the New Covenant by the sacrifice of Christ.

2. God is faithful to establish us in faith.

3. God is faithful to strengthen us for temptation.

4. God is faithful to answer prayer.

THE DIALOGUE

GOD IS . . .

SCENE 10

CHARACTERS:

Yusef, the Wise

Abdu, the Inquirer

Baseat, the Simple

Mayor Butrus

THE DIALOGUE

(Yusef and the Mayor are seated in Yusef's front room.)

YUSEF: We have missed you, Mr. Mayor.

MAYOR: Yes, I am very sorry to miss. Tell me, Yusef, what was the subject last night?

YUSEF: Last night we talked about the faithfulness of God.

MAYOR: Tell me, Yusef, about the lesson so I'll understand the whole story.

YUSEF: The story is very simple, Mayor. God is light. Light is faithful. Light does not trick us or deceive us. Light does not change.

MAYOR: True enough.

YUSEF: So we see God is like light in that God is faithful. So last night we looked at the Old Covenant to see how God was faithful to His people.

MAYOR: Indeed He was faithful to them, but they were not faithful to Him.

YUSEF: Very good, Mayor, but God remained faithful even when the people were unfaithful.

MAYOR: What then is the subject for tonight?

YUSEF: Tonight we will see how God is faithful in the New Covenant. We are more than His people, we are His family.

BASEAT: (Entering) Good evening, Mr. Mayor. Good evening, Elder Yusef.

YUSEF: Good evening, Baseat. Where is your friend, Abdu?

BASEAT: (Looking about rather guiltily) Do I know where he is?

YUSEF: What do you mean, do you know where he is? Of course you know where he is. Why will he not come?

BASEAT: Do I know? He is angry.

111

YUSEF: Why is he angry?

BASEAT: Do I know?

YUSEF: Baseat, go and tell him to come. Tell him not to be angry.

BASEAT: I will not go.

YUSEF: I see. He is angry with you.

MAYOR: I will go and bring him. Do not be afraid. (The Mayor goes out.)

YUSEF: Very well, Baseat. Tell me the story. What is the matter. Why are you and Abdu angry with each other?

BASEAT: It's nothing.

YUSEF: Come on! Tell me the story.

BASEAT: (Looking at the floor, clasping and unclasping his hands, drawing with his toe on the mud floor and looking down, he begins.) It is nothing, O Yusef. You know that Abdu has some palm trees.

YUSEF: Yes, I know.

BASEAT: Well, sometimes he asks me during the date season to guard them at night.

YUSEF: Yes, I know. I know. What happened?

BASEAT: Well, we heard from the Mayor that there were thieves in the area. Last night was my turn to guard Abdu's dates. Abdu told me to be on guard for thieves.

YUSEF: Did he give you a gun?

BASEAT: Yes, he gave me a rifle and a pistol.

YUSEF: What happened?

BASEAT: They came in the night, it seems, and they stole some dates.

YUSEF: Were you sleeping?

BASEAT: No.

YUSEF: Did you see them?

BASEAT: (Vaguely) I don't remember whether I saw them or not.

YUSEF: I see.

(The voices of the Mayor and Abdu are heard outside of the room.)

ABDU: Baseat is in there. I will not enter. I will not enter the room where he is.

MAYOR: (Quietly) But for my sake. Never mind. For my sake.

ABDU: (Still outside. Slowly) Very well, Mr. Mayor. For your sake, but only for your sake will I enter the

112

ABDU: room. (They come in and Abdu sits down angrily on the far side of the room from Baseat.)

YUSEF: Abdu, what's happened?

ABDU: Nothing.

YUSEF: What do you mean, nothing? Why are you angry?

ABDU: Baseat is not simple, he is an idiot.

YUSEF: Just tell us what has Baseat done?

ABDU: You know that sometimes I ask Baseat to guard my fields at night.

YUSEF: Yes, we know.

ABDU: When the dates are ripe, sometimes I ask him to guard my dates.

YUSEF: Go on.

ABDU: Yesterday I heard from the Mayor that there had been some stealing. So I gave my gun to Baseat last night and I asked him to be especially careful.

YUSEF: Then what happened?

ABDU: Do you see the point, Elder Yusef? I told him thieves might come. I gave him a gun. Then later the thieves came. And do you know what he did?

MAYOR: Was he sleeping?

ABDU: No. They came and Baseat sat down with them and made tea for them and served them tea.

MAYOR: My goodness!

ABDU: The thieves told Baseat that I had sent them to cut down a bunch of dates. Then this idiot, Baseat, believed them so they climbed one of my trees. They cut a fresh bunch of dates. Then they walked off.

MAYOR: Were they armed?

ABDU: No. The only man with a gun was Baseat.

YUSEF: (Turning to Baseat) Is this what happened, O Baseat? Did you serve them tea?

BASEAT: (Wailing) But I did not know that they were thieves. They appeared to be very kind men. I didn't know they were thieves.

ABDU: (Shouting) You didn't know that they were thieves! They steal my dates -- and you don't know they are thieves?

BASEAT: (Pleading) They were nice men.

113

YUSEF: (Interjecting) Now Abdu. I have many dates. Tomorrow I will send you a big bunch to replace the ones that Baseat has lost for you.

ABDU: No. Elder Yusef! I cannot accept!

YUSEF: It's all right. We'll work it out.

MAYOR: (Interjecting) It seems to me, Baseat, that you are in the wrong.

BASEAT: (Slowly) I guess I am.

YUSEF: (Turning to Abdu) Good - now everything is settled.

YUSEF: Shake hands, my sons. Shake hands. (Rather reluctantly they shake hands.)

YUSEF: Praise God. It is all finished. This is a very small matter and I think God will take this matter and teach us something.

Now, Abdu, what was last night's subject about?

ABDU: We talked about the faithfulness of God in the Old Testament.

YUSEF: And tonight, Baseat? What will be our subject?

BASEAT: I think it is the faithfulness of God in the New Testament.

YUSEF: Very good, but let us put it in another way. God is light. He is faithful to His family in the New Covenant. Say it now, Abdu.

ABDU: God is light. He is faithful to His family in the New Covenant.

YUSEF: Now, God is faithful to us in four ways. First, God is faithful to forgive by the sacrifice of Christ. Baseat, where is your brother?

BASEAT: You mean my brother, Bulis?

YUSEF: Yes, where is he?

BASEAT: You know where he is. He is in prison.

YUSEF: He killed a man didn't he?

BASEAT: Yes.

YUSEF: Do you go to visit him, Baseat?

BASEAT: Of course.

YUSEF: Very well, next time you go to him, say to him, "Brother Bulis, I know what is wrong with you. You are in prison."

BASEAT: How can I say this to him? He knows very well he is in prison.

YUSEF: Very well. Then say to him, "My brother Bulis, I have good news for you."

BASEAT: He will be happy to hear any good news.

YUSEF: Then say to him, "The good news is 'be good.'"

BASEAT: What is this? This is not good news for him.

MAYOR: (Interjecting) This is true. The only good news for a prisoner is how to get out. What is the point, Yusef?

YUSEF: The point is, that man is in a prison of sin. The Old Covenant is law. The law tells us we are in a prison of sin. We read the law. We see how righteous we should be. Then we see and understand how we are in a prison of sin. The law tells us to be good. But this is not good news. This does not help us. We wish to get out of the prison.

MAYOR: What then, Yusef?

YUSEF: So God makes a New Covenant with man. In the Old Covenant, God tells man to be righteous. But this covenant fails. Man is not righteous. He has no strength, so in the New Covenant, God forgives man and He gives men strength to be righteous. Abdu, read Hebrews 8: verse 6.

ABDU: (Reading) "For if that first Covenant had been faultless, there would have been no occasion for a second."

YUSEF: Now Baseat, read Matthew 26, verses 26 through 28.

BASEAT: (Reading) "Now as they were eating, Jesus took bread and blessed and broke it, and gave it to the disciples and said, 'Take, eat, this is my body.' And He took the cup, and when he had given thanks he gave it to them, saying, 'Drink of it, all of you, for this is my blood of the New Covenant which is poured out for many for the forgiveness of sins.'"

YUSEF: (Repeating) "'This is my blood of the New Covenant, which is poured out for many for the forgiveness of sins.'" Now, Mr. Mayor, honor us by reading I John 1:9.

MAYOR: (Reading) "If we confess our sins, he is faithful and just and will forgive our sins and cleanse us from all unrighteousness."

YUSEF: What does John say in the verses just before this, Mayor?

MAYOR: (Looking) He says God is light.

YUSEF: Very good. We see the two ideas together. God is light. God is faithful to forgive. What did your verse say, Abdu?

ABDU: It said the Old Covenant was no good and we needed a New Covenant.

YUSEF: Very good. Now, Abdu, why was the Old Covenant no good?

ABDU: I understand that the Old Covenant tells us to be righteous, but we can't do it.

YUSEF: Very good. So does the Old Covenant make us better, or make us worse?

ABDU: I think maybe it makes us worse, for now we find out how bad we really are.

YUSEF: Exactly right. Mayor, what did we say the New Covenant does?

MAYOR: The New Covenant forgives us and gives us strength for righteousness.

YUSEF: Now, Baseat, what did your verse say about the Covenant?

BASEAT: It said it is the New Covenant in the blood of Christ which is poured out for many for the forgiveness of sins.

YUSEF: Very good, Baseat. Now, Abdu, what did God call the people of the Old Covenant?

ABDU: He called them His people.

YUSEF: But in the New Covenant, we are not the people of God.

BASEAT: What are we then?

YUSEF: We are the family of God. We are closer than just the people of God. But God is not just faithful to forgive us. He does not forgive us and leave us. He helps us along the way. God is faithful to establish us in the faith. Abdu, read I Corinthians 1: verses 8 and 9.

ABDU: (Reading) "He will sustain you to the end, guiltless in the day of our Lord, Jesus Christ."

YUSEF: "He will sustain you to the end" - very good. Now, Mayor, read for us I Thessalonians 5: verses 23 and 24.

MAYOR: (Reading) "May the God of peace himself sanctify you wholly. And may your spirit, and soul, and body be kept sound and blameless at the coming of our Lord Jesus Christ. He who calls you is faithful, and he will do it."

YUSEF: Very good. "Your spirit, and soul, and body will be kept sound and blameless at the coming of our Lord Jesus Christ. He who calls you is faithful." Now, Abdu.

ABDU: Yes, Yusef.

YUSEF: God is faithful to establish us in faith, but we must rely on Him or He cannot. Now, are you ready to walk through the Mayor's garden at night?

ABDU: Impossible, impossible.

YUSEF: Why not?

ABDU: The Mayor has wild dogs he sets loose in the garden at night.

YUSEF: But, Abdu, there are dogs all over the village.

BASEAT: Not like these dogs! Once a donkey wandered into the garden and the dogs killed and ate the donkey. All of the village is afraid of these dogs.

YUSEF: Very well. Are you ready to walk, Abdu, through the garden if the Mayor walks with you?

ABDU: Ah - this is something else. I think the dogs will not bother you, Mr. Mayor.

MAYOR: It is so. They know me. They will not touch me. They will not touch the man who walks with me.

YUSEF: Very well, Mayor. What if Abdu walks through your garden with you at night, where must he walk?

MAYOR: He must walk behind me.

YUSEF: I think he must trust you for protection.

MAYOR: Indeed, he must.

YUSEF: What if he becomes afraid and runs?

MAYOR: The dogs will kill him.

YUSEF: What if he does not rely upon you, but walks on by himself.

MAYOR: They will kill him right away. Only if he trusts me and walks behind me can he walk safely.

YUSEF: Very good. Now my friends, life is like this. The devil is like the dogs of the Mayor. As we walk through life, these dogs are about us. God is faithful to establish us and protect us if we will trust in Him. If we are afraid and do not trust in Him, the devil will destroy us. If we trust in ourselves the devil will destroy us. Christ is ready to sustain us to the end, but we must trust in Him. Read your verse again, Mr. Mayor.

MAYOR: I think the verse in Romans is very good for this subject, too, Yusef.

YUSEF: Recite it for us, Mayor.

MAYOR: (Reciting) "Now in all these things we are more than conquerors through Him who loved us. For I am sure that neither death, nor life, nor angels, nor

MAYOR: principalities, nor things present, nor things to come, nor powers, nor height, nor depth, nor anything else in all creation will be able to separate us from the love of God in Christ Jesus, our Lord."

YUSEF: Very good. Christ is willing to sustain us to the end with one condition. What is it, Abdu?

ABDU: We must trust in Him.

YUSEF: Now, my friends, God is faithful to us in something else. He is faithful to strengthen us for temptation. Baseat, read II Thessalonians 3: verse 3.

BASEAT: (Reading) "The Lord is faithful. He will strengthen you and guard you from evil."

YUSEF: Now Baseat, read again I Corinthians 10:13.

BASEAT: (Reading) "No temptation has overtaken you that is not common to man. God is faithful and he will not let you be tempted beyond your strength, but with the temptation will also provide the way of escape that you may be able to endure it."

YUSEF: Now, Baseat, last night, did Abdu tell you the thieves might come?

BASEAT: Yes.

YUSEF: Did he give you his gun?

BASEAT: Yes.

YUSEF: Was the gun enough protection?

BASEAT: (Pleading) It was more than enough, but I did not know the men were thieves.

YUSEF: Exactly, O Baseat. We have a perfect parable here.

BASEAT: How?

YUSEF: When we are about to be tempted God comes to us. He says, "Look out for the devil, the devil is coming. The devil will tempt you." Then He gives us strength. He says, "Here's a gun. Here is my power. This is enough to drive away the devil. This is enough to drive away temptation."

MAYOR: I understand. Then when the devil comes we do not see that he is the devil. We do not use the power that God has given us. God gives us strength to overcome temptation, but we do not use it.

YUSEF: Correct. Then what do we do, Abdu? Do we blame ourselves?

ABDU: No. We do not. We make excuses. We say we are weak and had no strength to overcome. (Abdu raises his voice, suddenly getting the point.) That's right. This is exactly what Baseat said this morning. I

ABDU: gave him a gun to drive away the thieves which he did not use. The thieves tricked him, then he tried to blame me.

YUSEF: But you see, Abdu, Baseat has done this with you and you are both men. But all of us do this with God. We are tempted and we sin. Then we make excuses. But just like Baseat, we have power to drive off temptation, only we do not use it. Now, Baseat, read I Corinthians 10:13 again.

BASEAT: (Reading) "No temptation has overtaken you that is not common to man. God is faithful and He will not let you be tempted beyond your strength, but with the temptation will also provide the way of escape that you may be able to endure it."

YUSEF: Is this true, or not, Baseat?

BASEAT: (Sheepishly) It's true enough.

YUSEF: Now finally, my friends, how do we get this strength from God?

ABDU: I think we must pray. God says to us, "Ask and it shall be given unto you." He hears always, and He always answers.

YUSEF: Review for us, Abdu, the ways God is faithful to his family in the New Covenant.

ABDU: He is faithful to forgive our sins. He is faithful to sustain us in life, that is, in the faith.

YUSEF: Very good. And what else, Baseat?

BASEAT: He is faithful to strengthen us in temptation.

YUSEF: And finally, Mayor?

MAYOR: He is faithful to answer our prayers.

YUSEF: After all this, my friends, shall we trust in ourselves, or shall we trust in Him? Shall we lean upon ourselves, or shall we lean upon Him?

ABDU: We must lean upon Him. We must trust Him for He is faithful, as light is faithful.

QUESTIONS FOR DISCUSSION

1. Why is the law not enough?
2. Does the law save us, or condemn us?
3. What does Yusef suggest that Baseat say to his brother in prison? Why does this not help him? How is this like the law, when the law speaks to us?
4. In the New Covenant, God forgives us and He does something else. What else?
5. Christ says He will sustain us to the end, but He cannot sustain us unless we do something? What must we do?
6. What is the point of the story of the dogs in the Mayor's garden?
7. Baseat was guarding Abdu's dates. The dates were stolen. How is his excuse to Abdu like our excuse to God?
8. How did Abdu prepare Baseat for the robbers? How does God prepare us for temptation?
9. What excuse does Baseat use after the dates are stolen? What excuse do we use after we sin?
10. How can we get the strength of God?
11. What are the ways God is faithful to us? God is faithful. We can trust Him. How can we live day by day trusting God? If we really trust Him, what are the things we will do?

SUMMARY OF LESSON

God is faithful to us in Christ. He is faithful to forgive us and to give us power for obedience. He is faithful to sustain us if we will trust Him. He is faithful to strengthen us in temptation if we will accept His strength. He is faithful to answer our prayers, if we will pray.

Motto: On God - faithfulness: On us - trust.

11
GOD IS LIGHT AND HE WORKS LIKE LIGHT IN OUR HEARTS

SCRIPTURES TO BE READ: Psalm 36:9; John 2:45-46;
Revelation 3:20; John 1:5;
Matthew 5:14-16; Philippians 2:15

STATEMENT OF LESSON

God is light. He enlightens us in nature, in the prophets, and in Christ. We have seen that God is also faithful. Light is faithful, so God who is Light was faithful to His people in the Old Covenant. God is faithful to His family in the New Covenant. Now in this last lesson, in this section, we will see how God works like light in our hearts. God is light. Therefore, He must work like light. As we look to see how light works, we will begin to understand how God works. We see first that light is its own proof. As we look at light we do not ask for someone to prove to us that this is light. We look. We understand. We do not ask for proof. We see also that light does not tire. If we close the shutters to shut out the light, the light does not go away. It remains outside until we open the shutters again. But also, light will not enter the room by force. The wind comes and enters the room by force. The wind will blow the door open but light will not. Light waits patiently. Light enters only when we open the door. God works in this same way. Jesus said, "Behold I stand at the door and knock." Christ stands at the doors of our hearts knocking. He waits until we open and will not force His way in. If we do not open, He remains at the door knocking. Light also drives away the darkness. When we open the door, the light comes in. As the light comes in, the darkness goes. God works in this same way. He is light. When He comes, darkness goes. Lastly, light makes other things to

121

shine. So Christ has said that we are the light of the world. The light is not our light, but His light. His light shines through us to the world. Without His light, we are nothing. Because it is His light and not ours, all praise must be to Him and not to ourselves, so we see that we are responsible as lights in the world. God is light and He has enlightened us and thus we must enlighten others. God is light and He is faithful to us. Therefore, we must be faithful to others. God works like light in our hearts, we must work like lights in the world.

OUTLINE

GOD IS LIGHT AND HE WORKS LIKE LIGHT IN OUR HEARTS

1. Light is its own proof.
2. Light does not tire.
3. Light enters by invitation, not by force.
4. Light drives away darkness.
5. Light makes other things shine.

THE DIALOGUE

GOD IS . . .

SCENE 11

CHARACTERS:

Yusef, the Wise

Abdu, the Inquirer

Baseat, the Simple

(For this lesson, you must have at least two lamps or candles in the classroom. During the lesson, Baseat will have to carry one of the lamps out of the room. Thus, he will need another lamp in the room to read by.)

THE DIALOGUE

(Yusef is seated on the bench before his house. He is reading.)

YUSEF: (Reading) "You are the light of the world. A city set on a hill cannot be hid. Nor do men light a lamp and put it under a bushel, but on a stand, and it gives light to all in the house. Let your light so shine before men that they may see your good works and give glory to your Father who is in Heaven."

(Enter Baseat and Abdu.)

ABDU AND
BASEAT: Good evening, Elder Yusef.

YUSEF: Good evening, my friends. Good evening.

BASEAT: Where is the Mayor?

YUSEF: He cannot be with us tonight, but Abdu, did the dates arrive?

ABDU: Praise God. But Elder Yusef, you should not have done it. It was not necessary.

YUSEF: I have too many date palms anyway.

BASEAT: O Yusef, shall we begin a new subject tonight?

YUSEF: I thought first that we should, but I think we must talk again of God as light. This morning very early I came down to open the door of my house. The house was very dark. It was so dark I could not see the way. My wife had left a small table in the middle of the room. I almost fell over it.

ABDU: May God keep you, Elder Yusef.

YUSEF: And you, Abdu. Then I arrived at the door. I opened the door and the light filled the house. Then I began to think. All day I have thought of how light works.

123

YUSEF: Light works in a special way. God is light. God also works in this special way. Let us think together of how light works, then we will understand how God works in our hearts.

ABDU: This is the best thing, Yusef. Let us begin.

YUSEF: Very well, Abdu, open to Psalm 36 and read verse 9.

ABDU: (Reading) "For with thee is the fountain of life. In they light do we see light." What does this mean, Yusef?

YUSEF: All right now, Abdu, read also John 1: verses 45 and 46.

ABDU: (Reading) "Phillip found Nathaniel and said to him, 'We have found Him of whom Moses and the Law and also the prophets wrote, Jesus of Nazareth, the son of Joseph.' Nathaniel said to him, 'Can any good things come out of Nazareth?' Phillip said to him, 'Come and see.'"

YUSEF: Abdu, what does Phillip say to Nathaniel?

ABDU: He says, "Come, we have found Jesus of whom Moses wrote and the law and the prophets."

YUSEF: Then what did he answer?

ABDU: Nathaniel answered and said: "It's no use, nothing good can come from Nazareth."

YUSEF: Very well. Did he then begin to fight with him? Did he begin to argue with him? Did he try to prove to him that Jesus is the One of whom Moses wrote?

BASEAT: No.

YUSEF: What did he say, Baseat?

BASEAT: He said, "Come and see."

YUSEF: David says, "In thy light we see light." This means light is proof of itself. Abdu, do you remember Ishak, the cousin of the Mayor?

ABDU: I know who he is, but I have never seen him. He is originally from this village, but he has never been here.

YUSEF: Abdu, do you think he has ever seen a grain bin?

ABDU: Of course not.

BASEAT: Doesn't he have one in his house in the city?

ABDU: Of course not, Baseat. In the city they don't have grain bins in their houses. They buy bread from a bakery.

BASEAT: Really! Do you mean they buy their bread?

ABDU: (Impatiently) Do not bother us now, Baseat. Some day I'll explain to you what life in the city is like. Let Elder Yusef continue.

YUSEF: Abdu, supposing Ishak comes to the village.

ABDU: Yes, go on.

YUSEF: Supposing he wants to see a grain bin. So the Mayor takes him and shows him one, and says to him: "This is a grain bin." Then he says: "Prove to me that this is a grain bin." The Mayor would say: "You are looking at it. What can I say to you? Here is the wheat inside. Here are the side walls of the grain bin. What do you mean?" Then Ishak says: "No, no. I want proof. You must prove to me that this is a grain bin."

ABDU: That would be ridiculous.

YUSEF: Indeed! But this is what we do, my friends. Nathaniel wants proof that Jesus is the Christ. Phillip says to him: "Come and see." This is all Phillip can say. Jesus is proof of Himself. David says: "In thy light, we see light." Light is proof of itself.

ABDU: Yes, this seems to make sense.

YUSEF: Now, Abdu, can you prove to me that light is light?

ABDU: I don't understand.

YUSEF: Supposing I say to you, "Prove to me that light is light."

ABDU: I cannot. I can only show you the light.

YUSEF: Exactly right. The light is proof of itself. So what must you do, Abdu, if a man wants proof that Jesus is the Son of God?

ABDU: It seems I must show him Jesus and be finished.

YUSEF: Right. Exactly right. Do you understand, Baseat?

BASEAT: Yes.

ABDU: Pay attention, Baseat.

YUSEF: How then does light work? First, light is its own proof. Then, second, light does not get tired. Baseat, read Revelation 3: verse 20.

BASEAT: (Reading) "Behold I stand at the door and knock. If anyone hears my voice and opens the door, I will come in to him and eat with him and he with me."

YUSEF: Very well. Now Baseat, take this light and go out of the room.

BASEAT: Very well.

YUSEF: Abdu, stand on this side of the door after Baseat has gone out.

(Baseat goes out of the room. Abdu stands on the inside of the door.)

YUSEF: (Calling) Can you hear me, Baseat?

BASEAT: Yes.

YUSEF: Baseat, let the light come in by itself.

BASEAT: It cannot unless Abdu opens the door.

YUSEF: Abdu, is the light pushing on the door? Is there pressure on the door from the light?

ABDU: No, indeed.

YUSEF: If there was a wind, the wind would push on the door. Does not the light push on the door?

ABDU: No, indeed it does not.

YUSEF: But the light is not like the wind. The light will come in only if we open the door.

YUSEF: Very well, Abdu. Open the door and let the light come in. (Abdu opens the door. The light of Baseat's lamp shines in the room.)

The light has entered now that we have opened the door. Come on in, Baseat, and sit down.

Now, my friends, this morning I told you about how I opened the door to let the light into the house. Do you remember?

BASEAT: Yes, we remember.

YUSEF: Very well. Supposing I had not opened the door to let the light in. Would the light have gone away?

ABDU: How can it? It stays there at the door. It never goes away.

YUSEF: You mean if I waited for half a day and then opened the door, the light would still be there trying to come in?

ABDU: Of course, stupid!

YUSEF: Supposing I don't open the door for a year. Will the light still be at the door, or will the light get tired and not come back? Will the light be tired of waiting for me to open the door?

ABDU: No, the light never gets tired. The light will wait forever.

YUSEF: Very well. Baseat, what did you read from the Book of Revelation?

BASEAT: "Behold I stand at the door and knock. If anyone hears my voice and opens the door, I will come in to him and eat with him and he with me."

YUSEF: Very good. We see two things from this verse. Jesus stands knocking at the door. He does not get tired and He comes in only by invitation. Not by force! You see, my friends, this is the way light works. Baseat, do you remember the house of Bakhit at the south end of the village?

BASEAT: Of course, it is empty. No one has been in it for ten years. It is all closed.

YUSEF: Is there light within it?

BASEAT: Of course not. It is closed.

YUSEF: After ten years, if you open the door, will the light go on?

BASEAT: Sure, it will.

YUSEF: The door has been closed to the light for a long time. Will not the light be tired and angry and refuse to enter?

BASEAT: No. The light does not get tired. The light does not become angry. The light waits and waits until the door is open, then it goes in.

YUSEF: Exactly right, my sons. This is the way God works, for He is light. Just as the light waits at the door of the house of Bakhit to enter, so Christ waits at the doors of our hearts to enter. He will come in only when we open. He will not stop trying to come in. Now, Abdu, read John 1:5.

ABDU: (Reading) "The light shines in the darkness, and the darkness has not overcome it."

YUSEF: Now Abdu, when you spend the night in the fields, do you long for the coming of morning?

ABDU: Very much, indeed.

YUSEF: When the light comes in the morning, does the darkness stay?

ABDU: No. The darkness cannot stay.

YUSEF: As the light comes, does it push back the darkness?

ABDU: Yes.

YUSEF: Is it easy for the light, or is it very hard?

ABDU: It seems very easy for the light. The darkness cannot stand in its way.

YUSEF: Very well. Baseat, can light and darkness be in the same place.

BASEAT: No, I think it is impossible. Either there is light, or there is darkness.

YUSEF: So we see the fourth thing that light does. Light drives away the darkness. Here in John 3: verse 19 we read: "And this is the judgment, that light has come into the world, and men loved darkness rather than light because their deeds were evil. For everyone who does evil hates the light and does not come to the light lest his deeds should be exposed, but he who does what is true comes to the light that it may be clearly seen that his deeds have been wrought in God." Do you see, my friends, we must choose either darkness or light. When the light comes, what does it do?

ABDU: It drives away the darkness.

YUSEF: Then why do men like the darkness?

BASEAT: Because their deeds are evil.

YUSEF: Then why do men come to the light?

BASEAT: So everyone can see how clever they are.

YUSEF: No. No, Baseat. Listen to verse 21. "But he who does what is true comes to the light that it may be clearly seen that his deeds have been wrought in God." Now, Baseat, does a man come to the light to show that he is clever, or to show that God is clever?

BASEAT: We always want to stand in the center to show how clever <u>we</u> are.

ABDU: But Baseat, when we do this, we are not in the light. We only think we are in the light.

YUSEF: Good, O Abdu. That's exactly right and brings us to our last point. Light makes other things shine. Read, Abdu, Matthew 5: verses 14 through 16.

ABDU: (Reading) "You are the light of the world. A city set on a hill cannot be hid. Nor do men light a lamp and put it under a bushel, but on a stand and it gives a light to all in the house. Let your light so shine before men that they may see your good works and give glory to your Father who is in Heaven."

YUSEF: What does Jesus say that we are?

ABDU: He says we are the light of the world.

YUSEF: Ah, but the light which we have is from God. God's light shines on us and makes us shine. Paul says in Philippians that we are to shine as lights in the world. But this is not our light. Tell me, Abdu, does a mirror shine if there is no light in the room?

ABDU: No.

YUSEF: Does the river shine at night if there is no moon?

ABDU: No.

YUSEF: Do the eyes of a child shine if they are closed?

ABDU: No.

YUSEF: Does a new cooking pot shine if it is placed behind the oven?

ABDU: No.

YUSEF: Will the life of a man shine if the light of Christ is not within him?

ABDU: No. It will not.

YUSEF: Do you see, my friends? We are the light of the world. But our light is from God. The river shines in the moonlight, but it is not the light of the river. It is the light of the moon. A new pot shines in the sun, but it is not the light of the pot. It is the light of the sun. We must shine in the world. But whose light is it, Baseat?

BASEAT: It is the light of Christ.

YUSEF: Very well. Abdu, if we are pleased with the light on the river at night do we thank the river, or do we thank the moon?

ABDU: We must thank the moon.

YUSEF: If we are pleased with the beauty of a newly whitened pot in the sun, should we thank the pot, or thank the sun which makes it shine?

ABDU: We must thank the sun.

YUSEF: And if the light of God shines in a man's life, do we thank the man or do we thank God?

ABDU: I see that we must thank God. But Yusef, we are not like this. When we do good works, when we shine in the world, we want men to thank us.

YUSEF: I know, Abdu. But when we do, this is our light that is shining. This is not the light of God. What does Jesus say? "Let your light so shine before men that they may see your good works, and give glory to you." Is this what it says?

BASEAT: No. This is not what He says.

YUSEF: What does He say?

BASEAT: It says: ". . . and give glory to your Father who is in heaven."

ABDU: This is a new thought for us, Yusef.

YUSEF: It is new, but it is very old, my friends. Many times we have heard this, but we do not listen. Now Abdu, tell me the five ways that God works like light.

ABDU: I will try. Light is proof of itself. Two, light does not get tired. Three, light comes in only by invitation, not by force.

YUSEF: Very good! Very good! What else, Baseat?

BASEAT: Light drives away the darkness.

YUSEF: (Delighted) Very good! Very good, Baseat. And lastly, Abdu?

ABDU: Light makes other things shine.

YUSEF: What does this mean?

ABDU: It means he makes us into lights, so that we can be the light of the world.

YUSEF: And give glory to whom?

ABDU: We must give glory to our Father who is in heaven.

YUSEF: So my friends, we see that God is light. God is light, and He enlightens us. God is light, and He is faithful. God is light, and He works like light. O how great is our God.

QUESTIONS FOR DISCUSSION

1. Review. This lesson is somewhat shorter than the others. We have now finished the section on "God is light." Go back to the questions at the end of each of the last given lessons. Spend some time on each lesson. Review some of the questions of each lesson. See that everyone in the class understands the summary at least, of each lesson.

2. How do we prove that light is light?

3. What do we mean when we say that light is its own proof?

4. Jesus stands at the door and knocks, but He knocks only for a short time. Is this true or false? Explain.

5. Wind will enter a room by force. Light will not enter a room by force. What does this teach us about God? For God is light.

6. Can the darkness stand in the way of light?

7. If light is good, why do men love darkness?

8. Jesus says, "You are the light of the world." Does this mean that we are a source of light? Explain.

9. When we do good works, we always wish that men should give praise to us. Why? To whom should they give praise? Why?

SUMMARY OF LESSON

God is light and He works like light in our hearts.
If we look at Christ, we do not need proof that He is God.
He stands at the door of our hearts and knocks.
Like light, He does not get tired.
Like light, He enters only if we open the door.
When He enters, He drives away the darkness of our lives.
When He enters, He kindles a light in our lives, then we shine like lights.
When His light shines in us, we wish the praise to be to Him.

MOTTO: The light of God is in men; for this we praise God and not men.

SECTION III
GOD IS THREE IN ONE

12
ETERNALLY ONE GOD

SCRIPTURES TO BE READ: I Peter 1:2; I Corinthians 8:4-6; Thessalonians 2:13-14; Ephesians 4:4-6; II Corinthians 13:14; Matthew 28:19

STATEMENT OF LESSON

We have seen that God is great. We have seen that God is light. Now we must see that God is three in one. We will spend four lessons studying this deep subject. We notice first that many things around us are three in one. You look at a book. You see it has length, height and width. These are three different things, but the book is one. If you look at the mortar we use to build a stone house with, you see that the mortar is made of sand, cement and water. These are three things, but they are one. The lamp we use to light the room at night has fire, light and heat. These are three things, but they are one. Three winds can blow together in a valley. They are all one as they come into the valley. A person thinks. A person feels. A person wills. As he thinks, all of him thinks; as he feels, all of him feels; and he wills and chooses, all of him chooses, but he is only one person, not three. A man may be called by many names. His son will call him father, his father will call him son. His friend will call him friend, but he is not three people. He is one person. So it is with God. God has many names. Many names do not mean many Gods. We call God -- Father, Son and Holy Spirit. We do not know what these mean. To help to understand them, let us use different words. Let us call God - Creator, Redeemer and Sanctifier. This is part of what we mean when we say Father, Son and Holy Spirit. God is three, yet God is one. All through the Bible we see that this is true.

This is very hard to understand, but it is true. God is one -- just as the book, the mortar, the lamp, the wind and the person are each one -- from everlasting to everlasting He is one.

OUTLINE

ETERNALLY ONE GOD

1. Many things around us are three, and yet one.
    a. A book (length, width, height)
    b. Mortar (sand, cement, water)
    c. A lamp (fire, light, heat)
    d. Wind (three winds in a valley)
    e. A person (thinking, feeling, willing)
    f. A person (father, son, friend)
2. God is three and yet one.
    a. Many names do not mean many Gods.
    b. God is Creator, Redeemer and Sanctifier.
    c. God is eternally one.

THE DIALOGUE

GOD IS . . .

SCENE 12

CHARACTERS:

Yusef, the Wise

Abdu, the Inquirer

Baseat, the Simple

Sadeek

THE DIALOGUE

(Yusef is seated in his sitting room thinking out loud.)

YUSEF: (Speaking) It has been many days since Abdu asked me how God can be three and yet one. He and Baseat have been very patient. They have come for many nights. We still have many things about which we must talk. We have not yet seen that God is holy. We have not yet seen that God is love, but I think we must talk together, when they come, about how God is three and yet one. This is a very hard subject. May God give me understanding so I can explain it to my friends. We understand so little. Give us strength, O God.

(Enter Abdu and Baseat)

YUSEF: Good evening, my friends. Good evening.

ABDU AND
BASEAT: Good evening, Elder Yusef. We are glad to see you. All is well, God willing.

YUSEF: Praise God. Sit down my friends.

ABDU: Thank you, Yusef. What is our subject tonight, Yusef?

YUSEF: What has been our subject before?

ABDU: We talked of how God is light.

YUSEF: Baseat, what was our subject before that?

BASEAT: We talked about how God was great.

YUSEF: Good. You see, Abdu, Baseat is doing very well.

ABDU: Yes, I am beginning to see this Yusef. At first I thought he could learn nothing, but I see he is not doing badly at all. We must give him credit. His name is Baseat.

BASEAT: Indeed this is true. Indeed. What can I do?

YUSEF: What can you do? You can use what gifts God has given you, Baseat. Now -- tonight we must start a new

137

YUSEF: subject. We spent many nights talking about how God is great. We spent many nights talking about how God is light. Now we must talk about how God is three in one.

ABDU: Maybe now at last I will have an answer for the butcher. The next time I go to buy meat, I wish to be ready to speak with him.

YUSEF: I'm glad you have not forgotten about your friend. It will be very good if you can explain this to him.

ABDU: We are trusting in your knowledge, Elder Yusef.

YUSEF: No, trust in God's knowledge. This is a very hard subject, my friends. Paul says in Romans, "How unsearchable are his judgments and how inscrutable are his ways."

BASEAT: What does he mean?

YUSEF: He means many things we cannot understand.

BASEAT: I am right with you, Yusef.

YUSEF: But, my friends, we have to understand in order to believe.

ABDU: I like to understand, Yusef, if I can.

YUSEF: This is very good, Abdu. I wish all men tried to understand as you do. But let me ask a question. How did God create the world?

BASEAT: No one knows, of course.

YUSEF: Correct. We do not know how God created the world, but we know He did and we believe He did. How can God be everywhere at once?

ABDU: This is too much, we cannot understand it.

YUSEF: Indeed. But yet we know this is true and we believe it. Another question - what will life be like after death? Exactly, that is.

ABDU: We know that we will be in heaven with God if we believe.

YUSEF: Yes, but what will it be like?

ABDU: No one knows.

YUSEF: Exactly, but yet we believe. So it is with this subject. We will try tonight to understand as much as we can, but we know we can understand only a little. Now, Abdu.

ABDU: Yes, Yusef.

YUSEF: Many things about us are three, and yet one.

BASEAT: How is this true, Yusef?

YUSEF: Baseat, take a look at the book in your hand. How long is it?

BASEAT: Oh, I don't know -- maybe twenty centimeters.

YUSEF: Very well. How wide is it?

BASEAT: I don't know. Maybe twelve or thirteen centimeters.

YUSEF: And how high is it?

BASEAT: Maybe six.

YUSEF: Oh, I see. It has height. It has width and it has length.

BASEAT: Of course.

YUSEF: Then it must be three things. This is not one thing. This is three things. I understand height. I understand width. I understand length. I understand them as separate things. So the book in your hand must be three books.

BASEAT: No. No. This is only one book.

YUSEF: If it has length, width and height, how can it be one book?

BASEAT: Do I know? Here it is, it is one book.

YUSEF: Yes, I see it is one book, but I also see three things that are one thing. Abdu, go and call for us Sadeek across the square at work on the Mayor's house.

ABDU: (Goes to the window and calls loudly.) Sadeek. Sadeek. Uncle Sadeek.

SADEEK: (Answering from a long ways away.) Yes, Abdu. What do you want?

ABDU: (Again calling loudly.) Come, Sadeek. Talk. Elder Yusef wants you.

SADEEK: Very well, I will come, but let me finish the mortar I have mixed. One minute -- I will be there right away.

YUSEF: (From inside the room) Abdu, tell him to bring the mortar with him.

ABDU: (Calling out the window) Uncle Sadeek.

SADEEK: (Answering from outside) Yes, Abdu.

ABDU: Elder Yusef says for you to bring some mortar with you and come right away.

SADEEK: I am ready to do any service for Elder Yusef. I am ready to serve any of you, my friend Abdu.

ABDU: (Calling back) May God allow you to remain with us, Uncle Sadeek. Only hurry.

SADEEK: (Still from outside) I'm coming. I'm coming.

(Sadeek enters the room with a trowel in one hand and a short board in the other hand on which some mortar is mixed.)

YUSEF: Welcome, Sadeek, our good friend.

SADEEK: Welcome to you, Yusef.

YUSEF: We have a question, Sadeek.

SADEEK: Yes. Say on.

YUSEF: The mortar you have on your board. What is it made of?

SADEEK: I am building the Mayor's house of stone. Mud mortar is not good enough for stone. The mortar is made of cement so it will be stronger.

YUSEF: Yes, I know. But tell me what is in the mortar.

SADEEK: It has water, sand and cement.

YUSEF: Oh, I see. Three things!

SADEEK: Yes, three things -- water, sand and cement.

YUSEF: Then it must be three things. Mortar must be three things.

SADEEK: No, mortar is one thing.

YUSEF: Baseat, I'm thirsty. Take some of the water out of the mortar so I can drink it.

BASEAT: (Not knowing quite what to do) How will you drink it, Yusef? If you drink this mortar, you will die. If you drink the water, you will drink the sand and cement.

YUSEF: You mean if I touch the water in the mortar, I touch also the sand and the cement?

SADEEK: Yes. Yes. This is true. They are altogether one.

YUSEF: Oh, I see. You mean I cannot take the water out of the cement and drink it separately?

SADEEK: No. They are altogether.

YUSEF: Very well, my friends. What have you understood, Abdu?

ABDU: I see that three things have become one thing.

YUSEF: God is three, and yet God is one. But more than this, my friends, with the mortar, I cannot touch the water without touching the sand and the cement. I cannot touch the cement without touching the water and the sand. The mortar is all one. So with God. When I think of Christ, Christ says: "I and the Father are one." So when I touch the Holy Spirit, I touch all of God. That is, when I think of God in Christ, this is all of God. The Holy Spirit works in our hearts. This is all of God. God is like a Father to us. This is all of God. Yes, God is three, but He is one, like the

140

YUSEF:	mortar. To think of God is to think of all of God. Thank you, Sadeek, you have served us.
SADEEK:	Is it so? But I am ready to serve you in anything. Only excuse me, I must finish my mortar before it is dark.
YUSEF:	Go right ahead, Sadeek, and thanks again for coming.
SADEEK:	(Exiting) Goodby, my friends.
ALL:	Goodby, Sadeek.
YUSEF:	Very well, now let us think of something else. Baseat.
BASEAT:	Yes, Yusef.
YUSEF:	On the window sill behind you there is a village lamp. Get it down and light it for me and put it on the table.

(Baseat goes over, gets a village lamp from the window sill. He brings it and lights it and puts it on the table before Yusef.)

BASEAT:	Any service, Yuséf. Any service. We are all your servants.
YUSEF:	May God keep you, Baseat. Now, my friends, here we have a lamp. Abdu, what do you see?
ABDU:	I see a lamp.
YUSEF:	I mean now that it is lit, what do you see?
ABDU:	I see light.
YUSEF:	What else?
ABDU:	I see fire.
YUSEF:	What else?
ABDU:	(Thinking) I don't know.
YUSEF:	Baseat, give me your hand. (He takes Baseat's hand and holds it over the lamp. Baseat jerks his hand away.)
BASEAT:	What are you doing, Elder Yusef? This is hot.
YUSEF:	Did you feel something, Baseat?
BASEAT:	Of course, I felt heat.
YUSEF:	Very well. So from the lamp we see fire, light and heat. Is it not so, Baseat?
BASEAT:	Yes, it is so.
YUSEF:	Very well. Abdu, if you get rid of the fire, can we keep the light and heat?
ABDU:	No, it is impossible. If you get rid of the fire, if you put the lamp out, the light and the heat are gone too.

YUSEF: Well, then, can we have the fire and the light without heat?

ABDU: No, it is impossible. There is no light without heat.

YUSEF: Baseat, can we get rid of the light? Can we have fire and heat with no light?

BASEAT: No. You can't do that either.

YUSEF: Very well, my friends. Look at this lamp. We see three things, yet the three things are completely one. There is fire, light and heat. We understand fire, we understand light and we understand heat. These are separate things, but here they are completely one. God is like this. God the Father is like the fire. God the Son is like the light for He enlightens us. God the Holy Spirit is like the heat for heat is power and the Holy Spirit is power.

ABDU: (Delighted) I can use this story with the butcher. This is something he will understand. This is a very clear story. This is a great idea, Yusef.

YUSEF: Let us think of something else that is three and yet one. Baseat, can three stones become one stone?

BASEAT: No, I don't think so.

YUSEF: Very good, Baseat. This is right. But Abdu, can three winds blowing the same way become one wind?

ABDU: Yes, indeed.

YUSEF: Very well. God is a Spirit. God is not a thing like a stone. Because God is a Spirit, three Spirits can be one very easily. Have you ever thought of why the wind is sometimes stronger in the street than in the courtyard behind the house, Abdu?

ABDU: I never thought of this, Yusef.

YUSEF: But it is so. Sometimes you stand in the courtyard of your house and the wind is not very strong. Or even you stand on the roof of your house and the wind is strong, but not very strong. Then you turn and walk in the street and you find the wind very strong. Why?

ABDU: I don't know. Why is the wind strong in the street?

YUSEF: It is because sometimes two winds come together in the narrow street. They blow down the street as one wind and are very strong.

BASEAT: That makes good sense.

YUSEF: Very well. God is a Spirit. Therefore, it is very easy for three Spirits to be one.

ABDU: This is a good idea, Yusef, but the one about the lamp and the one about the mortar are better.

142

YUSEF: Each of these stories helps a little. But let us think of another. Abdu, you are a man who knows how to think.

ABDU: Thank you, Yusef.

YUSEF: Baseat, you know how to feel. Is it not so?

BASEAT: Of course, every man knows how to feel.

YUSEF: Every man knows how to choose. That is, he knows how to will to do something.

ABDU: What do you mean, Yusef?

YUSEF: I mean, a man can think and feel and will.

ABDU: Of course.

YUSEF: Very well. Abdu, when you are thinking, is this only part of you that thinks? Or does all of you think?

ABDU: All of me, of course.

YUSEF: When you think about selling your cotton, do you think with a part of you or is it your whole person that thinks.

ABDU: No, all of me thinks.

YUSEF: Very well, when you feel love to your son, is it only part of you that feels in your heart? Or do you feel all of you towards your son as you love him?

ABDU: No, my whole person feels when I feel.

YUSEF: Then you must be more than one person. If you can think, this is one Abdu. If you can feel, this is another Abdu. If you can will, this is a third Abdu.

ABDU: No. No. I am one person. How can you say this?

YUSEF: So here we have something else that is three and yet it is one. Every man is one person, but he thinks, he feels and he wills. But something else, Abdu.

ABDU: Yes, Yusef.

YUSEF: What does Khaleel call you, Abdu?

ABDU: He calls me "Daddy."

YUSEF: Very well. What does your father call you?

ABDU: He calls me "son."

YUSEF: Very well. And to me you are a "friend." Is it not so?

ABDU: Indeed it is. I am honored to be called your friend.

YUSEF: Very well. Here we have three names. You are father. You are son. You are friend. This means you are three people.

BASEAT: No. Abdu is only one person.

143

YUSEF: Explain to me. A father is one thing. A son is something else. A friend is a third thing. Abdu is a father. He is a son. He is a friend. Therefore, Abdu must be three people.

BASEAT: The story is not this way, Yusef. I do not understand the story, but I know that Abdu is one person.

YUSEF: Very well. Abdu, does Khaleel know you as only a third of a person? Or does he know you and deal with you as a whole person?

ABDU: He knows me as a whole person. I am his father.

YUSEF: Very well. Baseat and I are your friends. We know you as a full person, not as a third of a person. Is it not so, Baseat?

BASEAT: Yes, Indeed.

YUSEF: God is Father, Son and Holy Spirit. This is something like you as you are father, son and friend. But let us not forget, my friends, that every parable we use to try and explain God is not good enough. God does not have children as men have children. This is not what we mean when we say Father and Son. We will have to talk about these things another night. All I mean here is that again we have three things that are one thing. Even as God is three and He is one. I think it is not hard for us to understand this when we think of you, Abdu. We see you as a father, as a son and a friend. We know these are different, yet we know that you are one.

ABDU: I never thought of this, O Yusef. My goodness, you have mentioned many things about us that are three in one. A book, mortar, a lamp, a person as he thinks, feels and wills and a person as he is father, son and friend. All of these things about us are three and yet one, but we never thought of them in this way.

YUSEF: Indeed, God can teach us many things if we will but use what He has put before us. But let us go on. Last year when we ordained the preacher, we had a party afterwards for the village, did we not?

BASEAT: Of course. It was a very good party.

YUSEF: Indeed, it was. Many people offered congratulations to the Church. Do you remember even our good friend Sheik Ali from the next village came to offer congratulations.

ABDU: I remember. He is a very good man, a very good man.

YUSEF: How did he begin?

ABDU: He began by saying, "In the name of God the Merciful and the Compassionate..." Of course he began this way.

144

YUSEF: Very well. When our friends, the Muslims, say, "In the name of God, the Merciful and the Compassionate," does this mean that they believe in two Gods? One called the Merciful, the other called the Compassionate?

ABDU AND
BASEAT: (Excited and emphatic) No. No. Of course not! You know much better than this, Elder Yusef! How can you speak this way?

ABDU: You know very well, Yusef, that we and our friends, the Muslims, together believe that there is no God but God.

YUSEF: Yes, of course, I know, but stay with me. We can call God if we wish the Merciful and the Compassionate. This does not mean two Gods. Also, we can call God the Creator, the Redeemer, and the Sanctifier. This does not mean three Gods. God the Father is God the Creator. God the Son is God the Redeemer. God the Holy Spirit is God the Sanctifier. We call Him by three names. This does not mean that He is three Gods.

ABDU: It is beginning to make sense, Yusef.

YUSEF: You see my friends, we could begin our prayer by saying "In the name of the Creator, the Redeemer and the Sanctifier - One God, Amen." This is almost the same as saying "In the name of the Father, and of the Son, and of the Holy Spirit - one God, Amen."

BASEAT: My Goodness. We have said these things all our lives, but have never thought about what they mean.

YUSEF: But even here, the subject is very hard. For all of God is Creator just as all of Abdu is father. All of God is Redeemer and all of God is Sanctifier. We say God is Creator. Abdu, how does the Bible begin?

ABDU: (Quoting) "In the beginning, God created the heavens and the earth."

YUSEF: Abdu, open your Bible and read the second verse.

ABDU: (Opens and reads) "And the earth was without form and void, and darkness was upon the face of the deep; and the Spirit of God was moving over the face of the waters."

YUSEF: You see the Spirit of God was working in creation. Now, Baseat, read the second verse of the first chapter of Hebrews.

BASEAT: (Opens and reads) "But in these last days He has spoken to us by a Son, whom He appointed the heir of all things through whom also He created the world."

YUSEF: You see, my friends, in creation we see God created the heavens and the earth, the Spirit of God moved

YUSEF: over the waters and through the Son He created the world. That is, all of God was at work in creation.

ABDU: You mean Christ was at work in creation? I thought Christ was born in Bethlehem?

YUSEF: He was. But Christ said, "Before Abraham was I am." Christ is God and God is from eternity. Never, never think, Abdu, that the Son was created. No. No. God is eternal. So Christ is Creator, not created.

ABDU: This is a very hard subject.

YUSEF: Yes, I know. We must study this subject one night by itself. But think also of Redeemer. We said God was Creator, Redeemer, Sanctifier. Think of Redeemer. We know that the Son is Savior and Redeemer, but Abdu, open II Corinthians 5:19.

ABDU: I know this verse. It says, "God was in Christ reconciling the world to himself..."

YUSEF: Very good. So God was in redemption. God the Father. Then also in Ephesians Paul says, "Do not grieve the Holy Spirit of God in Whom you were sealed for the day of redemption." This means the Holy Spirit is at work in redemption.

ABDU: That is, all of God is the Redeemer.

YUSEF: Exactly right, Abdu. But think also of the Sanctifier. We know that the Holy Spirit is Sanctifier. Peter writes and says that we are sanctified by the Spirit for obedience to Jesus Christ. But, Abdu, read John 17:17.

ABDU: (Reading) "Sanctify them in the truth. Thy Word is truth."

YUSEF: Who is Jesus talking to?

ABDU: He is talking to the Father.

YUSEF: So we see the Father is Sanctifier. That is, He is One who sanctifies. Then in I Corinthians Paul says, "To the Church of God which is at Corinth, to those sanctified in Christ Jesus." So we see that Father, Son and Holy Spirit are all sanctified.

BASEAT: That is, everything is one.

YUSEF: That is, all of God is One. We know Him as Creator, Redeemer and Sanctifier, but all of God is Creator. All of God is Redeemer. All of God is Sanctifier. Abdu, what did Jesus tell the disciples on the mountain before He ascended into heaven? Into what name are they to baptize?

ABDU: The name of the Father, and the Son and the Holy Spirit.

YUSEF: And, Baseat, what name does Paul use in the blessing of the Apostles, which the preacher uses every Sunday?

BASEAT: Father, Son and Holy Spirit.

YUSEF: Abdu, open Ephesians and read Ephesians 4: verses 4 through 6.

ABDU: (Reading) "There is one body and one Spirit, just as you were called to the one hope that belongs to your call, one Lord, one faith, one baptism, one God and Father of us all, who is above all and through all and in all."

YUSEF: You see. One Spirit, one Lord, one God and Father of us all. Abdu is father, son and friend, but he is one. God is Creator, Redeemer, Sanctifier, but He is one. God is Father, Son and Holy Spirit, but He is one.

ABDU: The story of the mortar, and the lamp and the person helped me a great deal.

BASEAT: The idea of the book is good, too. It is length, width and height, but it is one book..

YUSEF: Tell me again, Abdu, how is the mortar three and yet one?

ABDU: The mortar is sand, cement and water, but it is one.

YUSEF: And the lamp.

ABDU: A lamp is fire, light, heat, but it is one.

YUSEF: And the person.

ABDU: A person can be father, son and friend, but he is one.

YUSEF: Baseat, what about the wind?

BASEAT: What about the wind?

YUSEF: Can two winds blow together in the village street?

BASEAT: Yes, of course they can.

YUSEF: So, my friends, let us not forget. Three names do not mean three Gods.

QUESTIONS FOR DISCUSSION

1. Many things around us are three in one. Name the illustrations Yusef uses.

2. Can you think of other illustrations of three in one from your world? Discuss them.

3. In the illustration of the cement mortar, to touch one part was to touch all three elements. How is this true of God? What difference does this make as we relate to Jesus?

4. Did God have a son before Jesus was born in Bethelem? Discuss.

5. God is Creator, Redeemer and Sanctifier. What does this have to do with the Trinity?

SUMMARY OF LESSON

Many illustrations around us in daily life are three in one. Thus we understand that the nature of God as three in one is not a unique problem for our understanding. A lamp has fire, light and heat. A person is thinking, feeling and willing. A person may be parent, child and friend all at once. It helps us understand the Trinity when we look at the work of the separate persons of the Trinity. The Father is Creator, the Son is Redeemer and the Spirit is the Sanctifier. Yet again, to touch one person in the Trinity is to touch all of God, and God is eternally one.

MOTTO: Relate to one person of the Trinity and you relate to all three.

13
FATHER

SCRIPTURES TO BE READ: Genesis 1:26; Matthew 6:24-26; Hosea 11:3; Luke 15:11-24; Ephesians 1:3; John 10:30; Galatians 4:7; John 8:35; John 4:21-22

STATEMENT OF LESSON

God is like a father. He is not like a master who rules us. But He is like a father who rules us, yet loves us. When we say, "God is like a father," we never mean that God has a wife and begets children. We mean that God feels and acts toward men like a father feels and acts toward his children. God is like a Father to all men. God creates us, cares for us, loves us, and yearns for our love. God is also Father to Christ and Father to the believers. We say that God is Father to Christ, but yet we know that Christ and God are one -- completely one. They are one from eternity. God in a special way is Father to the believers in His name. When we accept God as our Father, He accepts us into His family. God cares for us one by one. We are His children, not His slaves and thus are secure in the family of God. God can dismiss a servant. He will not dismiss a son. When we pray and worship we speak to a God that loves us like a Father. When we serve Him we find His yoke is easy because it is the yoke of our Father. God loves us so much that He suffers to redeem us. Only God can create and only God can redeem. Yes, God feels and acts toward us like a Father.

OUTLINE

GOD THE FATHER

(GOD FEELS AND ACTS LIKE A FATHER TO HIS CHILDREN.)

1. God is like a Father to all men.
    a. He creates all men.
    b. He cares for all men.
    c. He loves all men.
    d. He yearns for all men to love Him.
2. God is like a Father to Christ and to the believers in His name.
    a. God is Father to Christ.
    b. God is Father to the believers in His name.
        1. God cares for us one by one.
        2. We are children, not servants.
        3. We are secure.
        4. We worship and pray to a Father we know.
        5. We serve a Father we love.
        6. This Father loves us and redeems us.

The reader will note in all of the chapters of this section a tendency toward modalism. In trying to explain the Doctrine of the Trinity, one is faced with the basic inscrutability for the Doctrine. Abstractions are meaningless to the village people for whom this book is written. One must illustrate with concrete living illustrations. Yet with the Doctrine of the Trinity, there are no such illustrations that are adequate. Thereby, to illustrate the Trinity is to fall into one heresy or another. In the Middle East we are faced with a non-Christian community that accuses the Christian community with tri-theism. Thereby, the burden of this entire section is to demonstrate the Unity of God. The author quite readily admits the inadequacy of the illustrations used. Dr. Welch, in his excellent book on the Trinity, In This Name, points out that the Latin word *persona* used in the classical definition of the Trinity was a much more general term than our present word "personality." He says on Page 276, "I am increasingly persuaded that the most useful term for our purpose is 'modes of being' or 'modes of existence.'" Karl Barth's concept of the Trinity indicates concern in the same direction. William Temple mentions how the Trinity is a qualitative distinction and not a quantitative distinction understood numerically. Our concern in this section of the book is to say something that will help the simple village Christian understand his faith. We are quite aware of the inadequacies of the statement.

THE DIALOGUE

GOD IS . . .

SCENE 13

CHARACTERS:

Yusef, the Wise

Abdu, the Inquirer

Baseat, the Simple

Azziz, the Carpenter

THE DIALOGUE

(Abdu and Baseat are sitting waiting in Yusef's front room.)

ABDU: I wonder where Yusef went.

BASEAT: He went to speak to Azziz, the carpenter, next door. He said he would be right back. Here he is now.

YUSEF: (Enters) Good evening, my friends. I am very sorry not to be here to greet you.

ABDU: Never mind, Yusef. It is nothing. There is no strangeness in the house of our dear Elder Yusef.

YUSEF: Our house is your house indeed. You have honored us.

BASEAT: May God honor you, Elder Yusef.

ABDU: Elder Yusef, I have been thinking all day about the parables you used to explain how God is three in one.

YUSEF: I am glad you have been thinking, Abdu.

ABDU: Indeed, these parables help a great deal. A lamp is three in one, a book is three in one, a person is three in one. Three winds can be one wind.

YUSEF: But Abdu, we must be very careful. We must not forget that a parable is not good enough to explain our God.

ABDU: Of course, but these help a great deal to understand.

YUSEF: Is it so? Very well, then praise be to God. But tonight, my friends, we have a great subject which is also a difficult subject.

BASEAT: Say on, Elder Yusef.

YUSEF: We talked about how God was three in one. Tonight we must see how God is like a father.

ABDU: Very good. Very good.

YUSEF: Notice carefully, my friends, God is like a father, so we call Him Father. But He is not a Father as men are fathers.

ABDU: What do you mean, Yusef?

YUSEF: I mean that God does not have a wife. God does not have children as men have children.

ABDU: Of course. We know this very well.

YUSEF: Yes, but some do not know it. There <u>are</u> people who think that we Christians believe God <u>has</u> a wife and has children, but this is not what we believe at all. We call God Father. We mean, He feels and acts toward us <u>like</u> a good Father to His children.

ABDU: Go on.

YUSEF: God is a Spirit. A Spirit cannot give birth. We call God our Father, we mean He is <u>like</u> a father. Abdu, how does the Lord's prayer begin?

ABDU: "Our Father."

YUSEF: Very well. This is the New Testament. Baseat, what does David say about God in the 23rd Psalm?

BASEAT: I'm not sure.

YUSEF: You remember. He says, "The Lord is . . ."

BASEAT: Oh, yes, "The Lord is my Shepherd."

YUSEF: Very well. Does not the shepherd sometimes say, "I care for my sheep as though they were my sons?"

ABDU: Yes, indeed, sometimes he says this.

YUSEF: Does not the camel driver sometimes say about his camel, "I care for this camel very much. I look out for it as if it were my son?"

BASEAT: He feels that way too.

YUSEF: Does this mean he gave birth to the camel?

BASEAT: Of course not!

YUSEF: What does he mean?

BASEAT: He just means he loves it and he cares for it.

YUSEF: This is the point. God loves us and cares for us. Now, Abdu, you remember my pump in the field behind your house?

ABDU: Yes.

YUSEF: Does the pump care about the crops? If it does not pump water and if the clover dies, will it be sorry?

ABDU: Of course it cares nothing. It is only a pump.

YUSEF: Exactly right. This is the point. God is not just a great power like the pump. The pump does not care whether the plants live or die. God is not just a great power. He is like a Father, therefore He cares

152

YUSEF: about us very much. Now, Abdu, we pray, "Our Father Who art in heaven . . ." When we say, "Our Father," does this mean just the Christians?

ABDU: Of course!

YUSEF: I see! Then you mean God created the Christians and somebody else created the non-Christians?

ABDU: No. God created everybody.

YUSEF: Then if God created everybody, He must be the Father of everybody.

ABDU: (Puzzled) I never thought about it this way.

YUSEF: In Genesis we read that God created man in His own image. The Bible says, "Then God said, 'Let us make man in our image after our likeness.'"

ABDU: Then you mean that God is the Father of all men.

YUSEF: Of course. If God created all men, then God is the Father of all men. When we pray "Our Father," we confess that God is the Father of all men.

ABDU: I never thought of it this way.

YUSEF: But you must think this way, Abdu. A father cares for all his children. Abdu, read Matthew 6: verses 25 and 26.

ABDU: (Reading) "Therefore, I tell you, do not be anxious about your life, what you shall eat or what you shall drink, nor about your body what you shall put on. Is not life more than food, and the body more than clothing? Look at the birds of the air, they neither sow, nor reap, nor gather into barns and yet your Heavenly Father feeds them."

YUSEF: That is, God cares for even the birds. So if He cares for all the birds, does He not care for all people?

ABDU: I see this must be true.

YUSEF: God raises us like a father raises his boy, unless, of course, we rebel against him. Baseat, do you remember the story of the prodigal son?

BASEAT: Of course.

YUSEF: Very well. Did God still love the younger son who ran away?

BASEAT: I don't know.

YUSEF: Of course you know. Was He happy when he came back?

BASEAT: He was very happy.

YUSEF: Then He must have loved him all the time.

BASEAT: Yes, I guess this is right.

YUSEF: John says, "God so loved the Christians that He gave His only begotten Son . . ."

ABDU: (Breaking in) No. No, Yusef. The verse says, "God so loved the world" -- not the Christians.

YUSEF: Oh, I see. God did not just love the Christians. God loved everybody.

ABDU: Humm - yes - I see that this is true.

YUSEF: God is the Father of all men. Thus He loves all men. I remember when I was a young boy . . . .

BASEAT: Say on, Yusef.

YUSEF: The mayor of our town died. We did not know who they would appoint as Mayor. We were afraid. There were some men in the village who were very wealthy and very strong. A number of them tried very hard to be made Mayor. If one of them had been made Mayor, it would have been very bad for us. Then at the end, they picked my father as the Mayor.

ABDU: May God have mercy upon him. He was a great man.

YUSEF: We were very, very happy.

BASEAT: Of course.

YUSEF: We were happy because the power and authority was in the hands of our father.

ABDU: That was good for all of us.

YUSEF: But you see, my sons, the same is true of God. If God is like a powerful king, we would be afraid for he might be very harsh. If God is like a judge, we would be afraid. The judge may be cruel or unjust, but if God is our Father, we will not be afraid, but we will trust. This means the Power from on high loves us. This means we do not need to be afraid.

BASEAT: Indeed.

YUSEF: Now, Baseat, if you have a servant in the house who hates you, what do you do with him?

BASEAT: I would send him away of course.

YUSEF: But what if a man has a son who goes bad and hates his father. Does his father send him away like a servant?

ABDU: No indeed. He is still his father. Even if the boy hates his father, his father is still his father.

YUSEF: So God is the Father of all men. He loves all men. He is Father even to those who do not love Him. He loves them and He wants them to love Him.

ABDU: Just like the father in the parable of the prodigal son.

YUSEF: Exactly right. God yearns for all men to return His love. God is the Father of all men. When we pray "Our Father," we confess this.

ABDU: All my life I have prayed "Our Father," but I have never thought of this.

YUSEF: Now, my friends, we have a very, very hard subject.

ABDU: What is this, Yusef?

YUSEF: Paul calls God the Father of our Lord Jesus Christ. But Jesus says, "I and the Father are One." Jesus says, "I am the Father and the Father is in Me."

BASEAT: How can the Father be in heaven, and Jesus Christ the Son be on earth if they are one?

YUSEF: Do not think that God is only far away in the heavens. God is a spirit and is everywhere. But Baseat, the question you have asked is the question "How can the Father and the Son be One?" Jesus says, "I and the Father are One." Now, Abdu.

ABDU: Yes, Yusef.

YUSEF: The last time we talked together we saw that you were both a father and a son, is it not so?

ABDU: Yes, Yusef. To Khaleel I am a father, to my father I am a son.

YUSEF: This helps us some, but Abdu, step outside the house and call to Azziz, the carpenter. His shop is right across the street. I told him we would want him.

ABDU: Very well, Yusef. (Abdu steps outside the door and calls.) Oh, Azziz, O Azziz, O Azziz.

AZZIZ: (From some distance) Yes, Abdu. What do you want?

ABDU: Come and talk with Elder Yusef. He wants you.

AZZIZ: I'm coming right away. (The two of them enter the room together.) Good evening, Elder Yusef.

YUSEF: Good evening, our good friend Azziz.

AZZIZ: What can I do for you, Yusef?

YUSEF: I wish to ask you a question. Azziz, do you have a son?

AZZIZ: Yes, Hilmi is about eight years old now.

YUSEF: Does he help you in the carpenter shop?

AZZIZ: Yes, he does.

YUSEF: Have you taught him to do anything? Have you taught him to saw a board?

AZZIZ: Not quite yet. He is not yet ready to saw.

155

YUSEF: Well, what was the first thing you taught him?

AZZIZ: Let me see. I think the first thing I taught him was to light the fire under the glue pot to get the glue ready in the morning.

YUSEF: Very well. How did you teach him?

AZZIZ: Do I know? O- h-, I just taught him.

YUSEF: Very well. I will tell you how you taught him. First you knew it was not enough just to tell him, "Go light the fire and get the glue ready." To tell him is not enough. You must show him. You must show him how to obey yourself. Is it not so?

AZZIZ: Just to tell him would not be enough. Yes, that's right, I had to show him how to obey my order.

YUSEF: Very well. The first thing you did was to squat down so you could talk to him on his level. Didn't you?

AZZIZ: Yes, I did.

YUSEF: Then you changed your voice to a voice of a small boy. Then you began to use the words of a little boy.

AZZIZ: Yes, that's right.

YUSEF: I do not think you talked to him in classical Arabic.

AZZIZ: (Laughing) No. Of course not. He hardly understands village Arabic.

YUSEF: You talked to him in very simple words. You began to think like a small boy. That is, you became in a way a small boy eight years old to explain to him how to obey your command. Is it not so?

AZZIZ: (Thinking) Yes, this is right. I guess you could say it this way.

YUSEF: You said to him, "Hilmi, take the bricks and lay them like this, close together, then put the glue pot on the top and take these small chips and put them underneath. Don't get them too close together, and take a match like this and light them. Then put in more chips, etc." Is it not so, O Azziz?

AZZIZ: Yes, that's right.

YUSEF: So in a way you were the father and the son at once. You the man became a boy in order to teach the boy how to obey the man.

AZZIZ: Yes, indeed.

YUSEF: But were you not still a man?

AZZIZ: Of course.

YUSEF: What if I came by and said "Good morning" to you? Would you not answer me as a man?

AZZIZ: Of course.

YUSEF: So then you were father and son at once.

AZZIZ: Yes, I guess you could say so.

YUSEF: So you see, my friends, this is what God does. God tells us to obey Him. We do not know how. Someone must come and show us. So God comes in Christ. He makes Himself take upon the form of a servant to show us how to obey. Just as Azziz is son and father at once, so Christ and God the Father are One. Jesus says, "I and the Father are One."

ABDU: This is a great idea, Yusef.

YUSEF: Let us take something else. Today I went to the fields. We are planting wheat. I had a new workman in the fields. I tried to tell him how to throw the seeds of the wheat. I explained it to him many times. He tried, but he could not throw them properly. I stood on the dyke and shouted to him. I told him again and again how to throw the seeds. He couldn't do it right. So at last I took off my shoes. I took my robe in my hand and went down into the field.

BASEAT: There was no need for you to do this, O Yusef.

YUSEF: Baseat! This was the only way. I am a land owner. It is not expected that I should do this. But this was the only way. I, the land owner, became a peasant. I did this to show the peasant how to obey me, the land owner. So in the field I was land owner and peasant at once. Even so, Christ is God come down to show us how to obey God. So Christ says, "I and the Father are one."

ABDU: You make it very clear, Yusef.

YUSEF: Praise God. Now think of something else. When you want to know a person, how do you get to know him?

BASEAT: I don't know.

YUSEF: Baseat, you know a man by what he does and says. Isn't that right.

ABDU: (Thinking) By what he does and says? Yes, I think so.

YUSEF: Now, can we separate the man from his speech? Can we say the man is one thing and his speech is something else?

ABDU: I think not, Yusef.

YUSEF: Right. The man is known by his speech. The man and his speech are one. Now John says that Christ is the Word of God. We know a man by his speech. We know God by his Word. His Word is Christ. God and His Word are one. So The Father and Son are One.

157

ABDU: This makes it very clear.

YUSEF: So do not forget that there is more. But this helps us to understand. Christ is also the actions of God. That is, He is the <u>Living</u> Word. We said we know a man by his speech and actions. Well, we see the speech and actions of God in Christ. Christ is the Living Word of God.

BASEAT: I'm lost.

YUSEF: Never mind, Baseat. Never mind. Just remember this. God the Father and God the Son are one. What is the idea now?

BASEAT: God the Father and God the Son are one.

YUSEF: Is not Abdu both a father and a son?

BASEAT: Yes.

YUSEF: Very well. Put yourself at rest with this thought. Are not light and heat one in the fire?

BASEAT: Yes, Indeed.

YUSEF: Very well. God the Father and God the Son are one. Just like light and heat are one in the fire. Let us try from another side. When two men are very good friends, do we not sometimes say, "They have one spirit?"

ABDU: Yes, sometimes we say this.

YUSEF: But they are not really one because they have two bodies. But if they were just spirit, then they could be one. Just like two winds can blow together and be one.

AZZIZ: This is a very hard subject, but at least I understand how I can be a man and a boy at once. I do this when I become a boy to teach a boy.

YUSEF: Very good. You have understood something. The last time we met we said that God is Creator, and Redeemer. We said the Creator and the Redeemer are the same God. Do you remember?"

ABDU: Yes, I remember and it makes good sense.

YUSEF: I think maybe this is the hardest subject we have talked about yet, but let us go on to something not so hard. We said that God is the Father of all men. Now let us think of how God is Father, especially of the believers. That is, those who believe in His name.

BASEAT: Say on, Yusef.

YUSEF: In the story of the prodigal son can the father feed his younger son when he is far away?

ABDU: No, it is impossible.

YUSEF: Can he comfort him if he is sorrowing?

BASEAT: No.

YUSEF: Can he talk with him at all?

AZZIZ: No.

YUSEF: Can the prodigal son, who is in a far country feeding pigs -- can he serve his father?

ABDU: He cannot even serve himself.

YUSEF: Now - God is the Father of all men, but God is the Father of those who are in the family of God in a special way.

ABDU: Yes, this makes sense.

YUSEF: When we come home to God and live close to Him He can care for us one by one. When I want fifteen men to prepare a half-acre of ground for me, do I care about them one by one?

AZZIZ: I think not, O Yusef. You just want fifteen men. You do not care who they are. You just want workmen.

YUSEF: But with my sons it is different.

ABDU: Of course.

YUSEF: So, when we are close to God, living in the house of God and the family of God, God cares for us one by one. We are His sons. Now, Abdu, open and read Galatians 4:7.

ABDU: (Reading) "So through God you are no longer a slave, but a son and if a son, then an heir."

YUSEF: You see. We are not slaves, but we are sons.

AZZIZ: What precisely is the difference, Yusef?

YUSEF: Suppose a great king wants to build a palace. He brings thousands of slaves to work on the palace. Does he think about the slaves, or does he think about the palace?

ABDU: He thinks of the palace.

YUSEF: Does he care whether the slaves live or die?

ABDU: He wants them to live only so they will work for him.

YUSEF: But does he care about them as people?

BASEAT: No. They are just slaves. He thinks of his palace.

YUSEF: Exactly right. But you see, we are not slaves of a master, we are sons of a Father. There is a big difference. A father will use his sons to carry out his will, but he will do it in a way that is good for

159

YUSEF: his sons. A master will use his slaves to carry out his will, but he probably does not care what happens to the slaves. We are sons of God. We must serve God faithfully. God will use us to carry out His will. But because He is our Father we know He will carry out His will in a way that is good for us.

ABDU: That is, we do not need to be afraid of His will.

YUSEF: Why not, Abdu?

ABDU: Because He is our Father.

YUSEF: Exactly right. Now, something else. If I have a servant here in the house and he makes a bad mistake, if he insults me, what do I do?

AZZIZ: You dismiss him.

YUSEF: Very well. Now Baseat, read John 8:35.

BASEAT: (Reading) "The slave does not continue in the house forever. The son continues forever."

YUSEF: What does this mean, O Baseat?

BASEAT: I think this means if we are sons of God, God will not leave us.

ABDU: (Sincerely) Baseat, I have come to see that you are not a bad fellow after all. It seems you do have some brains.

BASEAT: I am a very simple man, but I try to use what I have.

YUSEF: (Delighted) Congratulations to you, Baseat, and congratulations to you, Abdu. I am glad you begin to see that Baseat is trying. You're right, Baseat. The point is that if we are sons of God, we have security. God will not throw us out. We keep trying to find security in money, in position, in land, in many friends, but this is not security.

ABDU: What do you mean, Yusef?

YUSEF: I mean that we must find our security in God. We are His sons. Nothing can harm us outside of His will. Paul says, "Nothing can separate us from His love."

AZZIZ: But we never think in this way.

YUSEF: But we must. This is what it means to be the Sons of God. Now, my friends, when we pray, do we pray to an unknown God? Jesus says to the woman at the well in Samaria, "You worship what you do not know." Are we this way?

ABDU: I think not, Yusef.

YUSEF: If we know Him, Who is He?

ABDU: I see. Yes, indeed, I see. We know Him because He is our Father.

YUSEF: Very good. Jesus says to the woman - "We worship whom we know. God is known because He is Our Father." But something else. Do we serve an unknown God?

ABDU: I think the answer is the same. We serve a God whom we know because He is our Father.

YUSEF: Very good. Jesus says, "My yoke is easy and my burden is light." Now, my friends, if I labor in the fields and I work for some stranger, is the work easy or is the work hard?

AZZIZ: It is very tiring, of course. It is tiring to serve a stranger.

YUSEF: Very well. What if I work in the fields and I know that I serve my father? The land I work is my father's land, so I am serving the house of my father. Is the work then easy?

ABDU: Yes, of course.

YUSEF: Very well. This is what Jesus means. He says, "My yoke is easy and my burden is light." His burden is light because when we carry it we are not serving a stranger, but we are serving God Who is our Father. What does John 3:16 say, my friends?

ABDU: (Quoting) "For God so loved the world that He gave His only Son that whoever believes in Him should not perish, but have eternal life."

YUSEF: This is what it means that God is our Father. God loves us so much, He is willing to suffer to redeem us. A master does not suffer to redeem his slaves. But a father will suffer to redeem his sons. God is our Father. This means His feelings and His actions are like a father. He loves us so much He comes Himself to redeem us. This is a big subject, my friends, and it is late. The next time we must think about this subject.

QUESTIONS FOR DISCUSSION

1. Is God the Father of all men?
2. When we pray "Our Father" in the Lord's Prayer, does this mean just the Christians?
3. When we say "God is Father," does this mean God begats us?
4. In what way is God a Father of all men?
5. Jesus says, "I and the Father are One." Can you explain what He means?
6. Explain how Azziz was a man and a small boy at one time.
7. Explain how Yusef was a land owner and a peasant at one time.
8. Are we sons of God or slaves of God? What is the difference?
9. Where must the Christian find his security?
10. We say, "God is our Father." How does this help us in prayer and worship?
11. Jesus says, "My yoke is easy and my burden is light." How can this be true?
12. God is our Father. What is the greatest way He used to show His love?

SUMMARY OF LESSON

God is the Father of all men because He has created all men, but in a special way God is the Father of those who accept Him as their Father. We cannot accept God as our Father until God comes to show us how, so God comes to us in Jesus. We call Him the Son, but God the Father and God the Son are one. Just as the Creator and the Redeemer are one. God is our Father. He shows His great love as a Father by suffering to redeem us.

Motto: A master has slaves, but a father has sons.

14
SON

SCRIPTURES TO BE READ:	Matthew 12:6, 41-42; John 1:1-3, 18;
II Corinthians 8:9; Philippians 2:5-11;
Luke 15:8-32; Ephesians 2:8-10, 4:24;
Colossians 2:9-10; II Corinthians 5:11;
I John 3:1

STATEMENT OF LESSON

God loves us like a Father. Like a Father, He wants us to return His love. So deep is God's love for us that He is willing to suffer to win our love. In the last lesson, we saw how the carpenter, a man, became a small boy. He became a small boy to teach a small boy how to obey him, the man. We saw how Yusef the land owner became a farmer to show the farmer how to obey him, the land owner. Even so, God becomes Man to teach man how to obey God. Man did not become God. This is idolatry, but God came down and entered into the form of Man. God in the flesh we call Jesus Christ, the Son. Christ claimed to be greater than the prophets. He claimed to be greater than the priests. He claimed to be greater than the kings. He is our Prophet, Priest and King. As Prophet, He teaches us. As Priest, He redeems us. As King, He leads us. When we studied the subject "God is Light," we saw that Christ reveals God. When we studied "God is One," we saw that Christ is the One through whom all things were made. In this lesson, we will see that Christ not only creates and reveals, but also redeems. Christ shows us how to enter the family of God. Christ has created us to be sons of God; we must be recreated. Only the Creator can create anew. We become children of God when Jesus Christ creates us anew.

OUTLINE

<u>GOD THE SON (THE REDEEMER)</u>

1. Who is God the Son? (God coming down - not man going up.)
    a. A greater than Jonah is here - Prophet.
    b. A greater than the Temple is here - Priest.
    c. A greater than Solomon is here - King.
2. What does God the Son do?
    a. He Creates.
    b. He Reveals.
    c. He Redeems.

THE DIALOGUE

GOD IS . . .

SCENE 14

CHARACTERS:

Yusef, the Wise

Abdu, the Inquirer

Baseat, the Simple

THE DIALOGUE

(Yusef, Abdu, and Baseat are already seated in Yusef's front room.)

YUSEF: Tonight, Abdu, I will ask you what is our subject.

ABDU: I think our subject must be "God the Son." The last time we talked about "God the Father." Next time I expect we will talk about "God the Holy Spirit."

YUSEF: Good. So let us begin with a question. Abdu, were the people of Jesus' time against idolatry?

ABDU: Of course. I think they were very much against idolatry.

YUSEF: Why?

ABDU: I don't know, but I think they must have been.

YUSEF: The reason is very clear, my friends. Since the time of Abraham, all of the people of God fought against idolatry. All of the prophets spoke against idolatry. This was very important to them. Now, was it easy for the disciples to look at a man and call Him God?

BASEAT: I think not.

YUSEF: Very good, Baseat. We are against idolatry. If a man came to our village and said, "I am God," would we believe him?

ABDU: No. We would beat him.

YUSEF: Very well. Now, Abdu, when you first married the mother of Khaleel what did you think she was like?

ABDU: An angel.

YUSEF: Very good. Then after you had lived with her for four or five years, did you still think she was an angel?

ABDU: (Smiling) No. After I had lived with her for a while, I found she was very naughty.

YUSEF: That is, when you lived with her you found out her mistakes.

165

ABDU: I certainly did.

YUSEF: This is true with anyone! When we get to know them we find out their mistakes. Now - did Jesus tell the disciples he was God?

ABDU: He must have.

YUSEF: No, my sons. He did not. He lived with them and He waited for them to decide themselves Who He was. He did not tell them He was God, but the longer they lived with Him, the more sure they were that He was more than just a Man.

ABDU: Really!

YUSEF: Then finally when Jesus asked them, "Who do you think that I am?" Peter answered, "You are the Christ, the Son of the Living God." Then what did Jesus say to him, Abdu?

ABDU: Let me see - he said - "Flesh and blood have not revealed it to you."

YUSEF: You see, the longer we live with a man, the more we are sure that he is a man with faults like us. But the longer the disciples lived with Jesus, the more they were sure that He was God. Now, Abdu, what does John say in the first chapter?

ABDU: (Quoting) "In the beginning was the Word, and the Word was with God and the Word was God."

YUSEF: Who is the Word of God?

ABDU: I don't know.

YUSEF: How is it that you don't know? The Word of God is Jesus Christ. And Christ was with God from the beginning. Paul says that Christ, existing in the form of God, did not count equality with God a thing to be grasped, but emptied Himself, taking the form of a servant, being born in the likeness of men. What does this mean?

ABDU: I think it means at least that Christ is present with God from eternity.

YUSEF: Exactly. Just as light and heat and fire are one, yet at a special time light can come into this room. Even so, God is one, yet at a special time God enters the history of man in Jesus Christ. Men saw Him, walked with Him, and talked with Him. Then they said, "This is God." And so Christ is not begotten. Christ is not created. Christ is not made. Christ is eternal with God. But at a certain time the Word became Flesh and dwelt among us. Now, my friends, we must look at two things. We must look at what this Word is like.

166

YUSEF: Then we must look to see what it does. Baseat, open and read Matthew 12: verse 41.

BASEAT: (Reading) "The men of Nineveh will arise at the judgment with this generation and condemn it; for they repented at the preaching of Jonah, and behold, something greater than Jonah is here."

YUSEF: Jesus says, "Something greater than Jonah is here." Who was Jonah, Baseat?

BASEAT: Jonah was a prophet.

YUSEF: Very well. Jesus says, "A greater than Jonah is here."

ABDU: About Himself.

YUSEF: Exactly. Jesus is saying, "I am greater than Jonah. That is, I am greater than the prophets." For Jonah was a great prophet. So first we see that Jesus Christ is greater than the prophets. Now, my friends, what did the prophets do?

ABDU: They told about the future.

YUSEF: Yes, they did this, but more than this, they gave to the people the Word of God. Didn't they!

BASEAT: Yes.

YUSEF: They told the people the Word of God. That is, they spoke for God to the people. They told the people about holiness, and righteousness. For example, they said to the people, "God wants you to do justly, to love mercy, to walk humbly with God."

ABDU: That sounds like them.

YUSEF: Now, my friends, were the prophets able to do this perfectly themselves?

ABDU: I think not. They were human.

YUSEF: Now notice carefully. Christ is the Prophet Who spoke the Word of God and *was* the Word of God.

ABDU: What do you mean, Yusef?

YUSEF: Then Christ said that God wants us to love all men perfectly. That is, He told men what to do, then He Himself did it. Do you get the point, Abdu?

ABDU: I think so.

YUSEF: Now, Abdu, read Matthew 12: verse 6.

ABDU: (Reading) "I tell you, something greater than the Temple is here." What does this mean, O Yusef?

YUSEF: Who were the people who served in the Temple?

167

ABDU: The priests.

YUSEF: Right. So Jesus says, "I am greater than the Temple." He means, "I am greater than all the Priests."

ABDU: That is, He was not only greater than the prophets, but He was greater than the priests.

YUSEF: Exactly. Now Baseat, what did the priests of the Old Testament offer on the altar?

BASEAT: I don't know. Was it a donkey or something?

ABDU: Shame, Baseat. The priests offered a bull or a lamb.

YUSEF: Right. Now Jesus is the _great_ Priest. What does He offer on the sacrificial altar?

ABDU: (Puzzled) I don't understand, O Yusef. Did He ever offer a sacrifice? Did He ever work in the Temple?

YUSEF: Think, my friend. Think! Jesus did not work in the Temple. He did not offer a sacrifice of a sheep or an ox. He offered a much greater sacrifice. What was it?

ABDU: I do not know, Yusef.

YUSEF: You know, Abdu, you just do not see. Stay with me, my friends. Jesus is the great High Priest who offers _Himself_ as a sacrifice. This is what He means when He says, "I am greater than the Temple."

ABDU: This is indeed a great sacrifice.

YUSEF: Yes. And it is a sacrifice for us. For Jesus is the Prophet Who speaks the Word of God and _is_ the Word of God. Jesus is the Priest Who is Priest and Sacrifice at once. Now Baseat, read verse 42 of the same chapter.

BASEAT: (Reading) "The queen of the South will arise at the judgment with this generation and condemn it; for she came from the ends of the earth to hear the wisdom of Solomon, and behold, something greater than Solomon is here."

YUSEF: So, now Jesus says, "I am greater than Solomon." Who was Solomon?

BASEAT: Solomon was a great king.

YUSEF: So what does Jesus mean when He says, "A greater than Solomon is here?"

ABDU: He means that he is greater than the king.

YUSEF: But, how is Jesus greater than Solomon? Was He richer than Solomon?

ABDU: No. He was very poor.

YUSEF: Did He have a bigger army than Solomon?

BASEAT: No. He had no army at all.

YUSEF: Then what does He mean?

ABDU: I do not know.

YUSEF: Well, let me ask a question. Long ago when there were many kings on the earth, did the kings serve the people, or did the people serve the king?

ABDU: The people served the king, of course.

YUSEF: Back in the days when there were many rich land owners, did the rich land owner serve the peasants, or did the peasants serve the land owner?

BASEAT: No. The peasants served the land owner.

YUSEF: Very well. How did Jesus come? Did He come asking that the people serve Him like the kings of the earth?

ABDU: No. He came as a servant.

YUSEF: Very good, this is the point, my friends. Jesus is the King Who comes as a servant. Is this not a strange kind of a King?

BASEAT: Very strange, indeed. We understand a King. We understand a servant. But a King who is a Servant is strange indeed.

ABDU: Yes, it is strange, but I remember that we talked for two nights about true greatness. We said that true greatness is in service.

YUSEF: Good, Abdu, I'm glad that you remember. So Jesus is a King and He is greater than the kings because He is the King Who is a Servant. So we see that Jesus is Prophet, Priest, and King. Abdu - what kind of a prophet is He?

ABDU: He is a Prophet who says the Word of God and is the Word of God.

YUSEF: Baseat, Christ is greater than the priests. As a Priest, what is He?

BASEAT: He is Priest and Sacrifice.

ABDU: It seems sitting with Elder Yusef has been very good for you, Baseat. You have begun to understand. I am surprised.

YUSEF: Did I not tell you that if you quit mocking Baseat he would begin to understand? Now Abdu, what kind of a king is Jesus Christ?

ABDU: He is a King who is a Servant.

YUSEF: Very good. So we see Christ is a Prophet Who teaches us, a Priest Who redeems us, and a King Who leads us. But do we accept this, Abdu?

ABDU: I hope so.

YUSEF: Sadly, often we do not. We accept Christ as a Priest who redeems us, but we do not accept Him as a Prophet to teach us, for we do not wish to learn. We do not accept Him as a King to lead us, for we wish to go our own way. But let us go on. We said we would look to see what Jesus Christ is like. We have seen that He is Prophet, Priest, King. Now let us look to see what the Christ does. We see He does three things. He creates, He reveals God and He redeems men.

ABDU: Indeed we have already learned that He is Creator. John says, "All things were made through Him, and without Him was not anything made that was made."

YUSEF: I'm glad you remember, Abdu. Now, look in Hebrews 1: verse 2.

ABDU: (Reading) ". . . but in these last days he has spoken to us by a Son, whom he appointed the heir of all things, through whom also he created the world."

YUSEF: Yes, and Paul says in Colossians, "For in Him all things were created in heaven and on earth, visible and invisible. All things were created through Him and for Him." So we see He is Creator. Do you remember also that we studied about how Christ is Revealer? The One Who reveals God to us?

ABDU: Yes, I remember. We talked for a long time about "How God is light." Let me see -- God is light. He enlightens us in nature, in the prophets, and in Christ.

YUSEF: I am very pleased with you, Abdu. You remember very well.

ABDU: May God keep you, Yusef. You make things so clear we cannot forget.

YUSEF: May God make all things clear to us. You are right, Abdu, we did talk for a long time about how Christ reveals God to us. John says, "No one has ever seen God, the only Son, who is in the bosom of the Father, he has made him known." But let us look at the third and most important question for tonight's lesson. Who is Christ? He is Prophet, Priest and King. What does Christ do? He creates, He reveals, and He redeems. Now, my friends, let us think together about this great subject. Baseat, who built the bridge at the edge of town over the canal?

BASEAT: Do I know who built it? Some engineer from the city built it.

YUSEF: Very well. If something breaks in the bridge, will the Mayor call in the water carrier to fix the bridge?

BASEAT: The water carrier? What can he do?

170

YUSEF: Oh - he can pour water on it.

BASEAT: I don't understand. This will do nothing.

YUSEF: Does the Mayor leave the bridge to fix itself?

BASEAT: No, of course not.

YUSEF: Then what does he do?

ABDU: He must call the engineer who built it. No one can fix the bridge except the engineer who built it.

YUSEF: Very good. Now, Abdu, you have a water wheel on your land. Right?

ABDU: Yes.

YUSEF: When it breaks, do you call in the brick-maker?

ABDU: No. What can the brick-maker do?

YUSEF: He can put some mud plaster on it.

ABDU: This is strange talk, O Yusef. The mud plaster will do nothing. The mud will melt in the water. The brick-maker cannot fix the water wheel.

YUSEF: Do you leave the water wheel to fix itself?

ABDU: No. It is impossible. What do you mean?

YUSEF: Who do you call then when the water wheel is broken?

ABDU: We call the carpenter who made it. Of course, only the carpenter who made it can fix it.

YUSEF: Very well, Baseat, when the farmer buys a cart, and when it breaks down, does the farmer call the town crier?

BASEAT: How is this? What can the town crier do to the cart?

YUSEF: Oh - he can cry to the cart and ask it to stand up again.

BASEAT: How is this? The town crier can do nothing to the cart.

YUSEF: Does he leave the cart to fix itself?

BASEAT: No. No. The cart cannot fix itself.

YUSEF: What then?

BASEAT: The man who made it must fix it.

YUSEF: If a man buys a boat and the mast of the boat breaks in the wind, does he call the village musician to play a tune? Does he leave the boat to fix itself?

ABDU: No. No. The village musician can do nothing. The boat cannot fix itself. He must call the boat builder to fix the mast.

YUSEF: If a potter is making a water jar with clay, and the clay is spoiled in his hands, does he call the carpenter to drive nails in it to fix it? Can the clay fix itself?

ABDU: No. No. Only the potter can fix the clay.

YUSEF: This is right, my friends. Who can rebuild the bridge if it falls down?

ABDU: Only the engineer who built it.

YUSEF: Who can repair the water wheel if it breaks?

ABDU: Only the carpenter who built it.

YUSEF: Who can repair the cart which breaks down?

ABDU: Only the farmer who built it.

YUSEF: Who can repair the mast of the boat which breaks?

ABDU: Only the boat-builder who made it.

YUSEF: Who can remake the water jar when the clay is spoiled in the hands of the potter?

ABDU: Only the potter himself.

YUSEF: Even so, my friends, God creates man. Man goes rotten and walks in the way of evil. Only God who created man can create man anew. Only God who made us can make us again. Only God can create. Only God can create again.

ABDU: We never thought of it in this way.

YUSEF: But this is the way we must think. Think of the prodigal son. Who can clean him up? Who can put a ring on his fingers? Who can put a robe on his shoulders and shoes on his feet and make him a son again? Can he do this himself? Can the men of the village do it? Can the servants do it?

ABDU: No. Only his father can do these things.

YUSEF: We are like the younger son. God has created us. Only He can create us again. Only He can restore us to the house of God. So Paul says, "God was in Christ reconciling the world unto himself."

BASEAT: All our lives we have never understood what this meant.

ABDU: Now we are beginning to understand.

YUSEF: Listen, my friends, to Paul, when he says, "If anyone is in Christ, he is a new creation." God creates us anew.

ABDU: But how does He do that?

YUSEF: I will explain. Abdu, have you ever seen me run in the streets of the village?

ABDU: No. Of course not. You walk very slowly through the village like a respectable man.

YUSEF: Well, what does the father do in the story of the prodigal son when his younger son comes home?

ABDU: I'm not sure what you mean.

YUSEF: He runs. He runs through the village. He humiliates himself before all in the village. He runs to greet his son. He kisses him before the whole village. He kisses him while he is dirty and in rags. Were there not many people from the village watching?

ABDU: Of course. Many people must have been watching.

YUSEF: Was it not very humiliating for the father to run through the village and kiss his son before all the village men? So he lowers himself and humbles himself so that he can make his son into a son again. He could have thrashed him.

BASEAT: Of course. He has every right to beat him badly.

YUSEF: Or ask him to work and pay everything back.

ABDU: Yes, he could do that too.

YUSEF: But he doesn't. He humbles himself so he can create a son again. Can the son reestablish himself as a son?

ABDU: Never!

YUSEF: His father knows this. If the father is to have a son, he must create a son again. Only he can do this. So he humbles himself and runs to the boy and takes the boy as he is, dirty and ragged, and he creates from him a new son. Does the boy deserve to be made a son?

ABDU: Not at all. All is from the generosity of his father.

YUSEF: Will the boy now love his father?

BASEAT: He will love him very much. He now knows he deserves nothing. All he has is from the generosity of his father.

YUSEF: Does he know that he is wrong?

ABDU: Yes, he comes very humbly. He comes saying that he is wrong.

YUSEF: But what is the wrong that he has done?

BASEAT: He has wasted the money?

YUSEF: Yes, but behind this what has he done?

ABDU: He has rebelled against his father and left his father's house.

YUSEF: Very good, Abdu, he has put himself first. He has not cared about his family. This is sin. When we

YUSEF: say, "I am first," we do not care about our neighbors, we do not care about God. This is the foundation of all sin.

ABDU: My goodness! I thought sin was adultery, drinking, murder and things like that.

YUSEF: Yes, this is sin. This is like the boy as he wastes his father's money in a far country, but behind this is something deeper. Behind this is his rebellion against his father and his father's house.

ABDU: Yes, I see.

YUSEF: When we put ourselves first and do not care about God and do not care about our brethren, sometimes we commit sins like murder and adultery. But then sometimes we become hateful, jealous and self-righteous. The foundation is the same. We say, "I am first, and after me comes God, after me comes my brother." This is what the prodigal son said.

ABDU: That's right. He did not care about his father or his family.

YUSEF: But don't forget that the older son said the same thing.

BASEAT: How is that?

YUSEF: The older son said, "I will look for myself first. I do not respect my father. I hate my brother."

ABDU: I don't understand. What do you mean, Yusef?

YUSEF: This is very clear. Does not his father make a banquet?

ABDU: Yes, he does.

YUSEF: Is the older brother willing to take part?

BASEAT: No. He refuses to go into the banquet.

YUSEF: Then the father humbles himself and humiliates himself before his guests and goes out in the field to talk to him.

BASEAT: The father is humiliated before his guests. It is a great shame that the older son did not obey.

YUSEF: Exactly right, Baseat. So we see that the older son did not respect his father and we see that he hates his brother for he will not go in. So again the father must humble himself to try to win his son back into his love.

ABDU: We have never thought of the parable in this way. But we see that this is true.

YUSEF: The father, by humbling himself and humiliating himself, tries to win his older son back. He tries to create a loving son out of his older son. Does he succeed?

ABDU: We do not know. Jesus does not say.

YUSEF: He does not say because it is much harder to make a new son out of the older son for he is very proud. When a man says, "I am first; I do not care about God; I do not care about my brother," he may commit the sins of the flesh of stealing, adultery and murder, or he may commit the sins of the spirit such as pride, anger, jealousy. Do you see, my friends, that they both have the same foundation?

ABDU: We never thought of that, Yusef.

YUSEF: The important thing is that the father must humiliate himself - must humble himself to try to create a new son out of his younger son and out of his older son. He only asks that the boys shall be humble, shall confess their sin - their pride, and begin to accept the father's love and return it to the father. And the two are the same.

BASEAT: They do look very much alike.

YUSEF: And so it is with God. God humbles _Himself_ and comes to us in Christ. He does this to try to create from us new sons. If we accept His love, we become new creatures. Can the younger son pay back what he has lost?

ABDU: We have already said that it is impossible.

YUSEF: Even so with us, we can but receive the gift of God's love. When we do this God creates us again and makes us His sons. Then we must live in grateful service for the gift.

ABDU: Only now have we begun to understand the meaning of God the Father and God the Son.

YUSEF: The subject is clear, my friends, if we think very deep. God in Christ has created us. Therefore, only God in Christ can create us new. Only God in Christ can make us sons in the House of God. This is what Paul means when he says, "God was in Christ reconciling the world unto himself." And in the parable we can say the father was in himself humiliating himself to win his younger son. Who can repair a bridge, Abdu?

ABDU: Only the engineer who had made it?

YUSEF: Who can repair the water wheel, Baseat?

BASEAT: Only the carpenter who had made it.

YUSEF: Who can repair the sail boat, Abdu?

ABDU: Only the workman who had made it.

YUSEF: Then who can repair us, my friends.

ABDU: Only God in Christ who has made us.

YUSEF: Exactly! God in Christ created us. God in Christ must create us again. He asks that we accept His love, and that we return His love. In humility we must admit that there is no hope in us, and we must spend our lives in grateful service for what He has done. Abdu, when the younger son is created anew in the house as son, do we expect him to serve his father because he has to?

ABDU: No. He will serve Him because He wants to from his heart, out of gratitude.

YUSEF: So, when we become sons of God, we do not love God and our fellow men because we have to. We do not serve God because He tells us in His law we must serve Him. We serve Him because we want to, because we are new creatures in Christ. Jesus says, "I am the Way, the Truth, the Light, no man cometh to the Father but by me." Abdu, why is this true?

ABDU: Because God in Christ has created us, so only God in Christ can create us anew to be His sons.

YUSEF: Right, Abdu. God says, "See what love the Father has given us that we shall be called children of God." Would that we might serve God even as we know the younger son will now serve his father.

BASEAT: Sadly, we do not serve Him in this way.

ABDU: A new creature in Christ. Only now have I begun to understand.

QUESTIONS FOR DISCUSSION

1. Was Christ created by God?
2. Were the Jews against idolatry?
3. At first, did Jesus tell His disciples He was God?
4. Jesus says, "A greater than Jonah is here." Explain.
5. Jesus says, "A greater than the Temple is here." Explain.
6. Jesus says, "A greater than Solomon is here." Explain.
7. Jesus is Prophet, Priest and King. What does this mean to us?
8. What are the three things that Jesus does?
9. Where do we read in the Bible that God creates in Christ?
10. What is the meaning of John 1:18?
11. Yusef uses the story of the bridge, the water wheel, the cart, the boat builder and the potter. What is he trying to illustrate?
12. How does the father humble himself in the story of the prodigal son?
13. Only God can create. Therefore, only God can create again. What does this mean?
14. God wants to create us again and make us His sons. What does He ask of us?

SUMMARY OF THE LESSON

Christ is greater than the prophets. He speaks the Word of God and is the Word of God. Christ is greater than the Priests. He is both King and Servant.

Christ does three things. He creates us. Then He reveals God to us.

Finally, because He has created us, only He can recreate us.

MOTTO: Only the Creator can create anew.

15
HOLY SPIRIT

SCRIPTURES TO BE READ: Luke 3:22; Luke 4:18; John 3:6-8;
John 7:37-39; John 16:8, 14; Acts 2:2-3;
Ephesians 1:13-14; Ephesians 4:30;
I John 2:20, 27.

STATEMENT OF LESSON

God is a Spirit and is everywhere in His Spirit. In the New Testament we have many symbols which are used to try and explain the Holy Spirit. The Holy Spirit is easy to understand. We know God only as we see Him in Jesus Christ and we know Jesus Christ only as the Holy Spirit shows Him to us. The Spirit is like the wind and like a dove. It is like the fire and the oil of an ointment. It is like water and it is like a seal. Each of these symbols shows us something about the Spirit. The Spirit of God is like the wind. We do not know where the wind comes from or where it goes. We know that the wind is all about us. We do not know how God's Spirit works, but we know that God's Spirit is everywhere. The dove is a sign of purity. The Spirit of God is called the Holy Spirit. When God's Holy Spirit is close to us we know that we are sinners. The Holy Spirit convicts us of sin. On the day of Pentecost, the people saw the Holy Spirit like tongues of fire on the heads of the people. Fire is power and fire is purifying. Even so the Spirit of God purifies us and empowers us. John says that because we are annointed by the Spirit, we are taught about everything. The Spirit annoints us for service. Also, the annointing of the Spirit teaches us about Christ. Jesus also says that the Spirit is like water. We are like a great pottery vase. The vase must be filled with water. Even so we must be filled with the Holy Spirit. Water

178

refreshes the thirsty man and the Spirit of God is refreshing to us. Paul also says the Spirit is like a seal. When wax is stamped with a seal, the image of the seal is left on the wax. When we are sealed by the Holy Spirit, the image of Christ is left on us. When something is sealed, anyone can look at the seal and know the owner. So when we are sealed by the Holy Spirit, we know that we are Christ's. We know that we belong to Him. Our security, thus, is with Him. We are sealed to the day of redemption.

OUTLINE

GOD THE HOLY SPIRIT

1. God is like the wind (God is present with us in His Spirit.)
    a. The Spirit is everywhere and works as it wishes.
    b. We must be born of the Spirit.
2. The Spirit is like the dove (God convicts us by His Spirit.)
    a. The Spirit is Holy.
    b. The Spirit convicts us of sin.
3. The Spirit is like the oil of annointing (God annoints us for service by His Spirit.)
    a. The Spirit annoints us for service.
    b. The Spirit teaches us.
4. The Spirit is like the fire (God gives us power by His Spirit.)
    a. The Spirit purifies us.
    b. The Spirit empowers us.
5. The Spirit is like water (God refreshes us by His Spirit.)
    a. The Spirit refreshes us.
    b. The Spirit unites us.
6. The Spirit is like a seal (God keeps us by His Spirit.)
    a. The Spirit stamps us with the image of God.
    b. The Spirit assures us that we belong to God.

THE DIALOGUE

GOD IS . . .

SCENE 15

CHARACTERS:

Yusef, the Wise

Abdu, the Inquirer

Baseat, the Simple

THE DIALOGUE

(Abdu, Yusef, and Baseat are seated in Yusef's front room.)

YUSEF: Are you ready, my friends, to complete our study of the Trinity?

ABDU: My goodness, Yusef, my head is still spinning from the last lesson.

YUSEF: What was it about, Abdu?

ABDU: It was about God the Son. God the Redeemer.

YUSEF: Did you understand it well?

ABDU: I tried. I learned many things, but I think I am just beginning to understand this deep subject.

YUSEF: I am happy, Abdu, that you see how deep it is. But praise God, our subject tonight is not as difficult.

BASEAT: Wonderful! My mind is worn out from the last three lessons.

YUSEF: Indeed, they were difficult lessons. We talked of how God is One. How God is like a father and how God comes in humility to redeem us. Now tonight, we must talk about how God is always with us in His Holy Spirit. Now, Abdu, how do we know God?

ABDU: We know God in Christ.

YUSEF: Very well and how do we know Christ?

BASEAT: I'm not sure.

YUSEF: When God was in Christ on this earth, men could see Him and talk with Him and know Him, but He is no longer here.

ABDU: Go on.

YUSEF: So, how can we know Him if He is not here?

ABDU: I don't know.

YUSEF: We know Him through the Holy Spirit. Abdu, read John 16, verses 13-15.

ABDU: (Reading) "When the Spirit of truth comes, he will guide you into all the truth; for he will not speak on his own authority, but whatever he hears he will speak, and he will declare to you the things that are to come. He will glorify me, for he will take what is mine and declare it to you. All that the Father has is mine; therefore, I say that he will take what is mine and declare it to you."

YUSEF: You see. Jesus says of the Spirit, "He will take what is mine and declare it to you." Do we not say it many times every day - "God is with us."

BASEAT: Yes, indeed.

YUSEF: We talk about many things and then at the end of the conversation we say, "God is with us." Now, how is He with us? I do not see Him.

ABDU: He is with us in His Spirit.

YUSEF: Exactly. I think this is a very easy lesson. God is Spirit. God is everywhere. God is with us, and so God is with us in His Spirit. The Spirit works in our hearts and teaches us all things about God. Abdu, can we not say that the spirit of the late Pastor Hanna is still in the village?

ABDU: What do you mean, Yusef?

YUSEF: I mean he was a very good man. He had great influence in the village. His influence is still here. Don't you think so?

ABDU: Everyone remembers him. Yes, you could say his Spirit is still with us.

YUSEF: Now, if the spirit of Pastor Hanna is in a way with us, the Spirit of God who is everywhere is really with us. Let us think of the prodigal son.

BASEAT: What about him, Yusef?

YUSEF: When he is in a far country, is not the spirit of his father within him?

ABDU: In a sense.

YUSEF: Does not the spirit of his father speak within him and tell him that his father loves him?

ABDU: He at least is sure his father will receive him.

YUSEF: Then after he comes home, does not the spirit of his father still work in him?

BASEAT: Of course.

YUSEF: This is what we mean by the Holy Spirit. God working in us -- through His Spirit.

ABDU: This is very clear.

YUSEF: Good. Now, my friends, the Bible uses many symbols for the Holy Spirit. Let us look at them and see what they teach us about the Holy Spirit. I have been studying the New Testament. I have found six symbols for the Holy Spirit. The Holy Spirit is like the wind. It is like a dove. It is like the oil of annointing. It is like the fire. It is like water, and it is like a seal.

ABDU: This sounds like a very interesting subject.

BASEAT: Let us go on with it.

YUSEF: So, first, the Spirit is like the wind. Now what does Jesus say to Nicodemus about the wind?

ABDU: He says we don't know where it comes from or where it goes.

YUSEF: Even so, the Spirit works as it wishes, but notice this.

BASEAT: Yes, O Yusef.

YUSEF: When there is a wind, the wind is everywhere.

ABDU: Which means - ?

YUSEF: When there is a wind in the village, can you say the wind is here or the wind is there? Can you say the wind is in this street, or the wind is in this palm tree?

BASEAT: No. When there is a wind, the wind fills everything.

YUSEF: Even when we close the door, does not some of the wind come into the house?

ABDU: Yes, indeed it does.

YUSEF: So the Spirit is like the wind. It works as it wishes and it is everywhere. Now, when Jesus was talking to Nicodemus at night He said to him, "That which is born of the flesh is flesh and that which is born of the Spirit is Spirit. Do not marvel that I said to you, 'You must be born anew.' The wind blows where it wills and you hear the sound of it, but you do not know whence it comes or whither it goes. So it is with everyone who is born of the Spirit."

BASEAT: What does He mean?

YUSEF: This is our subject for this evening. But think, my friends, we said that only God can create and only God can create anew. Right?

ABDU: This much we understand clearly. Only the carpenter who makes the water wheel can fix it. Only God who creates us can create us anew.

182

YUSEF: Very well. The carpenter works with his hands and with his tools to fix the broken water wheel. How does God work in us to create us anew? What are the hands of God? What are the tools of God?

ABDU: I do not know, Yusef.

YUSEF: The hands of God are the Holy Spirit. We are God's tools. The carpenter works with his hands to fix the water wheel. God works through His Holy Spirit to create us anew. This is what Jesus means when He says, "You must be born of the Spirit." God works through us by His Holy Spirit.

BASEAT: I don't understand.

YUSEF: Just stay with us, Baseat, and you will understand. Now, the Spirit is like the wind -- remember in the Book of Acts on the Day of Pentecost the people heard a great wind in the house?

ABDU: Yes, I remember.

YUSEF: So the Spirit is like the wind. The Spirit is also like a dove. Where do we read this, Abdu?

ABDU: When Jesus was annointed, the Bible says the Spirit descended on Him like a dove.

YUSEF: Now what was the dove a symbol of for the Jews?

ABDU: I do not know, Yusef.

YUSEF: It was the symbol of purity. The Spirit of God is like the dove in that the Spirit of God is called the Holy Spirit. Let me explain.

BASEAT: Yes, Yusef.

YUSEF: Yesterday I went down to the Village of Knowledge to see how Kamel was doing out in my fields. I spent the whole day in the field. I talked with Kamel and with my friends there. I walked around and sat in the field and had tea with the men.

ABDU: Sorry I missed it.

YUSEF: Now, as I sat there I did not notice that my shoes were dirty. Nor did I notice my hands and clothes. I did not see this because I was sitting in the field. Then last night I came home. On the way home, I stopped to greet the Mayor. We sat together in the Mayor's sitting room. The floor is very clean and the walls are newly whitewashed. The chairs are covered with white cloth. In the field I did not notice that my clothes had become dirty. But last night as I walked into the Mayor's sitting room, suddenly I saw that my clothes had become dirty. Then I was ashamed. Now, Abdu, what made me understand my clothes had become dirty?

ABDU: I think it is when you saw them next to the white covers of the Mayor's chairs and next to the white walls in the Mayor's sitting room. Then you saw them and saw that they had become dirty in the fields.

YUSEF: Exactly right. Now, what does Isaiah feel when he goes into the chapel and sees a vision of the Holy God?

BASEAT: I don't remember.

YUSEF: Open, Baseat, and look at the 6th Chapter of Isaiah and read verse 5.

BASEAT: (Reading) "And I said: 'Woe is me! For I am lost; for I am a man of unclean lips, and I dwell in the midst of a people of unclean lips; for my eyes have seen the King, the Lord of Hosts!'"

YUSEF: What did the seraphims cry one to another?

ABDU: They cried "Holy, Holy, Holy is the Lord of Hosts. The whole earth is full of His glory."

YUSEF: Notice that Isaiah never thought that he was unclean until what?

ABDU: Until he entered the Temple.

YUSEF: It is more than this. When he saw that God was Holy, *then* he saw that he was unclean. It is always like that. We think we are very good until God's Holy Spirit comes close to us. Then we see the holiness of God and we see our sin. God's Spirit is like the dove. This means that God's Spirit is pure. God's Spirit is a *Holy* Spirit. This spirit convicts of sin.

ABDU: Only when we come near to His Holiness.

YUSEF: Exactly right, Abdu. Now, third, the Spirit is like the oil of annointing. Read Luke 4: verses 18 and 19, Abdu.

ABDU: (Reading) "'The Spirit of the Lord is upon me, because he has annointed me to preach good news to the poor.'"

YUSEF: Now Baseat, read I John, 2nd Chapter, verse 20 and 27.

BASEAT: (Reading) "But you have been annointed by the Holy One, and you all know. But the annointing which you received from Him abides in you, and you have no need that anyone should teach you; as his annointing teaches you about everything, and is true, and is no lie, just as it has taught you, abide in him."

YUSEF: So we see, my friends, the Holy Spirit annoints us. Now, Abdu, why does the Holy Spirit annoint us?

ABDU: I do not know, Yusef.

YUSEF: Think, Abdu, about David. When was he annointed to be king?

ABDU: I think he was annointed when he was still a small boy and a shepherd.

YUSEF: Very good. Now, was he annointed so he could sit in a palace and get fat?

BASEAT: No.

YUSEF: Was he annointed to be lazy and have people serve him and have many wives and eat and drink and sleep? Was this why he was annointed?

ABDU: No.

YUSEF: Why, then, was he annointed?

ABDU: I think he was annointed because there was work for him to do.

YUSEF: Exactly right, Abdu. He was annointed king because there was a job for him. Even so God's Holy Spirit annoints us for <u>service</u>. Now John says His annointing teaches you about everything. Let us think again about David. When he was annointed by Samuel, did he understand everything?

ABDU: No.

YUSEF: Did he know everything he needed to know to be a king?

BASEAT: No. Of course not. He was still a boy.

YUSEF: There was a great service he had to do for his country. He was annointed to do this service, but was he ready?

ABDU: Not yet.

YUSEF: So it is with us. God creates us and then God creates us anew, that is, God makes us His sons. We are annointed to be sons of God by the Holy Spirit. When the prodigal son comes home, there surely is a lot of work for him in his father's house.

ABDU: Now he works with a willing heart.

YUSEF: But he must learn how to be a true son. He has not done this before so he must learn.

ADDU: Yes, I can see that, Yusef.

YUSEF: In this same way, God's Spirit teaches us. We are annointed for service in the house of God, but we are not trained. So the Spirit of God takes things of Christ and shows them unto us. That is, the Holy Spirit teaches us how to be loyal, obedient, fruitful sons in the house of our Father. Now, Abdu, what did the people see on the day of Pentecost?

ABDU: They saw the Spirit coming down like fire on the heads of the people.

YUSEF: So we see, fourth, that the Spirit is like fire. The Spirit is like the wind, the Spirit is like a dove, the Spirit is like the oil of annointing, and now the Spirit is like the fire.

BASEAT: I don't understand.

YUSEF: Patience, Baseat, when we explain, then you will understand. Now, Abdu, read Matthew 3 verses 11 and 12.

ABDU: (Reading) "I baptize you with water for repentance, but he who is coming after me is mightier than I, whose sandals I am not worthy to carry; He will baptize you with the Holy Spirit and with fire. His winnowing fork is in his hand, and he will clear his threshing floor and gather his wheat into the granary, but the chaff he will burn with unquenchable fire."

YUSEF: Who is talking?

ABDU: John the Baptist, I think.

YUSEF: That's right. John says about Jesus, "He will baptize you with the Holy Spirit and with fire." Now what does the fire do?

ABDU: I'm not sure.

YUSEF: This is easy. The fire purifies. Anything we put into the fire is purified. Is it not so, Baseat?

BASEAT: Yes, indeed this is right.

YUSEF: So the baptism of fire means that the Holy Spirit will burn out sin from within us, but it means more than this. Fire is also a sign of power. Is there power in the sun?

ABDU: Yes, indeed.

YUSEF: Is the sun not fire?

BASEAT: Yes, of course, the sun is fire.

YUSEF: Think of the engine which pulls the train.

BASEAT: What about it?

YUSEF: Do they not build a fire in its belly?

ABDU: Yes, indeed, I saw it once.

YUSEF: This fire gives it power and makes it go. Well, the Spirit is like fire. That is, the Spirit gives us power. Were not the people filled with power on the Day of Pentecost?

ABDU: Indeed, they were.

YUSEF: Think then, of something else. Baseat, read John 7, verses 37 through 39.

BASEAT: (Reading) "On the last day of the feast, the great day, Jesus stood up and proclaimed, 'If any one thirst, let him come to me and drink. He who believes in me, as the scripture has said, "Out of his heart shall flow rivers of living water."' Now this he said about the Spirit, which those who believed in him were to receive; for as yet the Spirit had not been given, because Jesus was not yet glorified."

YUSEF: Now, Abdu, what does Jesus say the Spirit is like here?

ABDU: He says it is like water.

YUSEF: Very good. Now Abdu, when a man travels a long way and has no water, what is it like?

ABDU: It's terrible. His mouth becomes dry like it was full of cotton. When he tries to swallow, it is like two pieces of sandpaper rubbing together. His body is like fire. He thinks his head will burst open.

YUSEF: Then when he comes to the water what is the water like?

ABDU: Like pure gold. He drinks and drinks and drinks. The water gives him life. He feels great peace and great joy.

YUSEF: Exactly right, Abdu. Now the Holy Spirit is like this to us. It is like water to a thirsty man. God comes to us in His Spirit. His Spirit refreshes us, deep within us. Now Baseat!

BASEAT: Yes, Yusef.

YUSEF: Do you go to the fields to work all day and take no water with you?

BASEAT: Of course I take water with me.

YUSEF: But if you take a big drink on Sunday, is this not enough for the whole week?

BASEAT: Of course not. I must drink every day -- many times during the day.

YUSEF: Ah, my friends, but we think that if we pray on Sunday this is enough refreshment of the spirit for us for all week.

ABDU: Too many people think that way.

YUSEF: But our souls need the Holy Spirit like our bodies need water. The Holy Spirit is the water of our souls. We need this water every day. Abdu, does your good wife fill the water jar in your house once a week?

ABDU: No. She fills it every day.

YUSEF: Does not the water stay in the water jar?

ABDU: No. Very slowly it runs out the bottom.

187

YUSEF: So with us, we must be refilled with the Spirit of God every day. All through the Book of Acts we read, "filled with the Spirit," "they were full of the Spirit." The Spirit is like water and we are like the water jar. If we are not filled afresh every day, the jar will be dry. Now, Abdu, do not the people who drink from the same well feel together some fellowship?

ABDU: Yes, I think they do.

YUSEF: We all drink from the same river. Does this not bring us together in fellowship?

ABDU: Yes, I think you can say this.

YUSEF: So we see that the Spirit which is like water united us in fellowship. We all need the same water. We all drink from the same well. That is, we all need the same Holy Spirit. As we take our life from the same place we find our fellowship with other men who also drink this water.

ABDU: I never thought of it this way.

YUSEF: The benediction says, "The fellowship of the Holy Spirit." We understand this when we understand that the Spirit is like water.

BASEAT: Have patience with me, Yusef. You have said many things. How can I remember them? You have said the Spirit is like water and it is like fire and it is . . . . I can't remember the rest.

YUSEF: Abdu, what is the Spirit like?

ABDU: (Thinking) Let me see. It is like the wind. It is like the dove. It is like the oil of annointing. It is like fire and it is like water.

YUSEF: (Pleased) Good, Abdu. Now we have one more. Take it easy, Baseat. Remember only what you can remember. Do not worry about what you forget. Worry about what you remember.

BASEAT: I will do as you say, Elder Yusef.

YUSEF: Now, lastly the Bible says the Spirit is like a seal. Paul says in Ephesians, "And do not grieve the Holy Spirit of God in whom you were sealed for the day of redemption." What does he mean?

ABDU: I do not know.

YUSEF: When a man has a very important paper and he wishes to put his seal upon the paper, what does he do?

ABDU: He gets some wax. He puts the wax on the paper and then stamps the wax with the seal.

YUSEF: Very good. And does not the image of the seal come off on the wax?

ABDU: Yes, it does.

YUSEF: Does not the seal shape the wax?

BASEAT: Yes, it does.

YUSEF: Now. We are like wax. If we wish, the Holy Spirit will press on our souls the image of Jesus Christ.

ABDU: Oh, that this might happen to all of us.

YUSEF: It is up to us, my friends. If we wish the Holy Spirit to do this, the Holy Spirit is ready. The Holy Spirit is like a seal. The Holy Spirit is ready to press us like wax and make us to be like Christ. We must be ready for the Holy Spirit to do this. Now, Abdu, when you see a sack of cotton, it has on it a seal. What can you learn from the seal?

ABDU: I look at the seal and I see from the seal who owns the sack.

YUSEF: Exactly. Even so, the Holy Spirit of God stamps us then on the day of redemption. That is, the Day of Judgment, we will be sealed to Jesus Christ. That is, we will not be afraid. Every one will see that we belong to Christ.

ABDU: This is a great idea.

YUSEF: Indeed it is. The trouble is we try to find security in things. We try to find security in wealth, or power, or position. God's Spirit will stamp us with God's seal. Then we will be secure because we belong to God. Abdu, if you see a sack of cotton that is stamped with the stamp of a very rich and a very powerful man, do you think about taking the cotton?

ABDU: No indeed. No one will think of taking the cotton. Everyone will see the seal and be afraid. They will say, "This cotton belongs to so and so, and he is very powerful."

YUSEF: Even so with God. If we have the seal of God, God is All Powerful; no one will be able to touch us. No one will be able to hurt us. The seal of God will be upon us. We will be secure.

BASEAT: These are great ideas, Yusef. But I cannot remember them.

YUSEF: Do not be upset, Baseat. Just remember one thing.

BASEAT: This is much better. I am ready to remember one thing.

YUSEF: Remember John 16:14. Jesus says of the Spirit, "He will glorify me, for he will take what is mine and declare it to you." Now Baseat, the Spirit will take what is of Christ and show it to us. What will the Spirit do?

BASEAT: (Repeating) It will take what is of Christ and show it to us.

YUSEF: That's enough -- just remember this and you will remember what the Spirit of God is like.

QUESTIONS FOR DISCUSSION

1. What is the most important thing the Spirit of God does?
2. The Spirit of God is like the wind. Explain.
3. How did the Spirit of God descend on Christ when He was baptized?
4. What is the dove a symbol of?
5. Why does the Spirit of God annoint us?
6. How is the Spirit of God like fire?
7. How is the Spirit of God like water?
8. How is the Spirit of God like a seal?
9. Go back and pick review questions from each of the three preceding lessons.

SUMMARY OF THE LESSON

God's Spirit convicts us of sin.
God's Spirit cleanses us.
God's Spirit gives us power for service.
God's Spirit gives us security.

MOTTO: We see God the Father in Jesus Christ by the Holy Spirit.

SECTION IV
GOD IS HOLY LOVE

16
GOD IS HOLY

SCRIPTURES TO BE READ: Leviticus 10:3; Leviticus 11:45;
Isaiah 1:15; 5:16; 6:3-4; 57:15; 59:2;
II Corinthians 7:1; Ephesians 4:22-32;
John 17:11

STATEMENT OF LESSON

We say that God is holy. This means three things. Holiness is first, majesty. We say God is holy, we mean God is most high. Therefore, we must worship Him with reverence and fear. We must be afraid, only of Him. But holiness also means purity. Thus, holy things are pure things. God is most pure. He is set apart from all things unclean. Only when we see ourselves in the light of God's purity do we see that we are sinners. Holiness also means righteousness. God is holy so He demands righteousness from us. We understand holiness when we think of a person like Jesus who is holy. Jesus was holy in the midst of people - not far away from them. We do not become holy by obeying laws. If this were true, then all the Pharisees would have been saints. We become holy through fellowship with the Holy One - even Jesus Christ.

OUTLINE

<u>GOD IS HOLY</u>

1. Holiness is majesty.
    a. God is most high.
    b. We must worship Him with reverence.
    c. We must fear only Him.
2. Holiness is purity.
    a. God is most pure.
    b. Holiness makes sin to be sin.
    c. We must be purified.
3. Holiness demands righteousness.
    a. Holiness demands righteousness.
    b. Holiness is found in the midst of people.
    c. The link between God and man is obedience to a person.
    d. We become holy through fellowship with the Holy.

THE DIALOGUE

GOD IS . . .

SCENE 16

CHARACTERS:

Yusef, the Wise

Abdu, the Inquirer

Baseat, the Simple

Mayor Butrus

THE DIALOGUE

(Yusef and the Mayor are seated in Yusef's front room.)

YUSEF: We have not seen you for a long time, Mr. Mayor.

MAYOR: I am very sorry to have missed these meetings with you, Yusef, but what is the subject this time?

YUSEF: Tonight we begin talking about the character of God.

MAYOR: What do you mean?

YUSEF: God is holy and God is love.

MAYOR: But I think the most important is that God is love.

YUSEF: Not so, Mr. Mayor. God is love - yes, but He is a special kind of love. God is holy love. But tell me, Mayor, how is Habib, the guard?

MAYOR: (Shaking his head) Sometime I must speak with you again about him. I do not know what to do with him. He is very tough. He disobeyed me. He is very proud. He has made himself greater than everyone in the village.

YUSEF: What do you do with him?

MAYOR: What can I do? He does not break the rules. If he were late for his work, I could fine him. If he would get one of the guns stolen, I could punish him. He does nothing for which I can fine him. Can I fine a man for pride, and anger, and jealousy?

YUSEF: Of course not.

(Enter Baseat and Abdu)

YUSEF: Welcome, my good friends. Our respected Mayor has honored us again tonight.

ABDU: Welcome, Mayor. We missed you.

BASEAT: You have honored us, Mayor Butrus.

197

MAYOR: May God keep all of you. I am happy to be with you again.

YUSEF: My friends, tonight we begin talking about God who is holy love.

BASEAT: What does that mean?

YUSEF: Very well, Baseat, open to John 17 and read verse 11.

BASEAT: (Opens and reads) "And now I am no more in the world, but they are in the world and I am coming to Thee. Holy Father, keep them in Thy name which Thou hast given Me that they may be one, even as we are one."

YUSEF: Now, Baseat, what is the name of God here?

BASEAT: Holy Father.

YUSEF: Good. Now, God is a Holy Father which means two things. What are they, Abdu?

ABDU: I'm not sure what you mean, Yusef.

YUSEF: It is very simple. God is holy and God is a father. A father loves His children. So God is holy and God is love. These two names summarize all the names of God.

MAYOR: Indeed, my goodness! All the names of God in these two names?

YUSEF: When we understand them properly, yes. Now, let us look tonight at the first. God is holy. Baseat, what do we mean when we say God is holy?

BASEAT: I remember some time ago we talked about this. I did not understand anything. You said we would talk about it again.

YUSEF: Tonight, Baseat, you will understand. Tonight we must talk only about the holiness of God. Now my friends, holiness means three things. Holiness means majesty. Holiness means purity. Holiness demands righteousness. Abdu, what does holiness mean?

ABDU: (Repeating) Holiness is majesty. Holiness is purity. Holiness is righteousness.

YUSEF: Very good. Now, first - holiness is majesty. That is, God is high and lifted up. Abdu, read Leviticus 10:3.

ABDU: (Reading) "This is what the Lord said, 'I will show myself holy among those who are near me and before all the people I will be glorified.'"

YUSEF: You see, my friends, glory and holiness go together. Remember Isaiah heard the Seraphim saying one to another, "Holy, Holy, Holy is the Lord of hosts. The whole earth is full of His glory." Then also Isaiah says in Chapter 57, "For thus says the high and lofty

YUSEF:	One Who inhabits eternity whose name is holy." So God's name is holy. This means He is high and lifted up. This means His name must be glorified.
ABDU:	Yes, we have always understood this.
YUSEF:	Good, but this is only a part of the holiness of God. In the beginning, in the old days, this is all the people knew. So holiness meant holy things, holy people, holy ceremonies, holy places and holy times. That is, the things belonging to worship were holy things.
MAYOR:	That's what we think.
YUSEF:	Very well, Mayor, Do you remember Pastor Hanna?
MAYOR:	May God have mercy on his soul. That man was a great saint.
YUSEF:	Aha. What did you say about him, Mayor.
MAYOR:	I said he was a great saint.
YUSEF:	Now, the saint has holiness, doesn't he?
MAYOR:	Yes -- yes, indeed. The saint has holiness.
YUSEF:	Very well, was Pastor Hanna just something to be used for worship?
BASEAT:	No, he was a holy man.
YUSEF:	Ah -- so we see that holiness is more than just holy things. That is, when we think of holiness, we think of a holy person.
ABDU:	I never thought of it in quite that way.
YUSEF:	Now, I have a question. Abdu, can my servant sit down before me at the table?
ABDU:	No, of course not.
YUSEF:	Very well, if I go in the presence of a great king, can I sit down before the great king?
ABDU:	No, indeed not.
YUSEF:	This is true also of God. God is King of kings and Lord of lords. He is high and lifted up. He is holy. He is not like a close friend that we can pat on the back and sit down with. We must come before Him with fear and reverence. Mayor, read Isaiah 8:13.
MAYOR:	(Reading) "But the Lord of hosts, him you shall regard as holy; let him be your fear, and let him be your dread."
YUSEF:	You see? The Lord of hosts is holy. We must fear Him. Let us think about fear. Baseat, if you are riding a boat across the Nile during the flood, and the boat upsets, what do you do?

BASEAT: When this happens, the people are terrified. Many of them drown.

YUSEF: Abdu, when you are coming back at night along the dyke, sometimes there is a strong wind. The strong wind blows in the sugar cane and makes a loud noise. When this happens, are you afraid?

ABDU: I am scared to death.

YUSEF: Very well. Mayor, when there is a great storm -- rain and thunder and lightning, is the village afraid?

MAYOR: Indeed! All the women of the village cry. They tear their hair and throw dust into the air. They think the end of the world has come they are so frightened.

YUSEF: Now, my friends, this is one kind of fear. This kind of fear leads many people to make charms, and this is idolatry.

MAYOR: My goodness. Is the use of charms idolatry?

YUSEF: Of course, the man who hangs a charm around the neck of his water buffalo is afraid of something else beside God. He is afraid of the evil spirits. Isaiah says, "The Lord of hosts, him you shall regard as holy. Let him be your fear. Let him be your dread." God is holy. This means we must be afraid of Him only. Now, Abdu . . .

ABDU: Yes, Yusef.

YUSEF: Supposing a great king came to our village, for instance, the King of Persia, or the Queen of England. We would wish to welcome the King of Persia in the right way. We would want him to be pleased with our village. Right?

ABDU: Of course.

YUSEF: Supposing he comes and the Mayor steps up to him and says: "O most honorable Shah of Persia, we have written many charms in your name in this village."

MAYOR: This would be a great shame. This would be an insult to the king.

YUSEF: Exactly right. But we do this to God. We must fear only God. If we are afraid of evil spirits or the evil eye, then we insult God.

ABDU: How do we insult Him?

YUSEF: We say to Him, "O God, you are weak! You are too weak to care for me. You are too weak to protect me. I must turn to these evil spirits so they will protect me."

ABDU: The people who use charms do not think of these things.

YUSEF: But this is what they mean. This is what they are saying to God. Now, to fear God in the right way means to worship Him with reverence. We must have reverence before God and before everything God has made.

BASEAT: What do you mean?

YUSEF: We must have reverence in God's house and before the world which God has created.

ABDU: We do not have reverence anywhere.

YUSEF: Yes, I know. We make God's house sound like the market place. All our lives we never have reverence for God's creation. Now, Baseat, would you take an ax and break down the house of God?

BASEAT: No, of course not.

YUSEF: Very well. God says that our bodies are a temple of the Holy Spirit. This means when one man kills another man, he has destroyed a temple of God.

MAYOR: When men take vengance in the village, they do not think of these things.

YUSEF: Let us see what we have said. God is holy. This means majesty. We must fear only God. This is how we make His name holy. Charms make His name unclean. Reverence before Him and before His creation makes His name holy. Is this understood?

ABDU: Yes, this much is clear.

YUSEF: Very well. Now, stay with me. Holiness is majesty. Holiness is purity. We said that Pastor Hanna was a saint. That is, he was holy. Was his life pure?

MAYOR: His life was very pure.

YUSEF: Read Leviticus 11, verse 45, Baseat.

BASEAT: (Reading) "For I am the Lord who brought you up out of the land of Egypt, to be your God; you shall therefore be holy, for I am holy."

YUSEF: The subject here is purity. God says, "I am holy. That is, I am pure. You must be holy. That is, you must be pure." Now, when we say something is pure, this means it has nothing unclean in it. Does that make sense?

MAYOR: Good sense!

YUSEF: A wall that has been freshly whitewashed is a clean wall. We could say it was a pure wall.

MAYOR: Yes, you could say that.

YUSEF: Even so, a cloak can be clean or dirty. A white tablecloth can be clean or dirty. Now, God is a Spirit.

YUSEF: He is not clean like the wall or like the cloak, or like the tablecloth. God is pure. This means there is no evil in Him. There is no sin in Him.

ABDU: Go on.

YUSEF: Now, Baseat, supposing you come in from the field and wish to go to town. You are in a hurry. So quickly you take off your old cloak and put on a clean cloak to go to town. Then, all of a sudden, you realize that you should have taken a bath. You feel that you are dirty and the cloak is clean. Have you ever done this?

BASEAT: Of course.

YUSEF: You did not feel that you were in need of a bath until you put on the clean cloak. Today, I went to visit the Mayor.

MAYOR: You honored our house, Yusef.

YUSEF: On the way in, I stopped and talked with the builder at work on the Mayor's house. I picked up a stone and lifted it up to him. I sat with him on the wall for a while. My hands became dirty. Then I went into the Mayor's sitting room. There the chairs are covered with clean white cloth. Outside I did not see that my hands were dirty. I got inside and saw my hands next to the clean chair covers of the Mayor. Suddenly I saw my hands were dirty.

MAYOR: We noticed nothing, Yusef.

YUSEF: Well, I noticed it. Now, my friends, last month I whitewashed the outside of my house. I did not think that the door of my house was dirty. Then I whitewashed the wall. Suddenly I saw that the door was very dirty.

ABDU: Of course, O Yusef. You saw the door next to the clean white wall, then the door suddenly looked dirty. Things of this kind happen to all of us.

YUSEF: Exactly right, Abdu. The same is true with us in our spiritual lives. A man sins very easily. He lies. He cheats. He hates. He is jealous. He is proud. He accepts bribery. He thinks nothing of it. He does not think he is wrong until he sees his life against the holiness of God. If he comes close to the holiness of God, he sees that his life is dirty. Abdu, what did Isaiah say after he saw that God was holy in the Temple?

ABDU: He said, "Woe is me for I am lost. I am a man of unclean lips and I dwell in the midst of a people of unclean lips, for my eyes have seen the King, the Lord of hosts."

YUSEF: Exactly right. Now why did he not think of this before?

ABDU: I do not know.

YUSEF: This is very clear. He saw the holiness of God and it was very pure. Then he saw his life beside it. His life seemed very unclean. This then is the work of God who is holy. A Holy God convicts us of sin. This sin separates us from God. Baseat, read Isaiah 59, verse 2.

BASEAT: (Reading) "But your iniquities have made a separation between you and your God and your sins have hid his face from you so that he does not hear."

YUSEF: You see. God is pure. Next to Him we see that we are very unclean. We see we are sinners, and this sin separates us from God. God is pure and we must be pure. Paul says in II Corinthians, the 7th chapter, "Beloved, let us cleanse ourselves from every defilement of body and spirit. Make holiness perfect in the fear of God." You see, because God is holy, we must cleanse ourselves from every defilement of body and spirit. Now, my friends, religious ceremony is not enough. We cannot make ourselves pure by religious ceremony.

MAYOR: What do you mean, Yusef?

YUSEF: Read for us, Mayor, Isaiah 1: verses 12 through 17.

MAYOR: (Reading) "When you come to appear before me, who requires of you this trampling of my courts? Bring no more vain offerings; incense is an abomination to me. New moon and sabbath and the calling of assemblies - I cannot endure iniquity and solemn assembly. Your new moons and your appointed feasts my soul hates; they have become a burden to me, I am weary of bearing them. When you spread forth your hands, I will hide my eyes from you; even though you make many prayers, I will not listen; your hands are full of blood.

"Wash yourselves; make yourselves clean; remove the evil of your doings from before my eyes; cease to do evil, learn to do good; seek justice, correct oppression, defend the fatherless, plead for the widow."

YUSEF: You see, my friends, Isaiah says to the people, "You have much religious ceremony. You have very little righteousness. Therefore, your religious ceremony is meaningless." We cannot cleanse ourselves by religious ceremony.

MAYOR: How then can we be cleansed?

YUSEF: We will come back to that. But think again of Isaiah. Did Isaiah purify himself?

ABDU: No. I think the Seraphim purified him.

YUSEF: That is right. What did the Seraphim do?

ABDU: The Seraphim took a coal from off the altar and brought it and cleansed his lips.

YUSEF: Do not forget this, Abdu. God cleansed Isaiah. God cleansed Isaiah with a coal from off the altar of sacrifice. But this is another subject. Tonight let us think only of holiness. We have said holiness is two things. What are they, Abdu?

ABDU: Holiness is majesty. Holiness is purity.

YUSEF: Now the third thing. Holiness demands righteousness.

MAYOR: I do not see the connection between holiness and righteousness.

YUSEF: Very many people do not see this connection, but this is the most important thing. Mayor, read Isaiah 5:16.

MAYOR: (Opening and reading) "But the Lord of hosts is exalted in justice, and the Holy God shows himself holy in righteousness."

YUSEF: You see. The Holy God shows Himself holy in righteousness. Now, Baseat, do you remember Jesus' story about the seven devils?

BASEAT: I can remember a story like this, but I don't remember how it goes.

YUSEF: Mayor, do you remember?

MAYOR: I think Jesus says that a man cleaned out one devil from the house and he left the house empty and seven devils came back in.

YUSEF: Yes, you are very close, Mayor. The story is about a man. The unclean spirit goes out of the man and then he comes back and finds the man empty, clean and orderly. So he goes back in and brings seven other devils with him more evil than himself. At the end the man is worse than at the first. We said holiness means purity. Purity means absence of evil. But it is not enough that a man's life shall be empty of evil. It must be full of righteousness. Now in 1st Peter we read, "He who has called you is holy. Be holy yourselves in all your conduct, since it is written, you shall be holy for I am holy." And Isaiah has said, "The holy God shows Himself holy in righteousness." This means everywhere. We must be holy in the shop. We must be holy in the market place, the field, the home - everywhere. But holiness is not obedience to law.

MAYOR: How is this? Holiness and righteousness surely mean obedience to laws.

YUSEF: Aha . . . if righteousness and holiness are obedience to law, then the Pharisees were of all men most holy.

YUSEF: All the Pharisees were then perfect saints. Is this right?

MAYOR: I think not.

YUSEF: Indeed not. The Pharisees crucified Christ. But the Pharisees obeyed all of the laws. Now, listen carefully. Holiness and righteousness mean obedience in love to the Holy One, that is, to Jesus Christ.

BASEAT: This is very hard to understand, Yusef.

YUSEF: Never mind. Keep trying Baseat. Now, we said a Holy God wants holy men. We said Pastor Hanna was holy. Even more, Christ is holy. Right?

MAYOR: Right.

YUSEF: Now, Abdu, is Christ holy by staying far away from men, or is Christ holy in the midst of men?

ABDU: No, Christ was holy in the midst of men.

YUSEF: Let us think together. Christ is holy. The Pharisees were not holy. We cannot become holy by merely obeying a law or a religious ceremony. We saw this in the first chapter of Isaiah which the Mayor read to us just now. In the Old Testament, the priests said, "Holiness is found in the religious ceremonies." The prophets said, "No, holiness is found in obedience and righteousness."

MAYOR: This follows. Obedience brings righteousness, but what is it we must obey?

YUSEF: Very good, Mayor. We said we must obey, not a law, but a holy person; we must obey Jesus Christ.

BASEAT: This is too difficult.

YUSEF: Very well, Baseat, I will tell you something. Christianity is not a list of "do's and don'ts." Christianity is not a series of rules.

BASEAT: What do you mean? This is all I understand! Some things are permitted. Some things are forbidden. I must learn the things that are forbidden and not do them. I must learn the things that are permitted and do them.

YUSEF: Ah, but if this is true, then the Pharisees were of all men most righteous as we saw. They very carefully obeyed the laws of what is permitted and what is forbidden. The Pharisee prays in the temple and says that he fasts, not just at fast times -- but every week. They were very righteous, as they thought. They obeyed the laws exactly. They gave a tithe of everything, clear down to mint and cummin, but were they holy?

BASEAT: I think not.

205

YUSEF: _Indeed_ not! They crucified Jesus. We cannot become holy by just obeying a religious ceremony. We cannot become holy by just obeying laws.

MAYOR: How then can we become holy? How can we become righteous?

YUSEF: We become righteous by fellowship with the Holy One. Remember, Mayor, when Pastor Hanna was alive? We used to sit and talk with him many hours. We would drink of his spirit. His spirit made us holy because he was holy. Don't you agree?

MAYOR: Yes, I do. Many of us would do this. My, O my, that man was a great saint.

YUSEF: Very well. If this was true of Pastor Hanna, is it not even more true of Jesus Christ? We must sit and drink of His spirit in fellowship with Him. Then we will become holy. Now, Abdu . . .

ABDU: Yes.

YUSEF: Think of the prodigal son. Think of when the young son was in a far country. Suppose his father wrote a set of laws for him . . . a set of rules. The father gave these rules to a servant, sent the servant to the far country to give the rules to the son. The servant went and met the son feeding pigs. He gave him the rules. He said to him, "Here is a set of rules from your father. Obey these rules and your father will be happy. Obey these rules and you will be a good man." Now, Abdu, if he did this - would it change the son from the inside?

ABDU: I think not.

YUSEF: The boy can obey the rules. He can become very proud that he has obeyed the rules which his father has sent. But inside he is not changed. He is not righteous. He is not holy. But in the parable his father does not do this. His father wants him in the house. Then, in fellowship with his father, the father's spirit will enter the heart of the boy. The boy will be changed from within because he will have his father's spirit. Then he will become, indeed, righteous. Now, Mayor, did Jesus come to challenge the people to improve themselves?

MAYOR: I'm not sure what you mean.

YUSEF: Did He say to the people, "Work hard and you can improve yourself?"

MAYOR: No, He didn't.

YUSEF: Exactly right. He said to them, "Repent."

BASEAT: I can't follow, Yusef.

YUSEF: Baseat, just keep trying. God is holy. Holiness is purity. Holiness demands righteousness. This holiness is not found far from people, but in the midst of the people. We cannot become holy by obeying a law. The Pharisees did that and they were not holy. We cannot become holy by obeying a ceremony. Rather, we become holy in fellowship with the Holy One, even Jesus Christ. Then we obey Him in love. We obey a person, not a list of laws.

MAYOR: But I wish to say something, Yusef.

YUSEF: Speak on, Mayor.

MAYOR: You say that holiness demands righteousness, but I see very little righteousness about me.

YUSEF: This is the problem, Mayor. God is holy and He demands righteousness, but men are sinners. They are not righteous so what is God going to do? This is the problem. God demands a special obedience from every creature. Baseat . . .

BASEAT: Yes, Yusef.

YUSEF: God has commanded that the fish must live in the river.

BASEAT: Yes, indeed.

YUSEF: Now what if the fish decides he will disobey? He decides he will live on the land so he jumps out of the river. What will happen to him?

BASEAT: He will die.

YUSEF: Are you sure?

BASEAT: Of course.

YUSEF: Very well, Baseat. What if the bird decides he will live in the river? So he dives into the river to swim like a fish. What will happen to him?

BASEAT: He will die.

YUSEF: Very well. What about the lion? What if the lion decides he will fly like a bird so he jumps off the top of a mountain. The lion decides he does not have to obey God. God has said the lion should walk. God has said the bird should fly. If the lion decides he will disobey God, what will happen to him?

BASEAT: He will die. He will fall and he will die.

YUSEF: Now, Baseat, what about man? If the fish disobeys, it dies. If the bird disobeys, it dies. If the lion disobeys, it dies. What if man disobeys? What will happen to him?

BASEAT: It seems to me it must be the same way -- he will die.

ABDU: But in what way, Yusef, has man disobeyed? In the parable, I see how the fish disobeyed. I see how the bird disobeyed. I see how the lion disobeyed. How did man disobey?

YUSEF: It is very simple, Abdu. God asks one thing of man. Man must put God first in everything he does. In everything he thinks, in everything he feels and in everything he wills, God must be first.

ABDU: Everything?

YUSEF: Everything!

ABDU: This is very hard.

YUSEF: But this is the way God created us. Then we decided we would disobey. We decided we would put ourselves first. When we put ourselves first, we try to take the place of God.

ABDU: I never thought of it in this way.

YUSEF: This is sin, my friends. No less - no more. This is sin. This is what we have done. God is the One who keeps the order of the world. If any creature disobeys, it will be punished. Now man has disobeyed. The honor of God is at stake. If He says, "Never mind," man will laugh at Him and say He is not God. Man will say that He is weak and that His commandments are meaningless.

MAYOR: What then can God do?

YUSEF: We will talk of this later, Mayor. Tonight we must think and remember that God is holy. He is not weak. God is the one who preserves the order of the universe. Holiness means majesty and purity. Holiness demands from us righteousness. God is holy and we must be holy in all our conduct. For a Holy God shows Himself holy in righteousness.

QUESTIONS FOR DISCUSSION

1. What was the first idea the people of the Old Testament had about holiness?
2. What does holiness say about how we should worship?
3. What is the wrong kind of fear?
4. What does this fear lead us to?
5. What is the right kind of fear in worship?
6. We must be reverent in God's house only. Is this right or wrong?
7. Holiness is purity. What is the work of purity?
8. When do we see sin for what it is?
9. Who does sin separate us from?
10. What makes sin sinful?
11. What does holiness demand from us?
12. How is God made holy?
13. Is Christianity a list of laws? Is it a list of "Rights" and "Wrongs?"
14. Can we become holy by obeying laws?
15. Were the Pharisees holy?
16. How do we become holy?
17. God is holy. What then is His problem with men?

SUMMARY

God is holy. Holiness is majesty. This means we must worship in fear and reverence. God is pure. In the light of God's purity we see our sin. Holiness demands righteousness. We become holy through a fellowship with a holy person, even Jesus Christ.

MOTTO: Holiness demands righteousness in all our conduct.

17
GOD IS LOVE

SCRIPTURES TO BE READ: John 3:16; Romans 5:6-8; 8:32;
Ephesians 2:4, 5, 8; Philippians 2:5-11;
I John 3:16, 17; 4:7-21

STATEMENT OF LESSON

God is Holy Love. If He were only holy, He would be cruel. But He is also love. We see this in many ways. The first is in mercy. Mercy means feeling <u>and</u> willing. Love is also grace. Grace means that what God does for us is a gift which we have not earned. Love is also forgiveness. Sin separates us from God. But this is not the end of the story. God so loves us that He is willing to pay a price to make reconciliation. There is no forgiveness without suffering. And there is no reconciliation without forgiveness. Lastly, we see that love is self sacrifice. God is willing to sacrifice to redeem. God's love is not the love that <u>needs</u>. God's love is the love that <u>gives</u>. It does not give <u>things</u>, rather God gives us Himself.

OUTLINE

GOD IS LOVE

1. Love is Mercy.
    a. Mercy is compassion.
    b. Mercy does not want judgment.
2. Love is Grace.
    a. God's love is a gift.
    b. God loves regardless of what men do.
    c. God gives us what we need, not what we want.
3. Love is Forgiveness.
    a. Sin cannot permanently separate us from God.
    b. There is no forgiveness without suffering.
    c. God is Love. Thus He is willing to suffer in order to forgive.
4. Love is Self Sacrifice.
    a. God's love is not love that needs.
    b. God's love is love that gives.

THE DIALOGUE

GOD IS . . .

SCENE 17

CHARACTERS:

Yusef, the Wise

Abdu, the Inquirer

Baseat, the Simple

THE DIALOGUE

(Yusef, Baseat, and Abdu are seated in front of Yusef's house.)

ABDU: We have waited a long time for this lesson, Yusef.

YUSEF: What lesson?

BASEAT: Do I know?

YUSEF: Of course you know. The last time we talked about holiness. Tonight we talk about love.

BASEAT: O yes, that's right. I forgot.

ABDU: We used to think that God was only Love. But now we have talked about many, many things. Let us begin, Yusef.

YUSEF: Very well. We said God is holy. This means God is majestic and pure. It means that He demands righteousness. Is this clear?

ABDU: Yes. This much we remember.

YUSEF: This means God must preserve order. He must preserve His honor.

BASEAT: Of course!

YUSEF: But His honor demands righteousness. We are not righteous. We are sinners. God has said, "The soul that sinneth, it shall die." So His holiness demands our death. So what can be done?

ABDU: But, Yusef, God is not only holiness!

YUSEF: Very good, Abdu - go on.

ABDU: God is also Love. He loves us. This is our subject tonight.

YUSEF: Exactly right. God is holy indeed. But God is also Love. If God were just holy he would destroy us and be finished with us. But God is Love. Tonight we must try to understand what this means. Let us take four words - mercy, grace, forgiveness and sacrifice. Say them, Abdu.

212

ABDU: Mercy, grace, forgiveness and sacrifice.

YUSEF: Good. Now Baseat - what does mercy mean?

BASEAT: Mercy? Mercy means - ah...ah - I can't explain it.

YUSEF: Never mind - I will tell you Baseat. Mercy is compassion, and compassion is feeling _and_ willing.

ABDU: What do you mean, Yusef?

YUSEF: I will tell you. Many times we think compassion is just feeling. We think feeling is enough. Baseat!

BASEAT: Yes, Yusef.

YUSEF: Suppose you are sitting beside the river, making rope palm fibers.

BASEAT: Yes!

YUSEF: A man falls into the river. He cannot swim. He shouts to you. He shouts, "Throw me the rope, have mercy! Throw me your rope." You feel very sorry for him. You even weep for him. But you do not throw the rope. Is this compassion? Is this mercy?

BASEAT: No! This is not mercy. This is cruelty.

YUSEF: But you felt very sorry for him. Your heart was with him. You even wept for him!

ABDU: This is not enough. You must throw the rope.

YUSEF: Suppose you are working in the threshing floor with your neighbor. He decides to make some tea. He lights the match and it falls into the wheat. The wheat is burned. You feel very sorry for him. You say, "Poor fellow, his children will starve." But you do not give him any of your wheat. Is this mercy?

BASEAT: His children cannot eat feelings. No, this is not mercy.

YUSEF: But you felt very sorry for him.

ABDU: This is not enough. You must give him some wheat.

YUSEF: The mayor is building some rooms for Magdi. Before us we see the builder at work. Soon he will have to tear down that old mud brick wall. Suppose we saw the builder fall from the old wall and break his leg. He cries for help. We sit here and do nothing. But we feel very sorry for him. Is this mercy?

BASEAT: No. No! This is not mercy.

YUSEF: But you feel very sorry for him.

ABDU: This is not enough. You must go and help him.

YUSEF: What if we saw a thief climb the palm tree beside the house of the mayor. We sit and do nothing. We do not

YUSEF: run over to the mayor and shout to him. We do not tell his guards that a thief has entered his house. We sit here and say, "Poor, poor fellow - the thief will take his money." Is this mercy?

BASEAT: No, no, this is not mercy! This is cruelty.

YUSEF: But you feel very sorry for him.

ABDU: This is not enough. You must help him.

YUSEF: The father of the prodigal son sees his son coming down the road. Does he say, weeping, "Poor fellow, he has nothing to eat. He is dressed in rags. I hope someone gives to him?"

ABDU: No! No! He runs down the road and welcomes him.

YUSEF: Does the Good Samaritan look at the man fallen among thieves and say, "Poor fellow!"?

BASEAT: No indeed. He helps him! He does everything for him.

YUSEF: God is love. This means God is merciful. God has compassion for us. He *feels* in mercy toward us. He also *acts* in mercy toward us. Feelings without actions are worthless. Feelings without actions are not mercy - they are cruelty. Many times we see a man in trouble. We say, "Poor fellow," then we do nothing. This is not mercy. This is cruelty. God is not like this.

ABDU: Explain this to us, Yusef.

YUSEF: God *is* merciful. And God *shows* mercy. We have fallen into the river of our own pride and self righteousness. We are about to drown. We do not know that we are drowning. We do not call for help. Yet God is merciful to save us from ourselves. God's feelings lead to action. He comes to show us mercy by saving us. In the Cross we see His great mercy. This is where the One who is mercy shows mercy. This is where the merciful is compassionate.

ABDU: This is strange new talk, Yusef.

YUSEF: Strange but true, my friend. Abdu, read Ezekiel 18:23.

ABDU: (Reading) "'Have I any pleasure in the death of the wicked,' says the Lord God, 'and not rather that he should turn from his ways and live?'"

BASEAT: What does this mean?

YUSEF: It means that God is mercy. Thus He wants us to live. He does not *want* to bring judgment on us. Jeremiah says, "He does not willingly afflict or grieve the sons of men." Suppose I have a servant and he disobeys me. What do I do?

ABDU: You punish him, of course.

YUSEF: Indeed I do. I punish him and it is finished. But if my son disobeys me, it is different. I will want to show him mercy. I will not want to punish him. Sometimes I have to. But I do not want to. God is like this. He does not want us to sin and die. He wants us to live. This is because He is love and love is mercy. Do you understand, O Baseat?

BASEAT: Not very much. Be merciful, Yusef. I am a very simple man.

YUSEF: Never mind, maybe you will understand the second point. God is love. This means mercy. But it also means grace. Abdu! - what is grace?

ABDU: Grace? Grace is - ah - love!

YUSEF: True, but it is more than this. Pay close attention, my friends. Love is grace. This means God's love is a gift. Sometimes we give gifts because someone has served us. Sometimes we give gifts in order to get people to serve us. Is it not so?

ABDU: Do not say sometimes, O Yusef, say always. Someone serves me in the village. Then I give him a gift. Or I give him a gift because I want him to serve me. I think these are the only reasons we have.

YUSEF: I am sorry to say that this is usually true.

BASEAT: Why are you sorry, Yusef?

YUSEF: Because God's gift is not like this. Love is grace. This means love is a gift. Now Baseat, let us think again of the drowning man in the river. Suppose you throw him the rope. Do you throw it because he has served you?

BASEAT: No, of course not.

YUSEF: Do you throw it hoping one day he will serve you.

BASEAT: No, I do not think of these things. I would just throw him the rope.

YUSEF: Suppose the builder across the street falls. Do we run to help him so that he will serve us?

ABDU: It would be a shame if we thought of these things. We should help him because he needs help. This is enough.

BASEAT: This is right. This is exactly right. God's love is like this. God's love is a gift. God does not love us because we have served Him. Never! Suppose God waited for us to serve Him before He loved us.

ABDU: He would wait forever!

YUSEF: Exactly right, Abdu. Paul says, "While we were yet sinners Christ died for us." This is the meaning of grace. Suppose the prodigal son comes home and his

215

YUSEF: father says, "He must have clean clothes before I can accept him. He must also return all the money he lost before I will love him."

BASEAT: Where could he get it from?

ABDU: This is the point, I think. This is impossible. He cannot help himself. I see it now. Yes, indeed! His father's love is a gift. He has done <u>nothing</u> to deserve his father's love.

YUSEF: Paul says in Ephesians 2:8, "For by grace you have been saved through faith; and this is not your own doing, it is the gift of God." You see my friends, grace means God's love is a gift. Now - if a servant is good, his master will love him. If a servant is bad, his master will not love him. Is it not so?

ABDU: Of course. This is very natural.

YUSEF: Very well. What about a son? Does a father say to his son, "My son, be good and I will reward you. Be evil and I will hate you?"

ABDU: No! The father will love his boy regardless of what he does. He is his son.

YUSEF: Right Abdu. God is like this too. God loves us even when we hate Him. He does not love us only when we are good. This is part of the meaning of grace. He loves us even when we are evil.

ABDU: "While we were yet sinners Christ died for us."

YUSEF: Excellent, Abdu. You remembered. While the prodigal son is in a far country his father still loves him. If he didn't the boy couldn't even think about coming home. This is grace. But think of something else about grace.

BASEAT: What is it, Yusef?

YUSEF: We said grace means God's love is a gift. But God gives us what we <u>need</u>, not what we <u>want</u>.

BASEAT: Are they not the same?

YUSEF: Sometimes, yes. Many times, no. Abdu, what if your boy asks to play with your gun. Do you give it to him?

ABDU: Indeed not!

YUSEF: Why not? Don't you love him?

ABDU: Of course I love him. But I won't give him a gun to play with. He might hurt himself.

YUSEF: I see. That is, you won't give him something that isn't good for him?

ABDU: That's right.

YUSEF: Very well, suppose in wheat harvest time he asks to ride the threshing sledge. Do you let him ride?

ABDU: Of course not. He might fall and be killed.

YUSEF: But he wants to ride it!

ABDU: I don't care. I won't let him!

YUSEF: You see, Baseat? We ask God for many things. He will not give us things that are not good for us. It is just like with Abdu and his son. One man asks for wealth. God knows wealth will destroy him. So God does not give it to him. Another man asks for many sons. God knows he will not raise them up in the fear of the Lord. They will bring much evil on others. So God does not give him many sons. Another asks for God's help against his enemy. He wants to get his rights. But maybe he is the one that is wrong. So God will not help him get his rights. I'll tell you a story.

BASEAT: Good! Good! - let us hear it.

YUSEF: Once a drunk got lost in the desert. He wandered for a long long time. He tried very hard to find his way. He couldn't find it. After two days he was very weak and thought that all was over. Then suddenly he saw a man riding on a camel a long way off. He ran as fast as he could to catch the man. "Stop! Stop!" he shouted. "Take me with you. Give me a drink! I am about to die of thirst!" Then the camel driver stopped. He waited for the man to catch up with him. Then the man said, "I want a bottle of wine. I am very thirsty." Then the camel driver shouted to him and said, "No! No! I will not give you such a thing. Are you mad? You do not need wine, you need water. You must drink water! Wine will kill you. You must drink water!" Then the drunk said, "What is this! Don't you want to help me? Give me what I want. Give me a bottle of wine." The camel driver refused. He said, "I will not give you what you want. You ask for the wrong thing. I want to help you. I will give you what you need, not what you want." So he untied the goat skin bag and gave the thirsty man a drink of water. He saved his life by giving him what he needed, not what he wanted.

ABDU: This is a good story. Indeed if the camel driver had given him what he asked for, the man would have died.

YUSEF: God's grace is like this. God in His grace gives us what we need, not what we want. He knows what we need. We must ask for what we think we need. He will grant what is best for us. Very well. Now we said God is Love. This means mercy. This means grace. It also means forgiveness. Now, Abdu.

217

ABDU: Yes, Yusef.

YUSEF: We said that sin separates us from God. Is it not so, Abdu?

ABDU: Indeed it is so.

YUSEF: Now, can sin permanently separate us from God?

ABDU: I don't understand what you mean.

YUSEF: The prodigal son went into a far country. His sin separated him from his father. But his sin did not _permanently_ separate him from his father because his father loved him. He loved him enough to forgive him. That is, _love_ is _forgiveness_.

BASEAT: (Pondering) Love is forgiveness, of course!

YUSEF: Now, Baseat, if I have a servant and he does wrong, I dismiss him. His wrong permanently separates him from me. I get another servant. But this is not true with my sons.

ABDU: Indeed not.

YUSEF: Even so with God. God is our Father. He loves us and wants to forgive us. Thus, sin does not permanently separate us from Him. Now Abdu, listen carefully. _There_ _is_ _no_ _forgiveness_ _without_ _suffering_.

ABDU: There is no forgiveness without suffering? I don't understand, Yusef.

YUSEF: I will tell you a story.

BASEAT: Good! Maybe I will understand something.

YUSEF: Once the hyena was sleeping in the grass in the forest. His young son slept beside him. In the middle of the day the elephant came by. The elephant stepped on the son of the hyena and killed it. The hyena jumped up and growled and growled and growled. Soon all the hynenas knew the story. They all met in the forest to see what they could do. They were very angry and wanted revenge. The leader of the hyenas spoke and said, "Who has killed the hyena's son?" They were all silent. Then an old hyena said, quietly, "The elephant has killed the hyena's son!" All the hyenas were angry. They said nothing. They didn't like what the old hyena had said. Then at last, a young hyena said, "The goats! The goats! Yes, it is the goats! The goats have killed the hyena's son!" Then they all began to shout against the goats. Soon they ran down into the valley and killed one hundred goats.

BASEAT: Wonderful story! Wonderful story!

ABDU: But Baseat, what is the point of the story?

BASEAT: O, I don't know what the point was. But it was a good story. What is the point of the story, Yusef?

YUSEF: Have patience and I will tell you. But think of something else. Suppose, a little boy decides to play a game with himself. He lives beside the canal and his father is building a new wall. He wants to play. So he takes some bricks and sets them on end beside the canal. He puts them close together. Then he takes a stone and throws the stone at the end brick. The stone knocks the first brick over. That brick knocks the next one over and so in a moment all the bricks are knocked over. The boy has fun playing in this way. Then once he throws too hard and the stone falls into the canal. But the canal does not act like the brick. The canal does not strike something else. When the brick was hit it struck something else. But when the canal was struck it did not strike something else. The stone and the stroke of the stone vanished into the canal.

BASEAT: This also is a good story Yusef, but I still don't understand anything.

YUSEF: I will explain, my friends. We said that there is no forgiveness without suffering. Now we don't like to suffer. So we don't like to forgive. We are like the bricks. We are like the hyena. The brick is hit and it falls and hits the next brick. Someone sins against us, we turn right away to pass on the sin. We sin against him or against someone else. If the man who has hurt us is too strong, we choose someone else.

ABDU: Oh, I see! You mean like the hyena! The hyena can't take revenge on the elephant. The elephant is too strong. So he takes revenge on the goats.

YUSEF: Exactly right, Abdu. But God is like a great river. He takes great sin unto Himself and does not strike again. Throw a great stone into the river and the river takes the stone and stops the movement of the stone. The river is not like the brick that turns to strike the next brick. Forgiveness is like this. Man in sin is like the hyena and the brick. Forgiveness is like the river that takes the stroke of the stone and does not strike again. Thus the movement of the stone is stopped.

ABDU: We have never thought like that.

YUSEF: Now, suppose someone curses me. Then I do not curse him back. I do not become angry and treat someone else badly. I do not seek to get even. I do not seek revenge. I still accept him as a true friend.

ABDU: This will be very painful.

219

YUSEF:	Indeed, deep within me I will suffer badly. Is it not so? If I do not strike back and do not think of these things, I will suffer.
BASEAT:	I have begun to understand. Yes indeed, you will suffer very much.
YUSEF:	This is the price of forgiveness my friends. We do not forgive because we do not want to suffer. So we seek revenge. For there is no forgiveness without suffering. Think of the father of the prodigal son when the boy comes home. Do you think it is easy for him to forget what the boy has done?
ABDU:	I think not.
YUSEF:	The boy asked for his inheritance while his father was still alive. We all know this means he cannot wait for his father to die. That is, he is anxious for his father to die. Will it be easy for the father to forgive this?
BASEAT:	This will indeed be very hard.
YUSEF:	Then when he comes home he comes with nothing. The wealth that the father gave him is all gone for nothing. Will the father easily forgive this?
ABDU:	This also will be very hard.
YUSEF:	But because of his great love he is willing to suffer to forgive. For there is no forgiveness without suffering. God's love is so great that He is willing to suffer in order to forgive us.
ABDU:	We have never thought of it in this way, Yusef.
YUSEF:	Paul says, "God, who is rich in mercy, out of the great love with which he loved us, even when we were dead through our trespasses, makes us alive together with Christ."
ABDU:	And John says, "For God so loved the world that he gave his only Son, that whoever believes in him should not perish but have eternal life."
YUSEF:	Exactly right, Abdu, and this brings us to the fourth thing we want to say about God's love. We said love is _mercy_, _grace_ and _forgiveness_. Now lastly we must say that love is _self-sacrifice_.
BASEAT:	This is too much; I can't remember all this!
YUSEF:	Very well, Baseat, just remember this last. God is love. Love is self-sacrifice. What is love?
BASEAT:	Love is self-sacrifice.
YUSEF:	Good. Now, we must think about two kinds of love. There is the love which _needs_ and the love which _gives_.

ABDU: I don't understand, as usual.

YUSEF: I will explain. Human love is the love which needs. A man loves a woman because he is in need. A man loves his friend because he is in need of a friend. Even the earthly father loves his children because one day he will need them.

ABDU: Indeed he will.

YUSEF: This love is like a cup that is empty and seeks water to fill it. But God's love is not like this. His love is like a cup that is so full it overflows.

BASEAT: I still don't understand.

YUSEF: The wind blows the boats on the river. Does the wind blow because it is in need?

BASEAT: No indeed!

ABDU: It blows because this is it's nature.

YUSEF: The sun shines and gives life to the earth. Does the sun shine because it is in need?

BASEAT: No indeed!

ABDU: It shines because this is its nature.

YUSEF: The mountain lifts its head high into the sky. Its beauty fills our hearts with joy. Many women dress beautifully because they seek lovers. Is the mountain beautiful because it needs a lover?

BASEAT: No indeed.

ABDU: It is the same. It is beautiful because this is its nature.

YUSEF: The river flows to the sea. It brings life to all who live along its shores. Does it bring us life because it is in need?

BASEAT: No indeed!

ABDU: It brings us life because this is its nature.

YUSEF: Even so, my friends, God gives us of Himself because this is His nature. God is not in need. God loves us because He _is_ love. This is His nature. God's love is the love that _gives_, not the love that _needs_. Do you understand, Baseat?

BASEAT: A little.

YUSEF: Good! Now, my friends, notice what it is that God gives us. When an uncle comes to visit, he brings a gift to his nephew. He may bring candy, fruit or garment. But the father is different. The father gives all these things. But the father gives also himself. Is it not so, Abdu?

ABDU: Indeed it is so, Yusef.

YUSEF: God gives us of Himself in self-sacrifice. In first John we read, "By this we know love that he laid down his life for us." And John, the disciple says, "God so loved the world he <u>gave</u> -- " Abdu, what does Paul say in Philippians 2?

ABDU: It says that, "Jesus Christ, though he was in the form of God, did not count equality with God a thing to be grasped but emptied himself, taking the form of a servant."

YUSEF: So God is Love. This means self-sacrifice. Now let us look at the problem. God is Holy. This means purity and righteousness. He demands perfect righteousness from us. But we have sinned. God said that if we sin we must die. But on the other side - God is love. Love is mercy and forgiveness. The Prophet says, "Do justly and love mercy." How can anybody do both? Justice is one thing. This demands punishment for disobedience. Mercy wants to grant forgiveness for disobedience. How can God be both holy and love? How can He do justly and love mercy?

ABDU: This is a very hard question.

BASEAT: I don't understand.

YUSEF: I know. Now, Baseat, suppose I am the headmaster of school. I want my school to be a good school where there is no cheating. So I make a rule that the student who cheats will be thrown out of the school. Then at examination time my brother's son cheats. What shall I do? I am headmaster. The rule must be for everyone. Yet this is my brother's son. I love him. I do not want to dismiss him. Justice says - throw him out. Love says - forgive him. What can I do?

BASEAT: Now I see. Yes, this is a hard question.

YUSEF: This, my friends, is God's problem with man. The last time we met we saw that God is holy. Tonight we saw that God is love. The next time we must try to see how God is holy love.

BASEAT: I don't understand!

ABDU: Patience, Baseat, Yusef has not explained this yet! Tomorrow we will talk of this.

YUSEF: Do not forget my friends - God so loved that He <u>gave</u>.

ABDU: We will remember.

QUESTIONS FOR DISCUSSION

1. We see a poor fellow. We say, "Poor fellow, may God help him." Is this mercy?
2. Compassion is two things. What are they?
3. Does God want to punish sinners?
4. What does grace mean?
5. Does God say, "Do good and I will love you. Do evil and I will hate you?" Explain.
6. Does God give us what we <u>want</u> or what we <u>need</u>? What is the difference?
7. Why must there be suffering for forgiveness?
8. Explain the story of the elephant and the hyena.
9. Explain the story of the boy and his bricks and the canal.
10. Explain the love which <u>needs</u>. Explain the love which <u>gives</u>.
11. Yusef talks of the wind, the sun, the mountain and the river. What was his point?
12. What is the greatest gift God gives us?

SUMMARY OF LESSON

God is Love. This means mercy that is compassionate and doesn't want to punish.

God is Love. This means grace which is a gift that we have not earned.

God is Love. This means forgiveness through suffering.

God is Love. This means the giving of self in sacrifice.

MOTTO: God so loves that He <u>gave</u>.

18
GOD IS HOLY LOVE: PART 1

SCRIPTURES TO BE READ: Luke 15:11-32

STATEMENT OF LESSON

We saw that God is Holy. We saw that holiness demands righteousness, but also we know that God is love and love seeks forgiveness. Love wants to show mercy. God is Holy and God is Love. Holiness by itself is meaningless. Love by itself is meaningless. God is Holy Love. In the Cross of Christ, we see this holy love. In the Cross of Christ, we see justice and mercy.

In this lesson, Yusef and his friends act out a play to show how God is holy love. The play shows how God preserves His honor and at the same time shows His love.

OUTLINE

GOD IS HOLY LOVE

1. The Parable (The problem of the rebellious son).
    a. The Mayor's answer is - "Punish him." (preserve honor)
    b. The Priest's answer is - "Forgive him." (show love)
    c. The Father's answer is - "Redeem him." (show love and preserve honor)
2. Interpretation of Parable.
    a. God is love (This is not enough.)
    b. God is holy (This is not enough.)
    c. In the Cross of Christ, God is holy love.

THE DIALOGUE

GOD IS . . .

SCENE 18

CHARACTERS:

Yusef, the Wise

Abdu, the Inquirer

Baseat, the Simple

Mayor Butrus

Azeez, the Carpenter

THE DIALOGUE

(Yusef, Abdu, Baseat and the Mayor are seated in Yusef's front room.)

YUSEF: You have honored us again, tonight, Mayor.

MAYOR: I can't stay away.

YUSEF: You are very kind, Mr. Mayor. Listen, Abdu.

ABDU: Yes, Yusef.

YUSEF: Go next door and get our friend the carpenter. We have something new tonight. I asked him if he would come and he said he would. He is waiting.

ABDU: Very well, Yusef, I will get him right away.
(Exit Abdu).

MAYOR: What do you mean, Yusef? What will we do tonight? What are these papers you have in your hand?

YUSEF: For some weeks, Mayor, I have been working on a play. It is a very little thing. Maybe it will help us understand how God is holy and yet Love.

BASEAT: You mean we will make a play here tonight?

YUSEF: Yes, indeed. Each of us will read a separate part and we will make a play together.

(Enter Abdu and the carpenter)

YUSEF: Good evening, Azeez.

AZEEZ: Good evening all. What's going on?

YUSEF: Very well, my friends. Tonight as I was saying to the Mayor, we must make a play. Now, all of you know the story of the prodigal son, don't you?

ABDU: Of course.

225

YUSEF: Very well, tonight we must act out the story of the son who stayed at home. The father held a banquet for the prodigal son.

MAYOR: Right.

YUSEF: And there were guests.

ABDU: Of course. I think at least he must have invited the Mayor and the priest from the synagogue.

BASEAT: At least these would be there.

YUSEF: Very well. Our Mayor Butrus has honored us again tonight. We will ask the Mayor to read the part of the Mayor in the play.

MAYOR: I will enjoy this.

YUSEF: Now, Abdu, you read the part of the Rabbi.

ABDU: A former priest - how about that.

YUSEF: You will make a good Rabbi, I'm sure. Here Abdu, take a copy of the play.

Now Azeez, we will ask you to be the older son.

AZEEZ: I am at your service.

YUSEF: But my friend, we do not see you in the play, we just hear your voice. You sit here by the door. Then when it comes your turn to speak, step outside the door and pretend you are calling from the courtyard. Is this all right?

AZEEZ: (In great delight) Very good.

BASEAT: And what can I do?

YUSEF: We have a very important place for you, Baseat. We will make you the head servant of the house.

BASEAT: Very good.

YUSEF: Baseat, you have a very important place in the play. Now, does everyone see what he is to do?

ALL: Yes, we understand.

YUSEF: Now, my friends, I will read the part of the father. I have called a banquet; we are seated at the banquet. The Mayor is on one side of me. Come, Mayor, sit here.

MAYOR: Very good. (He seats himself beside Yusef)

YUSEF: Now, Abdu, you come and sit here.

ABDU: My goodness, am I to sit there too?

YUSEF: Of course. You are the priest from the synagogue in the village. Now, Baseat, you stand over by the wall and pretend you are the servant. Here, hold this tray in your hand. (He takes the tray from a small table

YUSEF: before them and gives it to Baseat) Azeez, you stay by the door and pretend you are outside. Now -- is everybody ready? Everybody watch their papers closely. Each man must read his part in turn. Mr. Mayor, begin.

THE FATHER AND THE SON WHO IS NOT A SON

(The Play Within the Dialogue)

MAYOR: Congratulations. A thousand congratulations, Elder.

FATHER: Thank you indeed, Mayor. You have honored our house.

MAYOR: Congratulations for the safe return of your boy.

FATHER: Indeed. We were sure the boy was dead. He has been gone for a long time. We thought we would never see him again. Always we hoped that he might return. Now at last our hope has been fulfilled.

MAYOR: My good friend, all of us rejoice with you. But why have you prepared such a big feast? I see more meat before me than our village has eaten for a month.

RABBI: Not only meat, but <u>fat</u> meat as well.

FATHER: It is nothing, my friends. It is nothing but a piece of bread and some salt. Indeed you, my guests, are worthy of far more than this. But then, as the proverb says - "When you serve onions to your friends, they will say the onions are lamb's meat."

MAYOR: (Laughing) My goodness! Is all of this I see nothing but onions? We are not worthy of all this, Elder, but because of your son who has returned, for his sake, I think this is right.

FATHER: For you my friends, and for him. You have all honored us tonight.

OLDER SON: (From outside room - calling gruffly) Abdu, Abdu, come here.

FATHER: (Turning to servant) Abdu, go out and speak to him. Tell him the story of his brother's return. Tell him his father and his father's guests await him.

SERVANT: At your service, sir. (Servant goes out)

MAYOR: What's wrong with your older son? Is he angry, or something, Father?

FATHER: No. He always speaks that way.

(Voices come in from outside. The older son and servant are talking)

OLDER SON: (Angrily) What's the story, Abdu? What's going on? What is all the fuss about? Why have I not been consulted?

SERVANT: It is nothing, master Adam. Your brother has returned.

OLDER SON: My brother? Who do you mean?

SERVANT: Your brother who took his inheritance and left a long time ago. He has returned.

OLDER SON: Go on. Then what happened? Did he come back with much wealth? Did he bring a long camel caravan of cloth and spices? Is this it? Did <u>he</u> pay for this great banquet?

SERVANT: No, master Adam, I am sorry to report he did not.

OLDER SON: What then?

SERVANT: I am sorry to say it, but he came back in rags. He had nothing.

OLDER SON: Just what I expected. What happened then? Did my father beat him?

SERVANT: No indeed. Your father saw him at a great distance, for he was seated on the balcony on the second story. He came down quickly, took the edge of his robe in his hand, and ran through the village and down the road. Half the village ran after him. Then he fell on the neck of your brother and kissed him. Your father turned to us and asked us to dress him in clean clothes. He told us to put a ring on his hand and shoes on his feet and then he told us to prepare a great banquet and to kill the fatted calf.

OLDER SON: My father did all of this?

SERVANT: Even the Mayor and the Rabbi from the synagoge are at the banquet as guests of your father. They are waiting for you. Your father says for you to come and greet his guests.

FATHER: (From inside the room turning to the Mayor) Listen, Mayor, he will not come in.

MAYOR: How is this? He must.

RABBI: Be quiet, my friends, let us listen and see what he will do.

SON: (From outside room) I will not enter.

SERVANT: (Horrified) Your father will be very angry.

SON: Let him be angry and see if I care.

SERVANT: This is a great shame. This is a great shame. You must not do this before your father's guests. This is a great shame.

SON: He is responsible, not I. I will not go in. Go and tell him so.

SERVANT: Very well, if you wish.

(The servant comes in slowly and reluctantly and says:)

SERVANT: Master, permit me a word with you.

FATHER: It doesn't matter, Abdu. We heard everything here from the window. The story is very well known. My son will not come in. What is wrong with him?

SERVANT: He is angry.

FATHER: Why is he angry?

SERVANT: (Hedging) I don't know.

FATHER: Speak. Why do you think he is angry?

SERVANT: He is angry with you and with his brother.

FATHER: Why?

SERVANT: (Hedging) I do not know.

FATHER: Very well. That is all, Abdu.

(Servant exits)

MAYOR: Why is he angry, Elder?

FATHER: (Thoughtfully) He is angry tonight because I have welcomed his brother home.

RABBI: Well! Does this make him angry?

FATHER: Yes, it does, but there is more than this. You see, he has made himself higher than me in this house. He wants to be the head of the house.

MAYOR: How is this? How can he expect such a thing?

FATHER: I do not know, but this is what he wants. He feels that he is the most important. Tonight he is angry because he was not consulted about the banquet. He is very, very proud, but he thinks he is very, very righteous.

MAYOR: But he is not obedient.

FATHER: He is obedient to his own pride and ambition.

RABBI: But he cannot be the head of the house. You are the head of the house.

FATHER: (Slowly) Ah, but he thinks that he is. Deep in his heart, secretly, he wishes that I were dead.

MAYOR: (In great horror) May this evil be far from you. Shame! Great shame!

FATHER: He does not know this, but this is really what he wants. He has rebelled against me. Absolam rebelled

FATHER: against David. What he wanted was David's throne. It is the same with my son. He is very proud. He wants to be head of this house.

MAYOR: (Exploding) This is too much! This is too much! He must be punished! This is rebellion! This is sedition! I am a Mayor! I understand these things! Order must be preserved! The honor of this house must be preserved!

FATHER: Is this what you think, Mayor?

MAYOR: Yes, indeed. He must learn to respect his father. The boy is mocking you. If you are his father, you must act. Every father must have obedience. He has disobeyed. He must be punished. Is he not your son?

FATHER: Yes, by nature he is my son, but by the spirit, he is not my son. Everything I tell him to do, he does, but always he seeks one thing. He seeks to be first in this house. He seeks to make himself master of the house.

MAYOR: You _must_ beat him! This is the only answer. You must beat _him_. This way you will get from him what you want.

FATHER: But you see, Mr. Mayor, _I_ am not angry. _He_ is the one that is angry. I do not want revenge. I want a son who will know, accept, and return my love.

MAYOR: All of this I do not understand. I understand one thing. If there is disobedience, there must be punishment. Why don't you punish him?

FATHER: When he was small, many times I punished him. But now he is a man and punishment is not enough.

MAYOR: How is this? What do you mean, it is not enough?

FATHER: I can beat him, but this will make him afraid. I do not want him to be afraid of me. I want him to accept and return my love.

MAYOR: But he deserves punishment.

FATHER: Yes, he does. He deserves punishment, but you see, my friend, he does not _know_ that he is guilty. He does not know that he is _disobedient_. He thinks he is demanding only his rights. If I punish him, justice will be done, but he will be all the more angry. He will think I am unfair. He will then think of revenge. He will cry out in anger and say, "Why did you strike me? I have done nothing." _I_ am not angry, Mayor. _He_ is angry.

MAYOR: But the honor of the father must be preserved. The honor of the house must be preserved.

FATHER: Yes, you are right, Mayor. The honor must be preserved, but I want a son who will respond in love. He does not understand how great is his disobedience. Even now as he insults me before my guests, he thinks nothing of it. I can punish him, but this will not change him. He does not think that he is wrong so if I punish him he will seek to disobey all the more.

MAYOR: Then you must be strict with him. You must give him rules to follow. You must make him follow these rules.

FATHER: But my good friend, all this we have done since he was a boy. Every rule I give him he follows. He obeys the rule, but without love. He is very proud that he has obeyed the rules I have given him. He feels therefore that he is perfect. More rules would just make him more proud.

MAYOR: Very well then....then.....make him pay a fine. Make him pay a thousand pounds for his disobedience.

FATHER: And what will that accomplish? Supposing I asked him to pay a fine, for his disobedience. Maybe in the bottom of his heart he knows that he is wrong. I ask him to pay a fine. He pays the fine and believes that he has made up everything to me. Where is my response of love?

MAYOR: Yes, indeed, this is a very hard question.

FATHER: You are right, Mr. Mayor. He does deserve punishment. If he were a servant, I could punish him and be finished, but I do not wish a cringing servant, I wish a loving son.

RABBI: I have the answer, my friends. O most respected Elder, you must love him and forgive him.

FATHER: (Slowly) But, my friend, many times I have done this. When he was small, many times I forgave him. He would disobey and I would show him mercy, but now he is a man and this is not enough.

RABBI: What do you mean it is not enough?

FATHER: You see, my friends, he will not accept. I am ready to say to him, "You are forgiven." But he will answer, "Forgiven for what? I have done nothing. I ask only for my rights."

RABBI: Can you not say to him, "Never mind, it doesn't matter?"

FATHER: But what will this accomplish?

MAYOR: Rabbi, this is no good. If you do this, the boy will think disobedience is a very little thing.

FATHER: The Mayor is right. I cannot say "Never mind," but even if I did, this would accomplish nothing. He would

231

FATHER: still be in the field in rebellion. I still would not have a son who knows and returns my love.

RABBI: But you must show him your love.

FATHER: I am ready. But, Rabbi, if your young son takes kerosene and pours it on the back of your water buffalo, then lights the kerosene and stands laughing while the water buffalo burns to death, would you say to him, "Never mind?"

RABBI: Of course not.

FATHER: If you did - would it be love?

MAYOR: No indeed, this is showing weakness. This is not love, this is weakness.

FATHER: Rabbi, if your son takes his younger brother and fights with him on the roof and pushes him off the roof, would you say to him, "Never mind, it doesn't matter?"

RABBI: No. No. Of course not.

FATHER: Would this be love or weakness if you did this?

RABBI: I think ... yes, indeed, this would be weakness.

FATHER: Very well. Now, my son has insulted me before my guests. He refuses to love and welcome his brother. Shall I go and tell him, "Never mind, this is nothing?" Is this love, or is this weakness?

MAYOR: Indeed, indeed, it is the same. This is not love. This is weakness.

RABBI: Yes, I think I see what you mean.

FATHER: (Very intensely) I do love him! I am ready to forgive. But I must offer forgiveness in a way that will change him.

RABBI: Yes, I see.

FATHER: I must offer forgiveness to him in a way that will restore fellowship.

MAYOR: How is that?

FATHER: Forgiveness is not just letting the man who has done wrong go free.

RABBI: What is it then?

FATHER: Forgiveness is the return of fellowship.

RABBI: Then you mean you want reconcilation with your son?

FATHER: Yes indeed, but this is impossible until he stops disobeying. He cannot stop disobeying until he gives up his rebellious pride. But only as he does can we

FATHER: have reconciliation. Forgiveness that does not stop his rebellion is meaningless. Listen, Mayor.

MAYOR: Yes, Elder?

FATHER: What if a group of thieves come to fight against our village. We fight them. Then in the middle of the fight you, as Mayor, cry out and say to them, "I forgive you."

MAYOR: This is impossible. I would never say such a thing.

FATHER: Why not?

MAYOR: It would be meaningless. They would laugh at me.

FATHER: Would they not stop fighting?

MAYOR: Of course not, they would fight all the more.

FATHER: You see, Rabbi, it is the same with my son. Forgiveness means nothing if it does not bring the rebel to surrender.

MAYOR: I insist. The honor of the house must be preserved.

RABBI: But, Mayor, this is the father of the boy. He must show him love and mercy. This is his character.

FATHER: Don't be angry, my friends. Don't be angry. Both of you are right. Mayor, your opinion is correct. The honor of the house must be preserved. Punishment will preserve my honor for the moment, but it will not give me back a son. Rabbi, your opinion is right. I love him dearly, but I cannot say "I forgive you." Because he does not request forgiveness. I cannot forgive him until he requests it. He will not request it until he sees that he is wrong.

MAYOR: What will you do then?

FATHER: I will humble myself before him and go out to him.

MAYOR: No! How is this? There is no need for you to do this. But he is angry, and unpredictable. Send the servant again.

FATHER: Many times I have sent servants to talk with him.

RABBI: Then what happens? Does he listen to them?

FATHER: No. Rather he usually strikes them.

MAYOR: (Agitated) Then he may strike you as well.

FATHER: I have considered that.

MAYOR: (Agitated) Then you must not go out while he is angry.

FATHER: What then do you suggest? (They are both silent) (The father continues) Maybe it is necessary that I do this. Only then will he see what his pride really

233

FATHER: means. If he strikes me, maybe then he will see his rebellion for what it is. I do not want payment for his rebellion. I want his repentance. I will go out to him in love and humiliation.

MAYOR: But you must not do this. You may get hurt.

FATHER: Will my suffering be any worse than that which I now endure? Is my heart at rest with him in rebellion far from me?

RABBI: I do not understand.

FATHER: Now I suffer the suffering of one whose love is rejected. I go out to him. This is the only way I can make a path of reconciliation. Maybe then he will see what his evil really means and will repent. I go, my friends. (Very firmly) Please do not interfere with what I must do.

(Father goes out. The Mayor and Rabbi listen intently by the window. Voices come from the outside)

FATHER: Son, why are you angry?

SON: I'm not angry.

FATHER: Come into the banquet then. It is a shame to insult your father before his guests. We have music and dancing. The guests have asked for you. The Mayor is here. The Rabbi from the synagogue is here. They ask for you.

SON: I won't go in.

FATHER: Why, my son?

SON: I'm not getting my rights. I'm not being treated fairly.

FATHER: How do you mean?

SON: Lo, these many years I have served you. I have never disobeyed your commands, yet you never gave me a kid that I might make merry with my friends. But when this son of yours came who has devoured your living with harlots, you killed for him the fatted calf.

FATHER: Shame! Shame! Why do you speak of harlots? Have you heard anything? You have just come from the fields. We have not heard from him how he lost the money.

MAYOR: That's right. That's right. It is a shame for him to say such a thing.

RABBI: Sh - ush . . . Let us listen.

SON: (From outside) He's a criminal.

FATHER: Son, you are always with me and all that is mine is yours. It was fitting to make merry and be glad for

234

FATHER: this, your brother was dead and is alive. He was lost and is found.

SON: He is not my brother! He is a dirty criminal.

FATHER: I think if we heard that he was dead you would rejoice.

SON: Yes. This would be better. Now I must share the house with a criminal.

FATHER: If I had beaten him, you would be happy.

SON: Yes, this would be the best thing for him.

FATHER: But he is your brother.

SON: Him? I don't know him.

FATHER: (Very patiently) But he is your brother.

SON: (Angrily) What do you want me to do? Shall I go in and thank him for wasting our family's money?

FATHER: No, my son. I want you to go in and ask him to forgive you.

SON: (Exploding) Him forgive me? What do you mean? He must come begging my forgiveness. He is wrong and I am right. He is a dirty criminal. I am respectable, obedient and hard working. I have always obeyed you. All my life I have never done wrong.

FATHER: (Sorrowfully) No, my son. You must ask your brother to forgive you. You must ask me the same. You are part of the reason why he left the house in the first place. You have obeyed me, but you have never loved me. Your very obedience has made you proud. I do not want obedience to my commands in resentment and jealousy. I want you to serve in your father's house in love and great joy.

SON: (In great rising anger) How can you say this! How can you say this! Only I have labored. Only I have brought respect to my house. My brother wrongs me and you blame me. Always you blame me. You love him. You do not love me. Maybe if I ran away and spent the family's money on harlots -- then you would love me and reward me with a great banquet. Only I have labored day after day in the fields, but I receive nothing. You would destroy the honor of the house with all who are in it. All dignity, honor, respect is gone. It is your fault. Yet now you blame me. If my sister brought shame on our heads, I would save the family honor by purifying the house by her blood! There is only one thing left for me to do. Yes. There is only one thing for me to do. I must do it. I care nothing for myself. I want to save only the family honor. The family honor must be preserved. You are evil! (Wham) You are evil!

235

SON: (Wham) You have destroyed our house. (Wham) Yes. Yes. You have destroyed our house. (Wham)

(Sound of a heavy stick beating on a body. Inside the Mayor and the Rabbi jump up. A crowd quickly gathers outside. The Mayor shouts to the servants to go out and bring the father. A great crowd gathers outside. More and more voices are shouting. Over the top of them, the mayor shouts out the window)

MAYOR: Adam, where are you going?

SON: (The son answers from the outside) There is a service of worship in the synagogue. As you well know, I am a very religious man. I must not be late to pray. I am in a hurry! Goodbye!

(The servant enters)

MAYOR: Is he alive?

ABDU: Yes. He will live.

MAYOR: Did you hear him say anything?

ABDU: Yes, he said, "Never mind, my son. Never mind, my son. You do not know what you are doing."

MAYOR: Very well, Abdu. Go and see and care for your master.

(Servant exits)

MAYOR: (Shaking his head) Indeed. Indeed. We have never seen this in the village. The father should have beaten the boy for disobedience, but now the boy beats the father.

RABBI: But you see, Mayor, why he did it? He did it on purpose. He did it to show what rebellion means. He did it to show his great love. Maybe this will bring the son to repent. Now a way of reconciliation is open. Something has been done to bring the son to repentance.

MAYOR: (Shaking his head) Indeed. Indeed. I said there must be punishment for disobedience. I said there must be discipline and order. Honor and respect must be preserved. The father has preserved these things, but he did it in a strange, strange way.

RABBI: But was not this the only way?

MAYOR: I am beginning to see that it was.

RABBI: I told him he must show his love. Now he has shown supreme love. Now the son must decide what he will do. Surely he will accept the father's forgiveness. What do you think will happen, Mayor?

MAYOR: I don't know. What do you think?

RABBI: I think he will repent. He will see for the first time what his pride really means. He will see that his father should have beaten him, but now he has beaten his father. Now he cannot think of making up his rebellion to his father. He will see how much his father really loves him. Now he can accept his father's love. He will confess his sin and repent. Do you not think so, Mayor?

MAYOR: I hope that this is true, but I am afraid.

RABBI: What are you afraid of, Mayor?

MAYOR: He is very proud. I am afraid this great act of his father will harden him in his pride. If he does this, he will choose to be the enemy of his father and so he will be, indeed, his father's enemy.

RABBI: Then if he does this, the father will continue to suffer. He will still suffer the suffering of the one whose love is rejected.

MAYOR: I am afraid so! My friend, tonight we have seen a great work of reconciliation. We must think of these things.

YUSEF: The play is over, my friends. Baseat, come on in. Azeez! Where are you? Very good work, Mayor.

ABDU: Yusef, you were the best of all of us.

YUSEF: Now, my friends, tomorrow night we must come and talk about what this story means.

MAYOR: This story is very deep, Yusef.

ABDU: We have understood a little, but not very much.

BASEAT: I have understood even less.

YUSEF: Come tomorrow, my friends. Tomorrow night we will explain the story!

QUESTIONS FOR DISCUSSION

1. Who does the father in the play represent?
2. Who is the mayor in the play? What does he represent?
3. Who does the Rabbi represent?
4. Why is the solution of the mayor not good enough?
5. Why is the solution of the Rabbi not good enough?
6. What does the father want from his son?
7. What does the older son think about himself?
8. Why cannot the father send a servant to talk to his son?
9. The father says he used to punish him or forgive him when he was a little boy. The father says this is now no longer good enough. What does he mean?
10. What does the older son really want?
11. Who does the older son represent?
12. How does the father open a way of reconciliation?
13. The father suffers for his son. When he is finished, the son must do one of two things. What are they?
14. Explain the two choices before the son at the end of the story.

SUMMARY OF LESSON

Man rebels against God. Man tries to make himself first in his life. He does not let God be first. God is holy. This means He guards His honor. But God is also love which means He wants to love and forgive us. He must offer forgiveness in a way that will change us. He must lead us to seek forgiveness. So God comes to reconcile the world to Himself. In the Cross of Christ, God offers to us reconciliation. Thus He shows us that He is holy and He shows us that He is love.

MOTTO: Forgiveness does not mean forgetting the penalty. Forgiveness means restoring fellowship.

19
GOD IS HOLY LOVE: PART 2

SCRIPTURES TO BE READ: Luke 15:25-32; I Corinthians 15:54-57;
II Corinthians 5:21; Galatians 3:13;
Colossians 1:13; Hebrews 2:14-15;
Hebrews 10:11-15; Hebrews 10:26-31;
James 4:17; I Peter 2:14

STATEMENT OF LESSON

In the last lesson Yusef and his friends acted out a play. This play tells us something of what God has done for us. In the play, the Mayor said, "You must punish the boy." The father admits he should be punished. But punishment will not make him into a son. God is holy. Holiness demands holiness in us. We are sinners. Therefore, holiness requires judgment. In the play the Rabbi says, "You must forgive." The father is ready to forgive. But forgiveness is meaningless unless the sinner asks for it. If we do not see that we are wrong, forgiveness is meaningless. So God redeems us through holy love. God suffers in Christ to reconcile us to Himself. Now we have two choices. We can accept His love and return to Him in humility. Or we can be hardened by His love; then judgment falls upon us. We will be the enemies of God. This is because we have chosen God as our enemy. God still loves us, but we have chosen Him as our enemy.

In the New Testament, we see three parables trying to explain the cross of Christ. The first parable is from the law court. God in Christ became a criminal. That is, he took sin upon himself. He paid the penalty for us.

The second parable is from the altar. A Holy God demands holy men and we are not holy. We should offer to God perfect obedience, but we do not. We sin. Christ becomes priest and sacrifice. He offers Himself in perfect obedience to open a way of atonement. He opens a way of reconciliation between us and God.

The third parable is the parable of the battlefield. Sin brings death. This is what the devil wants. The devil leads men to sin so they will die. The devil does not want us to be redeemed so the devil fights Christ, but Christ is victorious. He is victorious over sin and death. Thus we cry with Paul, "Thanks be to God who hath given us the victory through our Lord, Jesus Christ."

OUTLINE

<u>GOD IS HOLY LOVE</u>

1. Interpretation of the Parable of the Son who stayed at home

   a. Holiness is not enough.

   b. Love is not enough.

   c. Holy love redeems us.

   d. We now have two choices before us.

2. The New Testament parables of the cross

   a. The parable of the law court

   b. The parable of the altar

   c. The parable of the battlefield

THE DIALOGUE

GOD IS . . . .

SCENE 19

CHARACTERS:

Yusef, the Wise

Abdu, the Inquirer

Baseat, the Simple

Mayor Butrus

THE DIALOGUE

(All four characters are seated in Yusef's front room.)

MAYOR: Yusef, that was a great play that you wrote.

YUSEF: Yes, but Mayor, did you understand it?

MAYOR: I understood a little, but you must explain the rest.

ABDU: It was a very strange play. Indeed you must explain it to us.

YUSEF: Baseat, are you listening?

BASEAT: Yes, indeed.

YUSEF: Very well. First we must see who the characters are. Who represents God in the play?

MAYOR: This is very easy. God is the father.

YUSEF: Very well. Who, then, is the Mayor in the play, Mr. Mayor?

MAYOR: This is what I don't understand.

YUSEF: Notice carefully. The father is God. The Mayor is holiness. Remember we talked about holiness? Holiness is purity which demands righteousness and justice.

ABDU: Yes, we remember.

YUSEF: Very well. The Mayor in the play is holiness. Now the Rabbi is love. Remember we talked about love and how God is love. Love seeks mercy and forgiveness. This is what the Rabbi in the play seeks.

BASEAT: Oh -- is that it?

YUSEF: The older son, then, is the religious sinner.

MAYOR: Indeed! Is there such a thing as a religious sinner?

YUSEF: Of course, Mr. Mayor. The Pharisees were very religious. They were the most religious people in the country. But they crucified Christ. We are religious

241

YUSEF: sinners. So the older son represents us. Abdu, are we not religious?

ABDU: Somewhat.

YUSEF: Are we not sinners?

ABDU: I think we are.

BASEAT: Who, then, is the servant in the play?

YUSEF: Oh yes -- the servant. The servant represents the prophets. God sends the prophets to us. We beat the prophet. So in the play, the father sends the servant, many times, out to speak to his son. His son rejects the servant. Now, does everyone understand? The Father is God. The Mayor is holiness. The Rabbi is love. The older son represents religious sinners. The servant represents the prophets. Now, Abdu, what happened first in the play?

ABDU: Les me see . . . First, the older son came and would not enter the banquet. He was angry and stood outside.

YUSEF: Why was he angry?

ABDU: He thinks he is not getting his rights. He is angry with his father and his brother.

YUSEF: Exactly right. But notice, he asserts authority over his father. This is what sin means. We make ourselves first, but only God should be first. What did the serpent say to Eve in the garden?

MAYOR: "You shall be as gods."

YUSEF: Exactly right. We are very proud. Now, what does the Mayor in the play suggest that we must do?

ABDU: He said, "Beat him."

YUSEF: Is this right or is this wrong?

MAYOR: There is no doubt he deserves beating.

YUSEF: Ah, but Mayor, will punishment bring restoration of fellowship?

MAYOR: Of course not.

YUSEF: So God is holy. Holiness demands righteousness. God must preserve His honor. A price must be paid for disobedience. What else does the Mayor suggest?

MAYOR: He suggests payment of a fine.

YUSEF: What else?

ABDU: He says give the boy rules he must follow.

YUSEF: But this is no good. God can give us rules to obey and in the Old Testament this is what God did. But this was not enough. Many people disobeyed the rules;

YUSEF: then they were far from God. Many people obeyed the rules. They became very proud. So they were far from God.

MAYOR: But I think the Mayor in the play is right. The Father has to assert his authority or he is lost.

YUSEF: Yes indeed. No one mocks God. But punishment is not enough. Punishment does not return fellowship. Now, Abdu, what does the rabbi say?

ABDU: The rabbi says we must love and forgive.

YUSEF: But is this enough?

ABDU: No indeed.

YUSEF: Why not?

ABDU: If the boy does not see that he is wrong, forgiveness is meaningless.

YUSEF: Very good, Abdu. Baseat, what if the father goes out to his boy and says to him, "You are forgiven"?

BASEAT: He will be angry and say, "I am not mistaken."

YUSEF: Good, Baseat. So God Himself is love. He is ready to forgive men, but forgiveness is meaningless unless men see that they are wrong and ask for forgiveness. So holiness is not enough, and love is not enough, but God is holy love. Christ did not come to <u>tell</u> <u>us</u> <u>about</u> salvation. He did not come to <u>give</u> <u>us</u> salvation. But He came to <u>make</u> salvation. This is reconciliation.

MAYOR: This is right. The father does not go out to <u>tell</u> his son about reconciliation. He does not go out to <u>give</u> his son reconciliation. He goes out to <u>make</u> reconciliation by suffering.

YUSEF: May God enlighten you, Mayor. You have understood exactly. The father goes out to suffer to make reconciliation with his son. God comes to us in Christ to make reconciliation with Himself. Paul says, "God was in Christ, reconciling the world unto Himself."

ABDU: Is this what this means?

YUSEF: Yes, indeed. In the story the son beats the father, but the father should have beaten the son. Even so, God should have punished us, but God comes and we punish Him. He comes to open a way of reconciliation to Himself.

MAYOR: Indeed, indeed. We are very evil.

YUSEF: Now, notice, my friends, in the story the father does this on purpose. He <u>chooses</u> to do this. The boy in the field does not trick his father into coming out. His father goes on purpose to save him.

BASEAT: I still don't understand.

MAYOR: (Impatiently) Be quiet, Baseat. Abdu will explain to you afterwards. Just listen.

BASEAT: Very well, Mayor.

YUSEF: Men do not seize Christ against His will. If this were true, we would say He was weak. Rather, God comes to us on purpose to save us. He comes to us <u>knowing</u> that this is what men will do to Him. He does this on purpose to open a way to reconciliation. On one side, God is not mocked. Holiness demands righteousness. On the other side, He does not deal with us according to our sins. That is, He is love. How can God be holy and demand righteousness and at the same time be love and offer forgiveness?

ABDU: He does both on the cross of Christ.

YUSEF: You are right, Abdu. How great a salvation God has wrought for us. God was in Christ, reconciling the world unto Himself.

MAYOR: We are very evil.

YUSEF: But think of something else. At the end the boy has two choices. What are they?

MAYOR: He can accept or he can reject the love of his father.

YUSEF: This is where we are. In the play, the rabbi says the boy may accept. So man can, if he wishes, accept the love of God offered in the cross. But he cannot accept until he admits his guilt.

ABDU: I am with the Mayor. We are all evil.

YUSEF: I'm glad you're beginning to see, Abdu. God suffers the deep suffering of the one whose love is rejected. If we accept the love of God, our pride must be broken. We see that Christ paid the penalty for us. In repentance we seek pardon.

MAYOR: But on the other hand the boy, if he wishes, can reject his father's love.

YUSEF: Yes indeed. So, some men in sin reject God's love. They reject the way of reconciliation that God Himself has made. They choose to become the enemy of God. Think of it, my friends, to be the enemy of God. Abdu, read Hebrews 10:26-31.

ABDU: (Opens and reads) "For if we sin deliberately after receiving the knowledge of the truth, there no longer remains a sacrifice for sins, but a fearful prospect of judgment, and a fury of fire which will consume the adversaries. A man who has violated the law of Moses dies without mercy at the testimony of two or

ABDU: three witnesses. How much worse punishment do you think will be deserved by the man who has spurned the Son of God, and profaned the blood of the covenant by which he was sanctified, and outraged the Spirit of grace? For we know him who said, 'Vengeance is mine, I will repay.' And again, 'The Lord will judge his people.' It is a fearful thing to fall into the hands of the living God."

YUSEF: Some men reject the love of God in Christ. Thus, they choose to live outside the love of God. This is hell. Hell is to live without God. So for some men, hell begins on this earth. Here on the earth they have part of hell.

BASEAT: I simply don't understand.

ABDU: (Kindly) Baseat, you must. This is the most important thing in your life. This you must understand. But don't worry. I'll explain it.

MAYOR: Yusef, in the play you explained to us the meaning of the cross of Christ. How does the Bible explain it?

YUSEF: I'm glad you asked, Mayor. We must think of this. In the Bible we have three parables. Each parable tries to explain the meaning of the cross of Christ.

ABDU: What are they, Yusef?

YUSEF: First is the parable of the law court; second, the parable of the altar; third, the parable of the battlefield.

MAYOR: I never noticed this, Yusef.

YUSEF: Let us look at them one by one. Each one answers a problem. We have three parables and three problems.

ABDU: What are they, Yusef?

YUSEF: First, what we have done; second, what we have not done; third, Satan, who wants sin to bring death.

ABDU: Carry on, Yusef.

YUSEF: It is very simple. First, what we have done. That is, the sin which we have done. This demands penalty. Second, what we have not done. That is, righteousness and holiness. God who is holy demands righteousness. He demands perfect righteousness. This means perfect obedience. This we have not done. This demands sacrifice. Third, Satan is like a cruel executioner. He wants men to sin because sin brings death. We want someone who will be victorious over sin and death. So Christ pays the penalty. Christ makes a sacrifice. Christ is the victor. So Christ saves us from all three problems. Let us look at them one by one.

ABDU: Not too fast, Yusef. We are not accustomed to thinking so deeply. Have patience with us.

YUSEF: I am ready to stay the whole night. Let us look first at the parable of the law court. The problem is the sin which we have done. The wages of sin is death. A price must be paid. The sinner cannot pay the price even if he wants to. Let me tell you a story, my friends.

BASEAT: Very good. Maybe now I will understand something this evening.

ABDU: Never mind, Baseat. Just listen to the story.

YUSEF: Last month a man came to me from the next village. He was very unhappy. It seems he heard something about someone in the village. It was a very little thing. He took the story and changed it. He made it sound like a big bad story. He went to all the village telling the bad story about the man in the village. After that his conscience was not at rest. So he came to me, asking, "What shall I do?" I told him to kill a duck and take the feathers from the breast of the duck and go very early in the morning and place one small feather before the door of every house, then to come back. He thought this was very strange. I insisted that he do this. So he went and killed the duck, plucked the feathers, and put a small feather before the door of every house very early the next morning. The following day he came back. Then I said to him, "Now, my friend, go back and pick up all the feathers."

ABDU: He can't, of course. It is impossible.

YUSEF: Exactly right. He cried and said to me, "How can I pick up the feathers? The feathers have gone all over the world. How can I find them and bring them back?" Then I began to explain to him what sin is like. We lie, cheat, become jealous, take bribes, are covetous, and envious. When we do these things, sin goes out from us to the whole world. My friend told an evil story in the village. The story went to the whole village and to many villages. He does not even know where the evil has gone. The evil is like the feathers. Each little sin is like a tiny feather placed before the door of a house. It goes many places. We do not know where it goes. I explained to him that he cannot make up for his sins. He understood and was very upset. He said, "Can I not repent? Can I not go to the man and say, 'I am sorry about the story I told about you'?" I told him, "Yes, this will help, but this will not bring back the evil that you have done."

MAYOR: That's for sure.

YUSEF: So, our sin is like this. The sin which we have done has gone to all the world. We cannot bring it back or cover it up. Repentance is not enough. This does not call back the sin which we have done. So what can we do?

BASEAT: (With great delight) I understood this story. This is the first thing I have understood tonight.

ABDU: Never mind, Baseat. Just pay attention. Yusef, I see that we cannot help ourselves from our sin.

YUSEF: That's right, Abdu. We cannot call back the sin which we have done. Abdu, read Galatians 3:13.

ABDU: (Reading) "Christ redeemed us from the curse of the law, having become a curse for us, for it is written 'Cursed be everyone who hangs upon a tree.'"

YUSEF: Baseat, read I Peter 2:24.

BASEAT: (Reading) "He himself bore our sins in his body on the tree, that we might die to sin and live to righteousness. By his wounds you have been healed."

YUSEF: Now, Mayor, read II Corinthians 5:21.

MAYOR: (Reading) "For our sake he made him to be sin who knew no sin, that in him we might become the righteousness of God.

YUSEF: This is the parable of the law court, my friends. There is a penalty on our heads. The price must be paid for our sins. We cannot do anything about it. Payment is not enough. Repentance will not cover what we have done. A Holy God passes a judgment on sin. Then God in Christ accepts this judgment and pays the penalty for us.

MAYOR: Say this again, Yusef.

YUSEF: (Slowly) A Holy God passes a judgment on sin. God in Christ accepts this judgment and pays the penalty for us. Let me tell another story so Baseat will be happy.

BASEAT: Please do.

YUSEF: About a hundred years ago, there was a man in Europe who made a revolution. He and his men were fighting against the government in the mountains. The leader's name was Shamel. He found out that someone in his group was taking the secrets of his group and giving it to the enemy. He was very angry. He said, 'When we catch the person that is doing this, we will beat him forty strokes of the whip." Then, after some days, they caught the man who was betraying them. It

YUSEF: was not a man. It was a woman. In great sorrow they found the betrayer was the mother of Shamel. Shamel had spoken. He said the betrayer must be beaten. How can he beat his mother? For two days he did not eat, or sleep, or drink. At last he came from his tent and said to his followers, "The penalty must be paid." They took his mother and began to tie her up. Then Shamel shouted and said, "No, no. Do not beat her. Tie me to the whipping post. Whip me in her place." So they took Shamel, the leader, and they beat Shamel in place of his mother.

MAYOR: This is a great story, Yusef.

YUSEF: This is what God has done for us. This is the parable of the law court. Sin demands penalty. God's holiness passes a judgment on sin. Then God in Christ accepts this judgment and pays the penalty Himself. But let us think of the second parable. The parable of the altar. We said we have three problems. What we have done is the first problem. The second problem is the things we have not done. That is, we have not been holy and righteous. We have a duty before God. Our duty is perfect obedience. This we have not done. Baseat, read James 4:17.

BASEAT: (Reading) "Whoever knows what is right to do and fails to do it, for him it is sin."

ABDU: We never thought of sin in this way.

YUSEF: But we must think of it in this way. God demands from us perfect obedience. Some things we do are sin. Many things we do not do are for us sins. What can we do about this? We owe God a debt. The debt is perfect obedience. But we never reach this standard.

MAYOR: We cannot. But does God really ask for perfect obedience?

YUSEF: Yes, of course. If we were not sinners, we would offer perfect obedience. We are responsible because we do not obey him. When you think a man has done something wrong in the village, Mayor, you catch him. You say to him, "Why have you done this?" What does he answer?

MAYOR: He says, "I have done nothing."

YUSEF: Even so, God comes to us. We say to God, "We are not wrong. We have done nothing." But our own words condemn us. This is the very point. We should have obeyed. We should have walked in perfect righteousness. But we haven't.

ABDU: But we can't.

YUSEF: That's right. So someone must do it for us. Christ comes from God to offer to God perfect obedience.

MAYOR: This is very hard, Yusef. Say it again.

YUSEF: (Slowly) Christ comes <u>from</u> God to offer <u>to God</u> perfect obedience. Stay with me, my friends. Christ makes an offering to God for us. The offering is perfect obedience. But this is a very hard offering. Sin is in the world. Sin is against obedience. Christ comes to walk in perfect obedience, but as Paul says, "He was obedient unto death, yea, even the death on the cross." That is, because of sin, this offering of perfect obedience leads to death. This then, is the parable of the altar. Christ is priest and sacrifice. Christ offers Himself as a sacrifice for us. Let us look at it from another way. The important thing is not <u>that</u> Christ died, but <u>how</u> Christ died. The important thing is <u>the way</u> He died.

ABDU: Please explain, Yusef.

YUSEF: Supposing Jesus in the upper room says to Peter, "Judas has betrayed us." Then He asks Peter to kill Judas. Peter draws his sword and kills Judas. Jesus plans their escape. They sneak out at night and get out of the city. Quickly they hurry to Bethany. Next day they start down the road to Jericho. The high priest hears that Jesus has escaped and sends soldiers after Him. They catch up with Jesus and His disciples on the road to Jericho. There is a great fight and some of the disciples are killed. In the fighting Jesus is killed also. Now, Abdu, if this had happened there would be for us <u>no</u> salvation. In this story, Christ <u>dies</u>, but He does not <u>save</u>. The important thing is not <u>that</u> Christ died, but <u>how</u> Christ died. Christ comes to make an offering of perfect obedience. The evil in the world is against this obedience. Christ obeys, even unto death. He goes to death willingly. He does this because only in this way can He offer the sacrifice of perfect obedience. Abdu, read Hebrews 10, verses 11 through 15.

ABDU: (Reading) "And every priest stands daily at his service, offering repeatedly the same sacrifices, which can never take away sins. But when Christ had offered for all time a single sacrifice for sins, he sat down at the right hand of God, then to wait until his enemies should be made a stool for his feet. For by a single offering he had perfected for all time those who are sanctified."

YUSEF: In the Old Testament, people would bring a pure, perfect, spotless animal. This pure animal was the offering to God of purity and holiness which man

YUSEF: could not offer. This was a symbol of what Christ would do. Now Christ comes. Christ does not offer a lamb. He offers Himself. He is pure and blameless. God demands holiness. God in Christ offers holiness to Himself.

MAYOR: These ideas are wide and deep, Yusef. We have never thought in this way.

YUSEF: All of this is just a beginning, my friends. We understand only a small part. But now, let us think of the third parable. We have seen the parable of the law court, and the parable of the altar. The third parable is the parable of the battlefield. Satan wants sin and death. He knows that sin brings death. This is what he wants. All Satan needs to do is to get Christ to disobey. This is what he did with Eve. This is what he tries to do with Christ. The battlefield is the world. Life begins with the temptations in the wilderness. It ends with the resurrection. Satan has two weapons. He can try temptation. He can try to tempt Christ, then He can make the way of obedience very hard. He works to make the way of obedience as hard as possible. He says to Christ, "You insist on obeying. I will make this path lead to a cross." These are the weapons of Satan. Jesus fights the battle with one weapon - obedience.

MAYOR: This is a strange, strange fight.

YUSEF: Strange indeed, but this was the fight of the ages. This was the great battle. Satan says, "If you walk this way, you will die and I will win."

ABDU: But he did not win. Jesus won.

YUSEF: How did He win?

ABDU: He arose victorious over the grave.

YUSEF: Exactly right. Abdu, read I Corinthians 15:54-57.

ABDU: (Reading) "'Death is swallowed up in victory. O death, where is thy victory? O death, where is thy sting?' The sting of death is sin, and the power of sin is the law. But thanks be to God, who gives us the victory through our Lord Jesus Christ."

YUSEF: Baseat, Read Hebrews 2, verses 14 and 15.

BASEAT: (Reading) "Since therefore the children share in flesh and blood, he himself likewise partook of the same nature, that through death he might destroy him who has the power of death, that is, the devil, and deliver all those who through fear of death were subject to lifelong bondage."

YUSEF: Then in Colossians we read, "He has delivered us from the dominion of darkness and transferred us to the kingdom of his beloved Son in whom we have redemption and forgiveness of sins." So my friends, the third parable is the parable of the battlefield. There is a great fight. Christ, our champion, is victorious. Thus we must cry with Paul, "Thanks be to God, who gives us the victory through our Lord Jesus Christ."

QUESTIONS FOR DISCUSSION

1. Who do the characters in the play represent?
2. How does Yusef explain sin?
3. What is a religious sinner?
4. Why is the answer of the Mayor not enough?
5. Why is love not enough?
6. How is God both holy and love at once?
7. What two choices do we have?
8. What happens if we accept God's love?
9. What happens if we reject God's love?
10. What are the three problems of redemption?
11. Explain the parable of the law court.
12. Why must a price be paid?
13. Explain the parable of the altar.
14. What debt do we owe that we cannot pay?
15. Explain the parable of the battlefield.
16. What are the two weapons that Satan uses?
17. What is the one weapon that Christ uses?

SUMMARY OF LESSON

God in Christ pays the penalty of sin. God in Christ offers the perfect sacrifice of obedience to a Holy God. God in Christ is victorious over sin and death.

MOTTO: The cross is for men by God to God!

20
GOD WANTS US TO KNOW, ACCEPT, AND RETURN HIS HOLY LOVE

SCRIPTURES TO BE READ: Luke 15:20-32; I Corinthians 13; Matthew 5:44,45; 6:14-15

STATEMENT OF LESSON

We saw that God is holy love. Holiness demands justice and righteousness. Love seeks mercy and forgiveness. God did both. He did this on the cross of Christ. What, then, does God require of us? In our play the father said to the mayor and the rabbi that he wanted three things. He wanted a son that would know, accept, and return his love. Each of the two sons in the story of the prodigal son must do this. God wants to restore fellowship. Only as we know, accept and return His holy love can we be fully restored to God's fellowship.

OUTLINE

TRUE SONS OF THE FATHER

1. We must <u>know</u> God's holy love.
    a. To the younger son - the father has offered forgiveness freely.
    b. For the older son - the father has opened a way of reconciliation.
2. We must <u>accept</u> God's holy love.
    a. The younger son must, in repentance, accept cleansing and restoration.

  b. The older son must, in humility, accept his responsibility for his father's suffering.
3. We must <u>return</u> God's holy love.
  a. The younger son must return thankful service.
  b. The older son must return love to his father <u>and</u> to his brother.

THE DIALOGUE

GOD IS . . .

SCENE 20

CHARACTERS:

Yusef, the Wise

Abdu, the Inquirer

Baseat, the Simple

Mayor Butrus

THE DIALOGUE

(Yusef is seated, reading, in his front room.)

YUSEF: "Beloved, let us love one another; for love is of God, and he who loves is born of God and knows God. He who does not love does not know God; for God is love. In this the love of God was made manifest among us, that God sent his only Son into the world, so that we might live through him."

(Baseat and Abdu enter)

YUSEF: Come in.

ABDU: Thank you. All day we have longed to come. You have made the cross of Christ very clear. That was a great play we had the other night.

BASEAT: I played a very good servant. I was very good indeed.

MAYOR: (Entering) Good evening, my friends.

ALL: Welcome, Mayor.

YUSEF: You have all honored us.

MAYOR: We are honored, not you, Yusef, but let us begin. What is our subject?

YUSEF: Does anyone remember what the father in the play wanted from his son?

MAYOR: He wanted him to come in.

YUSEF: Yes, but exactly what did he want? What did he say he wanted?

ABDU: O yes, I remember - he said he wanted a son who would accept and return his love.

YUSEF: Almost right. Very good, Abdu. Only you left one thing out. He said he wanted a son that would do three things. He wanted a son that would <u>know</u>, <u>accept</u>, and <u>return</u> his love. Baseat, what did he want?

255

BASEAT: He wanted a son that would know, accept, and return his love.

YUSEF: Good! Very good, Baseat! Now, Mr. Mayor, don't you think he wants this from the younger son as well?

MAYOR: Surely he does.

YUSEF: Very well, let us look at each of the sons to see what they must do to know, accept, and return their father's love. But first, Baseat, who are these two sons?

BASEAT: (Hesitantly) I don't remember.

YUSEF: Never mind, you will remember this time. The older son is the religious sinner and the younger son is the irreligious sinner.

BASEAT: What do you mean? How can a man be religious and a sinner?

YUSEF: (Somewhat sorrowfully) Not yet? Do you not yet understand, Baseat? The Pharisees were very, very religious. Yet they crucified Jesus. Religious people have the sins of pride, self-righteousness and envy. Irreligious people have the sins of drunkenness, adultery, and murder. They both are sinners. They both need to be cleansed and restored to the family of God.

ABDU: I will explain all of this to you later, Baseat.

MAYOR: This is clear in the play we had, Baseat. The older son was religious. Yet he was a sinner. He attacked his father.

BASEAT: Oh yes, that's right. I remember.

ABDU: Please begin, Yusef.

YUSEF: Very well, we must see how both sons can know, accept, and return their father's love. First, they and we must know of God's great holy love. Think about the younger son. He discovers his father's love little by little.

MAYOR: What do you mean, Yusef?

YUSEF: I mean he comes to know his father's love in three stages. First in the far country he thinks his father loves him. Maybe, he thinks, his father will be willing to feed him and let him work as a servant. He knows this is a lot to ask. For he thinks about what he has done. He never dreams his father loves him more than this.

MAYOR: But he does.

YUSEF: Yes, indeed. This is the second step. When he comes home, he finds his father loves him more than he ever dreamed. He is overwhelmed and shamed by the outpouring of his father's great love.

ABDU: Is this not the end? What is the third step?

YUSEF: Let the story go on in your mind. He stays in the house serving his father. But the longer he lives, the more he will find how deep and wide is his father's love.

BASEAT: I don't understand.

MAYOR: Neither do we, Baseat. Please explain, Yusef.

YUSEF: It is very clear, Mayor. The boy doesn't have any idea how much he has caused his father to suffer. He has caused his father to suffer in three ways. First, he asked for his inheritance before his father was dead.

MAYOR: Yes, this means he wanted his father dead. Go on.

YUSEF: Then he left his father's house. That is, he refused the love and fellowship of his father.

ABDU: And what is the third?

YUSEF: Third, he wasted the inheritance he received from his father. He came home with nothing. When he came home he did not think of these things. He did not think of how his father suffered the agony of one whose love is rejected. But notice carefully, the <u>longer</u> he stays in his father's house, the <u>more</u> he will see how deeply he has hurt his father.

MAYOR: And thus, the more he will understand his father's great love.

YUSEF: May God enlighten you, Mayor. Exactly right. The longer he stays close to his father, the more he will see how much his father has suffered for him. But my friends, the same is true with us. The longer we live close to God, the more we see how great is our pride and rebellion. Then we see how much this has hurt God. Then we understand how great is God's love. Now let us ask about the older son.

ABDU: Yes, what about him?

YUSEF: Notice also that pride never finds love. Only as the son was humble did he return to his father. He could not return in pride. Only humility discovers love. We are proud. Thus we find very, very little of the love of God. But let us think of the older son.

ABDU: Yes, what about him?

YUSEF: Here we must think about two kinds of love.

MAYOR: What do you mean?

YUSEF: Love says, "I want to help you and make you feel good." But holy love says, "I want to help you. I will help you in the way that is best for you."

ABDU: This is not clear, Yusef.

YUSEF: But it is very easy, Abdu. If the father had had plain love for the older son, he would have said, "No, no, my son, don't be angry. You must be happy. You want a banquet. Very well. I am ready to give you a banquet. Tomorrow night I will make the biggest banquet our village has ever seen. We will roast 12 camels and 8 sheep. I will slaughter 4 fatted calves. We will invite the governor of the province. You will be the only honored guest. I will make a great speech honoring you. No, do not be angry. Yes, you have worked hard. Indeed you deserve all this."

BASEAT: He would be very pleased with this.

YUSEF: But was this what the father did?

ABDU: No, indeed.

YUSEF: This would have made the older son prouder. He would despise his brother all the more. He would despise his father more. He would try all the more to make himself the head of the house. Don't you agree, Mr. Mayor?

MAYOR: I certainly do.

YUSEF: But the father does not love him with this kind of love. He loves him with holy love. Holy love does not seek to please. Holy love seeks to redeem.

ABDU: This is what the father does. In the play we saw the father seek to redeem the son.

YUSEF: Exactly right. Love says, "Let the beloved be happy." But holy love says, "Let the beloved be pure and righteous." Many times we seek the first kind of love from God. But God does not have this kind of love. All he has to offer is holy love. We don't want this kind. We do not want to be pure and righteous. Love seeks to please. Holy love seeks to redeem.

MAYOR: Your words strike us very deep, Yusef. We seek to be made happy. We do not seek to be redeemed.

YUSEF: I know, my friends, I know. But this is the holy love of God. This is the kind of love that the older son in our play is shown. He sees a love that opens a way of reconciliation. Now he must accept or reject it. Greater love has no man than this, that a man lay down his life for his friend. We too, my friends, must know of God's great love. We must see it through the eyes of both sons. Now, what was the second thing the father wanted?

ABDU: He wanted his son to <u>accept</u> his love.

YUSEF: Very good. How does he do this?

BASEAT: I don't understand. Does anyone reject love? Some call me an idiot. But even an idiot understands this. No one will reject love.

YUSEF: Ah, but Baseat, God's love is holy love. We want a love that will give us gifts and leave us as we are. Holy love is not like this. Holy love will change us. The father does not give his younger son more money and send him back to the far country. He does not give his older son a calf and send him off to his friends.

BASEAT: I never thought of this.

YUSEF: To accept God's holy love we must have three things: <u>repentance</u>, <u>cleansing</u>, and <u>restoration</u>. Let us look at each of them. The younger son must repent. Now let me tell a story about repentance.

BASEAT: Good! Good! A story.

YUSEF: A certain man had a big grove of palm trees. They all had good dates on them. The date harvest season came around. The man was anxious to cut his dates. Then one morning he went to the field to look at his dates. He came to one of his trees. The dates were gone. But there was a piece of paper nailed to the tree. The paper said, "Dear sir, I have stolen your dates. I am a poor man. I needed the dates very badly. I am sorry to steal your dates. I repent of what I have done. Forgive me." So the owner of the palm trees thought to himself, "Poor fellow. I will say nothing." Then the next day he went to the field and found a second palm tree with the dates gone. It also had a piece of paper nailed to it. It said the same thing. It also said, "Dear sir, I am very sorry I stole your dates. I will never do it again. I repent. Please, forgive me." The man was somewhat angry, but he still said never mind. Then, the next morning, he went quickly to the fields. Sure enough. There he found the third palm tree with the dates gone and the note nailed to the tree. Then the man said, "I will post a guard. I will catch this thief. I will deliver him to the police. He says, 'I repent.' But he uses this as an excuse to steal more. I will see that he is thrown in jail until he pays the last cent."

BASEAT: This is a good story.

ABDU: Explain it to us, Yusef.

YUSEF: This date thief says, "I repent." But his repentance does not mean a change within him. This kind of repentance is not repentance at all. The younger son repents and goes home. He changes. He can say, "I repent of what I have done," and then stay in the far

YUSEF: country feeding pigs. But this is meaningless. Many times we repent but do nothing. We go right back to the same sin. This is not repentance. This is mocking God, like the thief mocks the owner of the dates. Repentance means leaving sin and returning to God.

ABDU: Who is able for these things?

YUSEF: I am glad you see that they are hard. But we must see something else about the younger son and his repentance. He must admit to himself that his repentance will not make up for what he has done. That is, repentance cannot atone. Abdu, suppose your son breaks a tea glass. Then he says, "I'm sorry." Does this put the glass back together?

ABDU: Of course not.

YUSEF: Even so, our repentance. We must repent. But this does not make up for what we have done. The younger son repents. He returns to his father. Does this make up for the money he has lost?

MAYOR: No indeed!

YUSEF: Does it make up for the insult to his father?

ABDU: Indeed not!

YUSEF: So he comes home, admitting that there is no goodness or hope within him. He throws himself on the mercy of his father. This is the first thing he must do to accept his father's love. Then he is cleansed by his father. Is this his doing?

BASEAT: No! This is the work of his father.

YUSEF: Think of him in the far country, feeding pigs. He wants to go home riding a great powerful male camel. He wants to ride into the village with expensive gifts for all the leading men of the village. He wants to have a very expensive jeweled sword to give his brother, out of spite. Then he will be able to laugh at them. He will be able to say, "See, you thought I was wrong to take my inheritance. Now I have stopped your talk. Look at this long train of camels. Look at these spices. Look at this chest of silver, gold and jewels. Garments? I have more than all of us can ever use. You said I was wrong. But now you are silent."

ABDU: Surely this was his dream.

YUSEF: But he must give up his pride. He must accept cleansing from his father and admit to himself that he cannot help himself. But he must accept something else.

MAYOR: What is that?

YUSEF: He must accept restoration also. His father says he will make him a son again. The father wants to restore him to sonship.

BASEAT: He will accept, of course.

YUSEF: No, Baseat. It is not this easy.

BASEAT: How do you mean? It seems to me that this would be very easy indeed!

YUSEF: But it would be easier for his pride to return. Then he could talk like this: "No, no, Father. I <u>cannot</u> accept this great honor. O, I am <u>much</u>, <u>much</u> too humble to accept this great honor. I used to be very proud. I used to be so proud that I would never work with my hands. But now I return to you as a very humble man. I <u>insist</u> that I be made a servant. I cannot accept sonship. I am too humble. O, I will scrub floors. I will clean out the stables. I will spread manure with my hands in the fields. I will plow the fields with the day laborers. I am now a very humble man. Make me a servant."

ABDU: But what is wrong with this?

YUSEF: If you think about this long enough maybe you will understand. This is the speech of the proudest man in the world. This man is proud of his humility. He is so proud there is little hope for him. You see, Abdu, it takes a <u>very</u>, <u>very</u> humble man to accept an honor that he does not deserve. The younger son must do this. He must accept an honor that he does not deserve. Everyone knows that he does not deserve it. All the guests at the banquet know that he came home in rags. Now he is to be restored to sonship. Only if he is humble and broken in heart can he accept. The next thing he must watch is his repentance itself.

MAYOR: What do you mean?

YUSEF: Now he can talk like this: "Yes, I came home with nothing. Yes, I was dirty and in rags. But think of how <u>wonderful</u> was my repentance. Why yes, that speech I gave down the road was a <u>wonderful</u> speech. All the village was moved by my humility and repentance. No one in the entire village has ever repented so magnificently!"

MAYOR: What is wrong with this, Yusef?

YUSEF: (Earnestly) Don't you see, my friends? This is also the voice of great pride. We can be proud of our humility. We can even be proud of our repentance. The devil is very clever. He is ready to lead us into pride at every moment. Pride is what separates us from God. Pride is what leads us to serve the devil.

261

YUSEF: Pride is what destroys us. All this must be overcome before the younger son can accept his father's love.

ABDU: We are an evil people. All of us are like this.

YUSEF: (Thoughtfully) I know, Abdu, I know. But think now of the older son. What must he do to accept his father's love?

BASEAT: We cannot speak, Yusef. You must explain it to us.

YUSEF: It is very clear. He must see that <u>he</u> has caused his father to suffer and that his father has suffered for <u>him</u>. He cannot accept his father's holy love until he does. Think of our play. The father should have beaten the son. But the son has beaten the father. He must see and admit this. If he does not, he cannot accept his father's love.

BASEAT: I don't understand.

ABDU: (Impatiently) Your whole life you won't understand!

YUSEF: Don't say this, Abdu. Baseat, just think about it long enough and you will understand. Listen, Baseat, we say, "Christ died for our sins." Is it not so?

BASEAT: Yes, indeed.

YUSEF: (Very slowly) Very well, this means <u>our</u> <u>sins</u> <u>killed</u> <u>him</u>.

BASEAT: (Very slowly, pondering each word) Christ died for our sins. This means our sins killed him. Yes, Yusef, I think that this is right.

MAYOR: But, Yusef, we did not kill Christ. The Jews long ago killed him.

YUSEF: Mayor, if my sins did not kill Him then He did not die for my sins.

MAYOR: How do you mean this?

YUSEF: This is very hard to explain, but it is true. Let me try. In our play, the older son tried to make himself first in the house - remember?

MAYOR: Yes, I remember.

YUSEF: This meant that he wanted to be the head of the house. But he cannot be the head of the house as long as his father is alive. Thus, what he really wanted was the death of his father. Is it not so?

MAYOR: Yes, this much I understand. This is what he wanted - the death of his father.

YUSEF: Now, it is the right of God to be first in everything in our lives. Is that not so?

MAYOR: Of course.

YUSEF: God has the right to be first in all our thinking, in all our feeling, and in all our willing. But do we make Him first? Or do we make ourselves first?

MAYOR: No indeed, we make ourselves first. Each man seeks to serve himself first.

YUSEF: (Very earnestly) Very well, Mayor, then it is the same story. This means we have taken the place of God. This means that what we really want is that God shall die. We in our pride want God dead. It is His right to be first. We wish to be first in our lives. This means that, deep within us, we want God dead.

MAYOR: But no one thinks he wants God dead!

YUSEF: (Very earnestly) I know, Mr. Mayor, but this is what we really want. Now let us go on. Christ comes to save us from this. This is the sin of the world that He comes to take away. I am a part of this. I have this pride. Baseat, do you remember what the father said at the banquet table?

BASEAT: What do you mean?

YUSEF: He said that he was suffering the pain of one whose love was rejected. Remember?

BASEAT: Yes, I remember.

YUSEF: Very well, what if the older son, after the beating, still remains proud and arrogant? What if he refuses to be reconciled to his father? Even after his father suffers for him he still refuses to give up his pride and become a loving son. What then?

BASEAT: His father will be very sad.

YUSEF: He will be more than sad, he will be broken hearted. He will still suffer the pain of the one whose love is rejected. Is it not so?

BASEAT: Indeed it is.

YUSEF: Very well, we are like this. When we make ourselves first in our lives, we cause God to suffer in this same way. He has opened a way of reconciliation. If we accept it, we can make God first in our lives. When men reject it, God is broken hearted. That is, my rebellion and yours hurts God today! He is still a father. If we do not accept His great love after what He has done, He indeed will suffer. We are the cause.

MAYOR: These are hard, hard words, Yusef.

YUSEF: Yes, but they are saving thoughts if we will believe. Yes, if we will believe. You see my friends, we must know of God's holy love. And we must accept God's holy love. But this is not easy. His holy love is a consuming fire!

ABDU: (Pauses and then speaks) How, then, can we return his holy love?

YUSEF: Yes, Abdu, this is the third thing we must think about. If we do not return His love, we have not accepted it. If we accept it, we cannot help returning it. Let us look at the two sons again. The younger son will now return to his father a life of thankful service.

BASEAT: Indeed, he will.

YUSEF: But, pay close attention, Baseat. The son will serve his father because the father has already <u>done</u> something. He does not serve him so that he <u>will</u> <u>do</u> something.

ABDU: Your thoughts are very deep.

YUSEF: But they are very simple. Listen, does the younger son now serve his father so that his father may one day accept him?

ABDU: No indeed, his father has already accepted him.

YUSEF: The son thought that maybe it would be this way. He was ready to work as a servant. But when he got home he was ashamed to make this offer. He knew he could never make up for what he had done. But now he will offer thankful and sincere service because of what his father has <u>done</u>. He does not serve in order to get his father to <u>do</u> something. This is why the older son was working. This led him into great pride. But let us stay with the younger son.

BASEAT: Yes, let us finish with him first. I have just begun to understand.

YUSEF: We, my friends, serve people in order to get something from them. We visit people. We do so in order to make friends with them. We want friends so that some day they can be of service to us.

MAYOR: Go on.

YUSEF: We give gifts to people who will one day be of use to us. We help men in the field. We expect them one day to help us.

ABDU: Indeed, this is what we do.

YUSEF: So, we think the same must be true with God. We want God to prosper us and give us eternal life. We think that we must serve God so that He will be pleased. If God is pleased, He will give us what we want. So we pray a little in the church. We send a little money at the end of the month to the preacher. We make a banquet for the guests of the preacher. We send food to the house of the preacher. We buy a Bible and place it on the table in the guest room. We say to

YUSEF:	ourselves, "These are the things God likes. Now God will be pleased with me. Now God will make me prosperous. Now I will have many sons. The water buffalo will give more milk and the land will give more cotton. We serve God. Then God will reward us. If we serve him little, he will reward us little. If we serve him much, he will reward us much."
ABDU:	I guess most of us think this way, Yusef.
YUSEF:	We must serve God because of what He has already done for us. If we serve God to get Him to do something, then we are like the older son in the field. We still do not know anything of God's great holy love. We still have not accepted his holy love.
ABDU:	Your words burn within us, Yusef!
YUSEF:	May the light of this burning give light in your path to God, my son. If we know and accept God's love, we serve Him because we have received. Let us now turn to the older son. Think of our play. The father has opened a way of reconciliation. The older son can now know and accept his father's love. If he does, he will return his father's love. But he must love his father and his brother.
MAYOR:	Is it not enough for him to love his father?
YUSEF:	When you are very close friends with a man, Mr. Mayor, his spirit fills your heart. Right?
MAYOR:	Indeed.
YUSEF:	So, if we are reconciled to God, then God's spirit fills our heart. Fellowship with God means we become loving. It does not mean that now we will receive gifts. Abdu, read Matthew 6:14, 15.
ABDU:	(Reading) "For if you forgive men their trespasses, your heavenly Father also will forgive you; but if you do not forgive men their trespasses, neither will your Father forgive your trespasses."
YUSEF:	Why is this true, Abdu?
ABDU:	Why is what true? What do you mean?
YUSEF:	Why must we forgive others in order to be forgiven? This is what we pray in the Lord's Prayer.
ABDU:	I don't know, Yusef.
YUSEF:	Think of the older son, Abdu! The father wants to bring him into the love of the family. Can he really be in the family if he can't get along with his brother?
ABDU:	I see what you mean. No, he cannot. If he cannot get along with his brother, he is not really in the family.

YUSEF: Even so, with us and God. God wants to let us into the family of God. But if we cannot love and forgive our brothers, we shut <u>ourselves</u> out of the family. Baseat, listen, I will tell a story.

BASEAT: A story. Good!

YUSEF: Once a man had a piece of land beside the river. He decided to plant watermelons. He had to water the melons by hand. He had a good goatskin. He went every day to the melon patch. He would very carefully blow up the goatskin with air and then let the air out over the melon patch. For hours every day he did this. His neighbor filled his goatskin with water from the river and watered his patch of melon. The man thought this was not necessary. He said, "I will water my melons with my breath. This is enough." He wondered why his melons never grew up. He did not know that he was a fool.

MAYOR: He was a fool indeed. How can a man water his land with the breath of his lungs?

YUSEF: But, Mayor. We are like this. We try to love and forgive men. We find they are proud and do not ask for forgiveness. But we are like the fool with the melon patch. We are trying to love them by pouring out on them our own spirit. In our own strength we think we can love them. But we cannot. We must fill our lives with the water of life. This water we must pour out on their thirsty lives. This spirit, this water, will work in their hearts.

ABDU: How can we get this spirit?

YUSEF: Know and accept God's love in Christ and His spirit will fill your heart, Abdu. Then you will be able to love God with the very holy love that He has given you. Then you will be able to love men with the same holy love. If God's love does not flow <u>through</u> us, it cannot flow <u>to</u> us.

BASEAT: I think I understand. (Said very slowly)

YUSEF: We have talked of many things. God is great. God is light. God is one. God is holy love. O Lord, our Lord, how majestic is thy name in all the earth. Read for us, Abdu, I John 4:7-11. Then I will pray.

ABDU: (Reading) "Beloved, let us love one another; for love is of God, and he who loves is born of God and knows God. He who does not love does not know God; for God is love. In this the love of God was made manifest among us, that God sent his only Son into the world, so that we might live through him. In this is love, not that we loved God but that he loved us and sent

ABDU: his Son to be the expiation for our sins. Beloved, if God so loved us, we also ought to love one another.

YUSEF: (Praying) O Lord, we thank You for what You are. Out of Your greatness You granted freedom even to reject Your love. Out of Your greatness You revealed to us Yourself. Out of Your greatness You came to redeem.

Grant to us minds to understand Your love. Grant to us hearts to accept Your love. Grant to us wills to return Your love.

In the name of our Redeemer,

                                       Amen

QUESTIONS FOR DISCUSSION

1. Go back and pick at least two questions from each of the last four lessons.
2. God's love is free. Does this mean it is cheap?
3. How does the younger son earn his father's forgiveness?
4. What has the father's love opened for the older son in the play?
5. The younger son has hurt his father in three ways. What are they?
6. The younger son must accept two things from his father. What are they?
7. How must the younger son return his father's love?
8. How must the older son return his father's love?
9. Tell the story of the farmer and the goat skin. What is the point?
10. Tell the story of the camel driver and the drunk. What is the point?
11. How can _we_ know, accept and return God's love?

SUMMARY OF LESSON

We must know God's holy love. Then we will know that a way of reconciliation is open.

We must accept God's holy love. Then through repentance we can be cleansed and restored.

We must return God's holy love. Then we will serve with grateful hearts, for we have already received.

MOTTO: We have already received. Therefore, we must love and serve.

APPENDIX A
SUGGESTIONS FOR USE
IN THE YOUNGER CHURCHES

This book is a series of dialogues. They are dialogues out of village life about the Doctrine of God. They are written for the Village Church. But perhaps they will be meaningful to some of our city churches as well. Many of our city churches have many village people in them. Someone has said that the deepest things of the spirit cannot be said, they must be acted. This is certainly true. We can speak of our love for our neighbor, and for God. But the deep things of love must be acted in loving service. God wanted to show His love for us so he acted out His love in sacrificial service. He did this on the Cross.

Even so, God in the life of Christ, acts out a great and meaningful drama. At the birth of Christ, there is the song of angels, the visit of wise men from the East, and the shining of a great star. God was acting out something of the meaning of the wonder of the birth of the Son of God.

The Church all through the ages has used religious drama to show some of the deeper meanings of the Gospel.

So today, we have put these lessons in dramatic form. We hope they will be used in many ways. The following are a few suggestions:

BIBLE CLASSES

It is not easy for one villager to teach his fellow villagers. For him to stand and explain a lesson to a class is hard. But if he can get some of the members of the class to act out a story, the lesson teaches itself. The class together tries to find out the meaning of the lesson. Thus the teacher is really a supervisor, and the task is not as difficult.

NIGHTLY MEETINGS IN THE CHURCH

We praise God that we have this chance in the village church to worship nightly with our people. The task of preparing a new sermon for every night is very hard. Many pastors feel the need of some change. One night a week the church could have a play. If the church has one play a week, this book will last for nearly half a year. Or if the church wishes, the people could take a full month to study the Doctrine of God using these plays.

SPECIAL MEETINGS

Some of the village and city churches have special plays at special times of the year. The pastor could choose some of his young men and have them learn the parts in two or three of these plays and have a special program of as long as three hours. This, too, would be very helpful to the people. Perhaps the pastor could choose one section of this book and act it out in one evening.

Experts have said that we remember only ten percent of what we hear, but we remember sixty percent of what we see. We remember ninety percent of what we do. Nothing could be finer than to have the youth of the church learn about God by acting out plays that try to explain something of His holiness and His love.

YOUNG PEOPLE

So we suggest also, that this series of plays could be used for the young people of the church so that they might come to know and serve God.

PERSONAL READING

We suggest that the pastor may put this book into the hands of the people. They could read this for themselves and come to know privately more of the Bible, and more of our God Who inspired it, and of our Christ Who comes to save us.

SERMONS

If you cannot use these plays acted out in your Church, you can still use the book. You can take a month and teach the Doctrine of God. Each lesson has an outline at the beginning. The pastor can use this outline and preach, using this as an outline for his sermon. If he follows through the series, in one month, the people will have learned in an orderly fashion something of the Doctrine of God.

PLAY READING

The pastor can also read this play as a sermon. This can be very effective. The reader reads the play over four or five times. He reads all the parts himself. He turns his head one way for one character, and another way for another character. He changes his voice a little for each of the different characters.

For example, for Baseat, he talks through his nose and makes his voice sound silly. For Abdu, he speaks in a straight village accent. For Yusef, he speaks more slowly like an older man. He can change his speed of speaking, the accent, and the voice quality. He can turn the head one way for one character, and another way for another character. Thus, he can easily distinguish the different characters without having to repeat the name before each speech.

CITY CHURCHES

City churches are full of country people. Sometimes in the city church, we minister to the educated and leave the country people behind because they cannot understand. These plays could be used in the city church and all of the members of the Congregation will understand and benefit from them.

MOTTOS

At the end of each lesson, there is a motto. You could use these by making signs and putting them up in the classroom or in the Church. Also you could paint these slogans on the walls of the houses of the village. Many of the leading men of the village would be proud to have such fine statements about God written on the walls of their houses. This way the people of the village would see these things day after day after day and quickly learn them.

APPENDIX B
NOTE TO THE TEACHER

This series of lessons is a set of dialogues about village life showing something of the meaning of the Doctrine of God.

We have three main characters; they are: Abdu, the inquirer; Yusef, the wise, and Baseat, the simple.

You read at the beginning of the lesson the main points of the lesson.

There is also a series of Scriptures for each lesson.

The plays are to be read and acted out by the class.

Then the questions about them are to be discussed.

We suggest the sessions should go as follows:

1. Read the Scriptures called for in the lesson, then pray to God asking that His Holy Spirit shall lead you in the truth.

2. Read to the class the Statement of Lesson at the beginning.

3. Write the outline of the lesson on the blackboard. Point out the main points of the outline. Do not spend time discussing the outline at this point.

4. The teacher should read the whole play through first to the class.

5. Then he should ask members of the class to read the different parts.

6. Pick out people in the class who can read fairly well and ask them to read the different parts. If you can pick out these characters beforehand, do so. Get them together and have them practice at least once reading the play. With careful practice, the plays could be a good substitute for the sermon in the meetings in the evening.

7. Have the characters chosen read and act out the plays. Do not read the words between brackets. They are instructions for the actor.

8. If there is time, have some other members of the class act out the same play without their books. See if the class understands the main points of the play. This way you can get some of the people who can't read very well into the play.

9. Finally, discuss the questions at the end of the lessons. Try to answer them out of the story of the play. Then turn back to the outline on the blackboard and review the points of the outline itself.

10. If the class is large, or if the class is in the Church, perhaps you can divide into small groups to discuss the questions.

11. Try to get everyone to understand at least the summary statement at the end. Let each student go home with this thought ringing in his mind.

12. Close the class with prayer.

BIBLIOGRAPHY

Aulen, Gustaf, *Christus Victor*, London, S.P.C.K., 1931.

Baillie, D. M., *God was in Christ*, New York; Charles Scribner's Sons, 1948.

Barth, Karl, *Church Dogmatics, Vol. II, The Doctrine of God*, Edinburgh; T. and T. Clark, 1957.

Barth, Karl, *Come Holy Spirit*, New York; Round Table Press, 1933.

Barth, Karl, *The Doctrine of the Word of God*, Edinburgh; T. and T. Clark, 1936.

Barth, Karl, *Dogmatics in Outline*, London; SCM Press, 1952.

Bavinck, H. B., *The Doctrine of God*, Grand Rapids; Wm. B. Eerdmans, 1951.

Berkouwer, G. C., *The Triumph of Grace in the Theology of Karl Barth*, Grand Rapids; Wm. B. Eerdmans, 1956.

Brunner, Emil, *The Christian Doctrine of God*, Philadelphia; Westminster Press, 1940.

Brunner, Emil, *Our Faith*, London; SCM Press, 1936.

Burrows, Millar, *An Outline of Biblical Theology*, Philadelphia; Westminster Press, 1946.

Caird, G. B., *The Truth of the Gospel*, London; Oxford University Press, 1950.

Calvin, John, *Institutes of the Christian Religion*, Grand Rapids; Eerdmans, 1957.

Clarke, W. N., *The Christian Doctrine of God*, New York; Charles Scribner's Sons, 1909.

Conner, W. T., *The Work of the Holy Spirit*, Nashville; Broadman Press, 1949.

Cragg, Kenneth, *Sandals at the Mosque*, New York; Oxford University Press, 1959.

Cragg, Kenneth, *The Call of the Minaret*, New York; Oxford University Press, 1956.

Crawford, Thomas J., *The Doctrine of Holy Scripture Respecting the Atonement*, Grand Rapids; Baker Book House, 1954.

Crawford, T. J., *The Fatherhood of God*, London; William Bleckwood and Sons, 1867.

Denney, James, *The Death of Christ*, New York; A. C. Armstrong, 1907.

Dillistone, F. W., *Jesus Christ and His Cross*, Philadelphia; Westminster Press, 1953.

Easton, W. B., *Basic Christian Beliefs*, Philadelphia; The Westminster Press, 1957.

Eiler, H. B., *An Historical Survey of the Doctrine of the Covenant A. D. 100 -A. D. 1800*, M. A. Thesis, Pittsburgh - Xenia Seminary, Pittsburgh, 1958.

Ferre, N. F. S., *The Christian Understanding of God*, New York; Harper and Brothers, 1951.

Franks, R. S., *The Doctrine of the Trinity*, London; Gerald Ducksworth and Co., 1953.

Forsyth, P. T., *The Cruciality of the Cross*, London; Hodder and Stoughton, 1908.

Forsyth, P. T., *God the Holy Father*, London; Independent Press, 1957.

Forsyth, P. T., *The Person and Place of Jesus Christ*, London; Independent Press, 1948.

Forsyth, P. T., *The Work of Christ*, London; Independent Press, 1958.

Garvie, A. E., *The Christian Doctrine of the Godhead*, New York; George H. Doran Company, 1925.

Gordon, A. J., *The Ministry of the Spirit*, Philadelphia; American Baptist Publication Society, 1895.

Hodge, A. A., *Outlines of Theology*, New York; Robert Carter and Brothers, 1863.

Hodgson, Leonard, *The Doctrine of the Atonement*, New York; Charles Scribner's Sons, 1951.

Hubbard, J. F., *The Development of the Covenant Concept in Four Critical Periods of Hebrew History as Illuminated by Archaeology*, Pittsburgh, Pa., M. A. Thesis, Pittsburgh-Xenia Seminary, 1958.

Hughes, H. M., *The Christian Idea of God*, New York; Charles Scribner's Sons, 1936.

Lidgett, J. S., *The Fatherhood of God*, Edinburgh; T. and T. Clark, 1902.

Illingwroth, J. R., *The Doctrine of the Trinity*, London; Macmillan, 1907.

Kittel, Gerhard, *Bible Key Words*, New York; Harper and Brothers, 1951.

Knight, G. A. F., *A Biblical Approach to the Doctrine of the Trinity*, Edinburgh; Oliver and Boyd, 1953.

Knudson, A. C., *The Doctrine of God*, New York; Abingdon Press, 1930.

Kuyper, Abraham, *The Work of the Holy Spirit*, New York; Funk and Wagnalls, 1900.

Lewis, C. S., *The Four Loves*, New York; Harcourt, Brace & Co., 1960.

Morgan, G. C., *The Spirit of God*, London; Hodder and Stoughton, 1916.

Neill, Stephen, *The Christians' God*, New York; Association Press, 1955.

Neill, Stephen, *Christian Holiness*, New York, Harper and Brothers, 1960.

Newbigin, Lesslie, *Sin and Salvation*, Philadelphia; Westminster Press, 1956.

Pulliman, Paul R., *The Trinity in the Teachings of John Calvin and Karl Barth*, Pittsburgh, Pa., M. A. Thesis, Pittsburgh-Xenia Theological Seminary, 1960.

Richardson, Cyril, *The Doctrine of the Trinity*, Nashville; Abingdon Press, 1958.

Selbie, W. B., *The Fatherhood of God*, New York; Charles Scribner's Sons, 1936.

Shaw, J. M., *The Christian Gospel of the Fatherhood of God*, London, Hodder and Stoughton, 1924.

Spurrier, W. A., *Guide to the Christian Faith*, New York, Charles Scribner's Sons, 1952.

Stewart, J. S., *The Life and Teaching of Jesus Christ*, New York, Abingdon Press, 1960.

Strong, A. H., *Systematic Theology, Vol. I*, Philadelphia, Griffith and Rowland, 1907.

Stump, Joseph, *The Christian Faith*, New York, The Macmillan Co., 1932.

Temple, William, *Christ's Revelation of God*, London, S.C.M. Press, 1925.

Temple, William, *Christian Faith and Life*, London, SVM Press, 1931.

Temple, William, *Christus Veritas*, London, Macmillan and Co., 1954.

Temple, William, *Nature, Man and God*, London, Macmillan and Co., 1953.

Temple, William, *Readings in St. John's Gospel*, London, Macmillan and Co., 1955.

Thomas, M. B., *The Biblical Idea of God*, New York, Charles Scribner's Sons, 1924.

Tillich, Paul, *Systematic Theology, Vol. I*, Chicago, University of Chicago Press, 1951.

Torry, R. A., *The God of the Bible*, New York, George H. Doran Co., 1923.

Vidler, A. R., *Christian Belief*, Charles Scribner's Sons, New York, 1950.

Welch, Claude, *In This Name* (the Doctrine of the Trinity in Contemporary Theology), New York, Charles Scribner's Sons, 1952.

Whale, J. S., *Christian Doctrine*, New York, Macmillan, 1941.

Whale, J. S., *Victor and Victim*, Cambridge, At the University Press, 1960.